THE FACTORY

A JOURNEY THROUGH
THE PRISON INDUSTRIAL
COMPLEX

CHRISTOPHER LORDAN

&

ROBERT DELLELO

Dedication

This book is dedicated, with respect and gratitude, to all the men and women who endured unspeakable pain and suffering growing up behind the walls of the Massachusetts reform schools and state prison system. It is for those resilient individuals who put their lives on the line in this struggle, but always held fast regardless of the hardships they faced. It is for those still living within those walls, and for those who died there. It is for those who are finally out, and struggle daily to retain their freedom.

Acknowledgements

Though there are too many to name individually, there are several for whom special recognition is necessary: Dr. Jerome Miller for his courage and leadership in shutting down the hellholes operating under the guise of "reform" schools; the first black commissioner John Boone, for his courage and leadership as he attempted to reform the racist Department of Correction; Ralph Hamm, who still remains behind bars after over 46 years because of his political activity and leadership during the troubled times at Walpole; Larry Rooney, who along with Ralph Hamm, helped keep the peace and maintain the order when the guards abandoned their posts; Reverend Ed Rodman for his courage and compassion in leading the Observer Program in a hostile and racist environment, which he saved the lives of both prisoners and guards; all of the Observers who had the courage to step between the prisoners and guards, and, despite severe harassment from the guards, never abandoned their posts; Fr. Russell Carmichael and the NPRA External Board of Directors for their tireless efforts; the NPRA Internal Board of Directors for staying on the front line and not backing down; Phillis Ryan who was always there whenever we called, never hesitating to offer advice and give assistance; Susannah Sheffer for her friendship and work to prepare me for release from prison; and last but not least, my brother Louis Dellelo and his wife Lois. Without their unconditional love and support I would undoubtedly still be in prison today.

This book would not have been possible without the time, patience, effort, and assistance of Jessica Lordan, Gary Farrow Jenn Soucy, Matthew Levenson, Ryan Murphy, Thos Niles, Mike Hill, Paul Piantedosi, Chris Mountain, Rich LaMarche, Kathleen Dennehy, Margaret Luciano, and Brenda Fredericks. Thank you for your very different kinds of help.

A special thanks to Brian Caldwell for going far above and beyond small favors.

Preface

My name is Robert Dellelo. I was released from Walpole prison this past Nov. 19th after serving forty years. In those forty years I have been actively involved in the politics of the prison. I have lived through the policies and practices of the numerous past administrations and have watched from a personal perspective as the current policies and practices have evolved into what they are today.

Unfortunately, it is nearly impossible to adequately articulate these experiences and insights in any meaningful manner, nor is it possible to even give a brief summary of the policies and practices regarding governance, operations, budget, security and treatment, let alone giving any concrete suggestions for improving the system, in five minutes.

Time is not of the essence. Simply giving you a laundry list of issues would be tantamount to a whitewashing. There are profoundly important issues that go to the very heart of public safety, issues that are correctable and address the unnecessary attack and destruction of our communities. This Committee must re-evaluate the necessity of allowing only five minutes, at least for those like myself, who have spent many years in the system and lived through these conditions.

If you are sincerely interested in addressing and remedying the issue of classification and want to know how the present classification system is actually corrupting any meaningful efforts to rehabilitate prisoners, why the classifications system is not a workable or viable concept, why it is corrupting and being corrupted by other aspects of the system, how incompetence is preventing efforts to adequately address and remedy the situation, then I am the man who can tell you these things.

If you are sincerely interested in addressing and remedying the issues of the disciplinary practices and procedures, knowing and understanding how and why these practices and procedures are corrupting the entire system to the severe detriment to all concerned, then I am the man that can tell you these things.

I have spent five years and one month in solitary confinement in Walpole's Departmental Disciplinary Unit. If you are sincerely interested in knowing and understanding how detrimental this unit is to

7

the communities, inside and outside of prison, if you want to know how the DDU serves to emasculate, dehumanize, and psychologically destroy the minds of men through severe sensory deprivation, which manifests itself as paranoia, disorientation, and confusion, causing bizarre and irrational thought processes, having devastating consequences to the communities, inside and outside of prison, if you want to understand why this is an abomination that serves no social purpose or function and is the clearest example of the utter breakdown of corrections, if you want to understand the insanity of releasing men so traumatized directly into the community, and why this unit must be shut down for public safety, then I am the man who can tell you these things.

If you are sincerely interested in knowing and understanding how the cult of guards beating prisoners evolved and was sanctioned by the prison administration, how the guards' union became the tail that wags the dog, then I am the man who can tell you all these things and much, much more.

However, I simply cannot tell you these things in five minutes. If you are sincerely interested in not covering up and whitewashing the root causes of what brings us here today, then I implore you to reconsider the necessity of limiting the time for testimony and allow these issues to be presented in a truly transparent committee and not be covered up as they have been for all these years.

-Bobby Dellelo, Harshbarger Committee testimony, 2004

PART I

CHAPTER ONE

A decade before receiving a natural life sentence for first-degree murder, young Bobby Dellelo's run of second chances with the law was about to come to an abrupt end. In September of 1953, he stood in front of a juvenile court judge, charged with breaking and entering into the Jordan Marsh department store in downtown Boston. Although he was young, he had been arrested before and had a typical adolescent attitude, combining irresponsibility with an unrealistic sense of invulnerability. Prior experience led him to believe that this arrest would turn out the way all the others had; the charges would be dropped or, at worst, he would receive a stern lecture from the judge and a slap on the wrist. This attitude hadn't sprung from nowhere. In the past, his family connections had allowed him to avoid any serious consequences for his misbehavior. He had always had a seasoned lawyer who was able to persuade the judge that Bobby was a good kid hanging out with the wrong crowd. To him, it was all just a game, and he was confident he would win it once again and the judge would give him another chance. Previous experiences had gradually developed in him a sense of entitlement; arrests had become mere inconveniences.

I got banned from the City of Boston by Judge Connelly when I was a kid. I think I might have been about twelve years old. He pointed at me and said in a loud voice, 'I am banning you from the City of Boston!' He told the cops in the courtroom, 'If you find him in downtown Boston, you bring him to this courthouse and I will put him into reform school until he's twenty-one years old!' When I walked out of the courthouse, guess where I went? Straight to the penny arcade on Washington Street in the heart of Boston. I never really paid attention to authority.

Bobby had heard scary stories about reform school from older boys around the neighborhood, and it sounded pretty frightening. But in his head, the possibility of actually going there was non-existent. Only *other* kids got sent to places like that. The *really* bad ones. The judge's threats were meant to scare him straight, but he laughed it off. Adults always talked tough but never seemed to follow through.

In his mind, the charges against him shouldn't apply because he didn't actually break into Jordan Marsh—he had broken *out*. Bobby and his friends had hidden themselves within the department store during hours of operation, then, after closing, emerged from hiding to leisurely shop around and pass goods out to friends waiting outside designated windows. Therefore, he reasoned, he had never broken in and the charges must be dropped.

This time, though, Bobby had pushed his luck too far and the judge intended to adjust his carefree attitude. Bobby was completely stunned when it was announced that he was to be committed to a term at the notorious Lyman School for Boys.

He was thirteen years old and weighed only 79 pounds.

* * *

Bobby Dellelo grew up with his family on Leland Street in Boston's Roxbury neighborhood. Some white families used a bit of revisionist geography in calling it Dorchester, by stretching the border of the heavily white-populated area to include them. Just about all the families in his neighborhood were either working-class poor or subsisting on welfare. In the late 1940s and early 1950s, this crowded neighborhood, the city streets lined with triple-decker homes, served as the only available playground. Without money to go to the movies, camp, or baseball games, kids played street games and modified versions of team sports. For Bobby, though, those activities held little appeal. He found his entertainment by running the streets looking for adventure, which in Roxbury, more often than not, meant looking for trouble.

Bobby was surrounded, not so much by criminals, but by bored kids looking to get a rise out of adults to make each other laugh. He and his friends would descend on a pet store, running through the aisles while letting all the parakeets out of their cages. The birds rampaged all through the store while the boys would make a fast escape, laughing as they ran. Sometimes, when the owner wasn't paying attention, they'd pluck the fish from the tanks and slowly fill up one single bowl with all of them. They had a lot of fun.

At home, Bobby lived with his mother, Jeannette, and his brother, Louie, two years his senior. Jeannette was loving, but tough, and tended to direct her attentions elsewhere, usually to whoever happened to be her boyfriend at the moment, often a local wiseguy. Bobby and Louie, though close in age, ran with different crowds. Louie was hardworking, holding down various jobs, and was an avid baseball and football fan. But Bobby's lack of interest and frequent asthma attacks prevented his participation in athletics; he preferred roaming the city.

Compared to some of the neighborhood kids, Bobby's life was cozy. For those kids, home life could be a violent, nightmarish existence and the streets, as tough as they could be, were the only refuge. In those days, it was not unusual for children as young as ten years old to be out running the city streets until late at night, totally unsupervised. Some parents knew where their children were and couldn't be bothered to care; others weren't aware of their child's whereabouts at all.

We lived in Roxbury, Leland Street. A couple streets over were the other kids that I had met. There was one kid, Willy, who I began hanging around with. Another older kid, Billy, he started hanging out too and was a little more sophisticated in stealing things. In those days when you broke into a store, the money was in the cash register, they didn't stash it in a safe. We used to just break into places.

I was really small when I was a kid, and all the guys could fit me through little holes and windows that chickens could barely get through. Then I would open the doors. We broke into this shoe store one time and both Billy and Willy were grabbing shoes and trying all kinds of shoes on and stuff. I wouldn't put those shoes on because if I got rid of the sneakers my mother had bought me, she'd kill me. I didn't really have a need for the shoes, I had shoes and sneakers and good clothes. I never personally needed to break into places, but those guys were very poor and had the need for these things. They were trying to survive.

Shoplifting, theft, and burglary weren't crimes in Bobby's eyes, they were adventures. His intent wasn't malicious; it was all about the thrill, the rush of getting away with it. It was exciting to be somewhere he shouldn't, taking things that didn't belong to him. He was drawn to breaking the rules, especially as his respect toward adults and authority began to decline. Every time he got away with something, there was a desire to push it a little further. And for the few times he was caught, the consequences were a joke.

Bobby liked people and genuinely enjoyed social interactions with others. He was a "give you the shirt off his back" kind of a kid, never hesitating to help out a friend in need. In his early years, he was also known as being sympathetic and soft-hearted, and would strongly react to anyone's tales of woe. He was especially compassionate toward pets and other animals. Once, his mother, who followed the horse races carefully, mentioned a racehorse having to be scratched. Bobby overheard

13

the conversation and instantly burst into tears, failing to understand why the animal had to be put down. He felt hurt when the adults laughed at his uninhibited display of emotion, and later came to understand that, in his world, sensitivity and compassion could be a serious liability.

Young Bobby's sympathetic disposition did not indicate softness; he had plenty of street smarts and had developed a physical toughness even before he was a teen. His lessons began at home, where Bobby's mother had no time or patience for a sissy. In her view, bigger or tougher kids were always going to be a problem if he didn't take a firm stand. She advised him that a problem with a bully was never an excuse to back down or, even worse, run away.

> *She told me to pick up a stick or you kick him in the balls. She made it clear that if I got my ass kicked on the street, do not come sniveling home looking for comfort and sympathy, because none would be given. In fact, I just might get my ass kicked again.*

Standing up for oneself was a virtue on the street. With his physically slight build, Bobby knew that he was going to have to be willing to fight, even when it meant taking a beating. And he did; he never shied away from fighting a bigger kid. It was that willingness which would eventually gain him respect, not the ultimate victory or loss.

* * *

> *I didn't like school. I'm a very right-brained thinker and the schools taught left-brained methodologies. It didn't work for me. I didn't care for a lot of the subjects they taught, but I did love science—it entertained me.*

> *We went to the Sacred Heart, we went from there back to the public school. The grade difference was almost a year. So when I get back to the public*

14

school system they're teaching things I already know, and it's just really boring to me. So I did a lot of hooky. I was supposed to go over near Mass. General Hospital, there used to be a school building there. You'd have to go there twice a week, they'd give you bus transfers. You just sat in this room, waiting for the time to go by. Transfers, hell. Scollay Square was right up the street. In-town Boston was there, so you got out of there as fast as you can then went up and played. It just got to the point where I didn't bother going any more. So I quit school in the seventh grade, didn't complete it. I became street wise, street smart in that time. That's basically how I grew up.

While Bobby had trouble learning within a traditional school setting, his neighborhood life provided an entirely different type of education, one in which he thrived. By hanging around older kids, he absorbed their criminal knowledge; shoplifting, breaking and entry skills, fighting, eluding police, and scamming. Bobby evolved into a classic street kid, and as his experience deepened, by age twelve he had become criminally sophisticated. He ran the streets constantly, leaving his Roxbury neighborhood to hustle in downtown Boston's Scollay Square, with both cops and criminals as his mentors. In the 1950s, the area was bustling with theaters, bars, restaurants, and department stores lining the crowded sidewalks where Boston City Hall is located today. The square was always packed with city officials, cops, ex-cons, shoppers, businessmen, all of whom converged upon the area for either business or pleasure and sometimes both. Most noticeable were the hundreds of sailors docked in Boston Harbor at any given time, looking for a weekend of women, fights, and booze. From a criminal's viewpoint, Scollay Square was a great place to hang out, a goldmine of criminal opportunities loaded with suckers waiting to be had.

15

Bobby started out with hustling tourists, and occasionally some minor theft on the side. Taking cues from the many homeless men in the area, Bobby found it was easy for a kid to beg small change. "We'd put on the puppy dog eyes and say, 'Hey Mister, you got a quarter?' When you're a kid, people give you money real quick. So we used to get whatever money we needed." While adult beggars were routinely ignored, Bobby knew that a kid with his hand out tugged at most adults' heart strings. He understood that it wasn't necessary to appear destitute to scam people, as the mere act of a child begging implied his family was struggling through hard times. It never took long before he begged a large amount of change, and it was also never used to put food on the table. Bobby always ran straight to the penny arcade on Washington Street to blow the money on an afternoon of movies and games. He and his friends laughed about it. If someone was foolish enough to hand over their money, there was nothing to feel bad about.

> *There were older people that were using us. There was this Mary, a blonde old blauser, we used to go shoplifting with her. She had made these jackets with a lip on the inside cuff, so if you took a ring and you snapped it up, it went up under the cuff. Then you scratched your head, when you put your hand down, it rolled back into the pocket. Then she had a shoebox and there was a cut on the top of it, like a lip. It was all cotton lined and it had this string around it so it looked like it couldn't be opened. Well, she'd be looking at jewelry and stuff and put something on the box. Simply press it, the lip went down, the jewelry fell inside, the cotton was in there so there was no noise. We would create a distraction, or sometimes put it on the box and she would get the guy's attention and we would push it into the gig. Of course, she was abusing us; but I mean we had carte blanche at her house. You had a little sex, drinking*

16

booze and all that other stuff, so it was a big score as a kid.

Then we had hustles that we learned through that experience. E.B. Horn's, a jewelry store in Boston, we would get their labels, their price tags with their name on it. And you go into a five and dime store like Kresge's, there were fifty cent rings, dollar rings, dollar-fifty rings. So when you look at them all together they look real cheap. But when you take it out and polish it, because it's that gilded stuff, it looks good by itself. It doesn't look as cheap as when you get it in with a bunch of them. So one of the gigs we used to do was to put a $150.00 tag on the smaller one, and put a $450.00 tag on the other one. Then we drove to Scollay Square because that's where all the sailors were from all over the world. Scollay Square was an awesome place! And we would grab a sailor. The routine is looking suspicious, looking back and forth, and one of us says, 'Look, I got two rings, I can't give you the $450.00,' and you give him the $450.00 like you gave it to him by accident. Then you'll say, 'I'll give you this $150.00 one for fifty bucks.' One time, one mark was an uptight kind of guy grumbling about our stolen stuff. His friend looked and saw $450.00 tag. His greed takes control, and he's trying to shut the other guy up. He said, 'No, it's a good ring, it's a good ring!' It's so obvious what they're doing, right? Then the other guy finally sees the $450.00 tag. They give us the $50.00 and they screw!

The sailors, because they are foreigners, they're easy targets. And if they run to the cops, it's not going to help because you're just out of the neighborhood, then they're on their ship and gone. And then we're back up there the next night selling stuff to their shipmates or the next ship. Those were the types of little hustles that we used to do. I'm a young kid

17

doing this. You kind of get used to that kind of world, you think that it's a normal world. You don't really make sense out of it yet, but you see the hustle that's going on in life.

Most people in the neighborhood had a positive view of law enforcement. Growing up, Bobby was taught to believe that cops were the good guys, always friendly and helpful. But as Bobby got older and ran the streets with increasing frequency, his arrests piled up, and his thoughts about police and authority began to change.

That was part of the attitude I get toward cops. There was a cop named White. I'd be in Uphams Corner, he'd say, 'Hey Bobby, c'mon get in the car, I'll drive you home.' He'd drive me home, alright. I thought everything was cool, he was just being nice. Then eventually my mother smacked me. She said, 'You see that asshole again, you run!' What was happening was he was picking me up, bringing me home, and talking to my mother on the side. He was telling her I was into shoplifting, but I wasn't actually doing anything. She'd duke him twenty bucks for looking out for me, for being a good guy. When it kept happening, she caught on that this guy's abusing his power, looking for a payout. That was the nature of cops in those days.

Later on, in my teens. Somebody had broken into an ice cream place, on Washington Street, somebody had broken the window. Me and Billy, we were coming back from in town, walking back toward Dudley Street, and the trains were closed. As we came up to there the cops grab us. They said, 'The place was robbed,' but they're sitting there eating ice cream. So they are trying to blame us for doing this, right. Then there was one cop who says, 'Why did you break into a place like this?' We just looked at him confused. He says, 'Why don't you throw something

18

through the window of the jewelry store, ya know, where there's money.' I looked over at the jewelry store, and there was a milk crate on the ground. Now those milk crates were those old heavy wooden metal ones, I mean they were heavy. So I said to the cop, 'You want me to throw one through that window over there?' He looked at the other guy, then back at me, and said, 'You'd throw that through that window over there for me? You'd do that for me?' I said, 'You'd let me go if I did that?' He said yeah. He grabbed all the other cops, said, 'Hey let's go.' They all got in their cars, there are two or three cars there and they drove away. I picked the milk crate up, walked over, threw it through the window. The alarm went off, we grab a few things and we boogied. The cops came back up there after we left and emptied the place out.

That was the cops. To me, as a kid, they were the biggest thieves. They had their own rules. They had their guns and they did what they wanted. You get in the police station and they'd beat the shit out of you. The concept of law and order was a myth, it was just nonsensical. There were people that believed that, but most people I knew didn't go along with that after a while. The court systems were a joke, and the cops were a joke.

CHAPTER TWO

When Bobby arrived at reform school, it didn't look like he had imagined. In fact, rather than a jail, its appearance had more in common with a private college. Founded in the 1840s, Lyman School for Boys in Westborough, Massachusetts, a suburb thirty-five miles west of Boston, was the first established reform school in the country. Theodore Lyman, Boston's mayor from 1834 to 1835, championed the idea of a boys' reform school, and became the school's namesake after he contributed large sums of his personal wealth towards its construction. Built upon a vast spread of rural farmland, the Lyman School's campus sprawled across hundreds of acres of land surrounding Powder Hill. Lyman's bucolic setting was by design, intended to be the best location for inner-city kids to reform themselves; it was the opposite of the crime-ridden neighborhoods from which the prisoners tended to originate. For some kids, it was their first time outside of the city. The rural environment was intended to strip away the distractions of urban living, allowing the boys to focus on the more meaningful aspects of life.

Lyman provided a strict structure for troubled kids, built around a regimented schedule of positive discipline and rigorous schooling. Instead of the usual drab, cement institutional monstrosities, boys lived in a collection of four-story brick buildings spread across green grounds, surrounded by colorful trees, a lake, and farmland. Lyman's ten buildings were referred to as "cottages," each of which housed about forty boys apiece, as well as administrative offices and staff residences. Kids typically slept on the top floor in clean but uncomfortable bunks, thirty to forty beds spread across an open floor plan. Administrative offices, a kitchen area, and headmasters' quarters were located on the second floor, and were strictly off limits to the boys. In the basement were showers, toilets, lockers, wooden benches, and a recreation area. Despite the stately exteriors, the cottages were not designed for the residents' comfort or visual pleasure, with drab tan walls, dusty shelves and floors, musty air, and temperatures too hot or too cold.

Bobby's introduction to institutional life was far from the reformative experience Lyman alleged to provide. Like all new boys arriving at Lyman, Bobby was brought directly to Lyman Hall where he was processed, tested, and eventually assigned to a long-term cottage to serve his term. Lyman wasted no time acquainting boys to their new reality; everyone was put to work on his very first day.

The Lyman Hall is where you went for a while before they found out where they were going put you. You used to scrub floors, you had these big wooden brushes with bristles. And you scrubbed on your knees one, two, one, two, one, two, back and forth. There was a line of kids, and they threw water on the floor and you backed up as you scrubbed, it's what you did. Your knees were all bruised by time you were done.

Bobby quickly learned that discipline was a top priority. The rules of behavior were clearly stated and strictly enforced. Corporal punishment was the norm for even minor violations and was limited in neither frequency nor severity. Misbehaving kids were routinely struck with a wooden paddle across the behind, palms of the hands, bottoms of the feet or any other available body part. All kids feared the paddle, which was often drilled to create aerodynamic holes for maximum striking velocity. If no paddle was available, staff used open-hand slaps, hair pulling, kicking, or even closed fists.

They used something called the 'three-inch punch' or sometimes a 'six-inch punch' which is exactly what it sounds like. They held a fist three inches from your jaw and let loose. Not as much impact as a full punch, but it still did damage. A six-inch punch was usually to the chest or stomach. Even if you tried to follow the rules you got hit. Everyone got whacked at some point. It hurt like a bastard.

Nothing short of total obedience and strict compliance with all rules and regulations was acceptable. Even unreasonable personal requests from the staff—sexual favors—had to be honored. Earning credits took time and discipline; loss of credits came easily, allowing the potential for any boy to languish in Lyman indefinitely. Lyman's behavioral guidelines were disciplinarian, almost militaristic in nature; rigid and inflexible rules which were to be respected without question. Talking was not allowed other than at specific designated times. This included normally social times such as meals, work details, and after lights out. For young kids, this rule was often the hardest to follow, despite its strict enforcement. More serious offenses such as fighting and insubordination were dealt with in typically swift and severe fashion—usually a trip to the disciplinary cottage, physical punishment of some sort, and loss of credits. Every boy's clothes and appearance, as well as personal effects, were to be kept clean and neat at all times. Showers were required at designated times, and toilet use was limited to just a few minutes in order to allow time for everyone. Institutional control was on constant display in order to permeate every facet of the boys' lives. At Lyman, boys were expected to respond to the structured schedule and disciplined lifestyle, which in turn would theoretically spark a positive adjustment in their behavior.

All boys were required to perform physical labor. They were responsible for the upkeep of the grounds, assigned to tasks such as raking leaves, mowing grass, weeding and planting gardens, tree and shrub pruning, ditch digging, painting, and shoveling snow. Laziness was not tolerated; all boys were expected to work to physical capacity, and all work was to be performed in silence. Though much of the assigned work was utilitarian, housemasters could assign tasks with no purpose, either as punishment or simply to occupy boys when no meaningful jobs were available. Sometimes boys were given spades and directed to dig large holes, only to fill them back in immediately upon completion, or made to move heavy rocks from one location to another for no reason at all. Skill development was not a part of the Lyman experience. Instead, a steady regimen of hard labor intended to wear down the boys down both physically and mentally, to the point where they would be too exhausted to rebel.

For whichever work assignment a boy received, the conditions were consistent: safety precautions were ignored, no limits on work hours, and no wages were paid. Cooking was left mostly to staff, but the cleaning and food prep was assigned to the boys. Kitchen work generally was not as difficult as other types of jobs, but nobody wanted the duty of peeling potatoes, a monotonous task which was expected to be performed both quickly and precisely. Usually, neither happened. The potato peelers were old and dull, and the kids were never properly instructed in how to correctly use one. A peeler ended his shift with cuts all over his fingers and hands, the basin pink from blood mixed into the water.

The kitchen produced food on par with most prisons. Cornbread was made on long baking sheets, and stored on open counters where rats could easily feast. Lyman veterans knew to check all food carefully before eating; it was not unusual for boys to be served cornbread with their meals, flip it over, and find rat feces caked on the bottom. A common dinner was creamed codfish made in large vats, a horrible smelling concoction that would turn the stomachs of even the hungriest. From the vats, buckets of the slop would be distributed out to the cottages. Once there, the codfish mush was served straight from the buckets to the boys' food trays. Many kids opted to go hungry, and those brave enough to eat the dish had trouble keeping it down. If a newcomer voiced an opinion about the food quality, a whack from a headmaster ended the discussion quickly. Older kids knew better than to complain.

For all its rigidity, though, Lyman had a level of security much less restrictive than any jail. In an effort to appear less penal in nature, the institution had no locked doors, checkpoints, visitor restrictions, fences, alarms, or other standard security measures typically associated with a lock up. Lax security, however, sometimes allowed for problems such as fights, smoking, thefts, vandalism, and so on. Most boys realized that even without having an elaborate escape plan, they could simply walk away from Lyman if they chose to do so. However, Lyman staff didn't worry much about escapees, knowing most of the boys had nowhere safe or comfortable to go, and no money or survival skills to make it on their own in the streets. Some went straight home and waited for Lyman personnel to show up. Most often, runaways didn't plan an escape in advance; it was usually an impulsive flight without a destination in mind. Those boys could be found walking down the road in broad daylight, not attempting to hide themselves or resisting when apprehended. Even without a destination, they desperately fled toward the unknown, thinking it was a better option than spending another day at Lyman.

Bobby's first escape came a few months after his arrival. He was living in Westview Cottage, working as an orderly, cleaning up around the institution's hospital. Though the job required undesirable early morning hours, awake by five a.m. and reporting to work by six, there were perks. The nature of the position allowed him to move about freely and he was often out of the direct supervision of a housemaster. He was even allowed to walk from the cottage down to the hospital alone. The first time he was granted this rare privilege, he felt the staff eyes on him, watching to see if he could be trusted. He walked slowly until he reached the crossroad, equidistant from both the water tower and the main hill. Prior to that morning, he hadn't given much thought toward escaping, but he now saw an opportunity too good to pass up.

Stopping there for a moment, I knew it was decision time. Turn back or go for it. I looked around, said, 'Go!' Made the break down the hill. Now I don't know about the supervisor, Jackman, and his crew yet. So I went down that hill, there's a road there. I just got across that little road, went down the hill, and they're there with the pickup truck. They're out of the truck chasing me. There's a lake and you can't go across it. So you're limited to go left or right. I don't know all this yet, I just got to this place. I run down the damn thing and I take a right, which is bringing me toward the highway. And they're chasing me, Jackman's yelling, 'Stop now, stop now, you won't get beat if you stop right now, I won't beat you!' And that's just making me run all the more.

Now, I get up to this fence, it's a cow fence. I'm a city kid; I don't know this. There are porcelain balls on top of the posts and I kind of recognize that this is a different kind of fence. It's not like barbed wire, it's just a thin wire, there are two strands of it, and there are cows. The thing was, they're right behind me chasing. My choices are go in between the two wires or just grab them and jump and go over. I opted for the leaping over the damn thing. It's an electric cow fence, it's like 12,000 volts. I grab that thing and was instantly on my knees. And once I got down low enough the weight of my body pulled me off. Jackman and the others almost killed themselves laughing; it's what saved me from getting a beating.

25

They thought that was the funniest thing they had ever seen in their lives. I mean it shocked the hell out of me! That was my introduction to a cow fence. I really got an appreciation for what those porcelain balls were. You see porcelain balls, this sucker's electric! Do not touch it. So now that puts me in the disciplinary cottage.

So many of Lyman's kids came from abusive environments that the physical pain they suffered at Lyman seemed almost normal. Nobody blinked if a boy was yanked out of line by his hair, removed from a room by the ear, or given a swift kick. Slapping and shoving were commonplace for minor offenses, and staff members were allowed to beat kids with closed fists, a leather strap, or any other convenient object when the offense was more serious. Discipline was not only harsh, but was also meted out arbitrarily. Housemasters frequently punished all of the boys for the actions of one. A typical scenario involved the boys being forced to kneel on concrete floors for prolonged periods of time, all because one boy spoke out of turn. If the housemaster noticed boys displacing their body weight from the knees to relieve pressure, more time would be added. And if that didn't get the message across, he would have the boys place a small object, usually a pencil, under their knees to maximize discomfort and pain. The boys well knew that if anyone complained or cried, there would be yet more time added to the punishment.

Abuse at Lyman included psychological manipulation as well. Boys were punished in front of the others to maximize humiliation. Staff members often tried to embarrass and degrade boys by focusing on specific insecurities such as physical appearances, learning disabilities, bedwetting, or other private issues. The use of threats to maintain constant fear was institutional policy. All boys knew that at any time their lack of obedience could get them sent to Oak Cottage and stripped of privileges.

As in prison, a total lack of privacy stripped away any sense of dignity. This was especially difficult for developing young boys who lacked confidence in the first place; they would have to shower and use the toilet in full view of others. Lyman leveraged the boys' often fragile emotional states, constantly reinforcing the idea that they were complete failures. These relentless reminders conditioned the boys to submit to authority, fair or not. Fighting back, they were taught, was not an option.

While most boys were sent to Lyman for criminal offenses, there were some who landed there due to behavioral issues, usually nonviolent kids. Labelled by the court as "status offenders," they were the boys with no place to call home and no responsible adults looking after them. Juveniles were often stamped with a status offender label for a variety of offenses, which if committed by an adult would not be considered a crime. Boys who perpetually ran away from home were sent to Lyman. Boys with uncontrollable behavior and negative attitudes, usually from a single parent home, were sent to Lyman as incorrigibles. Kids who refused to attend school were shipped off to Lyman as truants. Even orphaned kids, who had done nothing wrong, ended up at Lyman by default. These were the boys who typically landed in reform school because of circumstance, mostly beyond their control, rather than as the result of intentional wrongdoings. Regardless, they were locked up alongside the juvenile delinquents, and by all accounts, the Lyman staff treated them with no distinction.

Many of the boys did not fare well in their post-Lyman lives. Mark Devlin, who gained national attention for his memoir *Stubborn Child*, wrote extensively about his time spent at Lyman and other reform schools. Devlin believed, at least initially, that the Lyman staff cared about him and wanted to help. Devlin chronicled his emotional ups and downs, starkly describing his overwhelming fear, anxiety, and distrust which blossomed into anger and hatred. He was constantly put down and humiliated, and like most boys, suffered physical punishment.

[The housefather] called me to his desk and made me take down my pants. He then whacked me hard across my bottom with a long flat board and told me that it was for nothing, but just to wait until I did do something.

Devlin's constant bed wetting, nightmares, or wrong answers in class earned him more verbal abuse and beatings, and he admitted with painful honesty the details of suffering rape at the hands of older boys. Out of desperation, Devlin escaped at one point, but was quickly caught and returned. As an adult, Devlin's years were marked by unemployment, broken relationships, impulsive decisions, and abuse of drugs and alcohol. He never rebounded from the trauma of his youth, dying homeless at age fifty-seven. His memoir is testament to the enduring damage reform schools inflicted upon thousands of young boys.

One of the most well-known alumni of the Lyman School for Boys was the infamous "Boston Strangler," Albert DeSalvo, who was believed to be responsible for raping and brutally murdering thirteen women in the Boston area during the early 1960s. Like many other Lyman boys, DeSalvo had lived in an extremely abusive home. In addition to suffering sexual abuse throughout his childhood, his father encouraged his criminal behavior by ordering him to steal for the family. At age thirteen, DeSalvo landed at Lyman after a series of petty thefts. On his first stint, he served approximately seven months before his release. Two years later he returned to Lyman for stealing cars. During that second term he successfully escaped, but like most Lyman escapees, had nowhere to run and was returned to Oak Cottage. Years later, DeSalvo spoke of his hatred for reform school and how it fueled his desire to join the Army to get as far away from Boston and Lyman as possible.

Bobby later served time with DeSalvo in Walpole State Prison. While Bobby and many other inmates believed he was not the Boston Strangler, it was clear he was a violent and sexually dangerous individual. In 1973, he was stabbed to death in Walpole.

Some reform school graduates immediately launched criminal careers. Vincent "Jimmy the Bear" Flemmi aspired to work in organized crime circles like his brother, Boston mob boss Steven "The Rifleman" Flemmi. Like his brother, the Bear had established his reputation for hair-trigger violence from an early age. Whether as a professional hitman or just to settle a personal problem, the Bear loved killing. In fact, his violence became so rampant that Boston's mafia underboss Jerry Anguilo personally called him in to warn that nobody was to be killed without prior approval. The Bear ignored the order and continued with his violent streak. Despite getting away with most of his crimes, he was eventually charged for the barroom murder of another street thug. After shooting the victim, the Bear decided to destroy the evidence by removing the head from the body and disposing of it. The head was never found, but he received a life sentence anyway. He died of a heroin overdose at Norfolk Prison in 1979.

Joe Barboza, Jimmy Flemmi, all your big killers in the Commonwealth, guess what? All went to reform schools. Reform schools did one of two things to young boys. It either broke them, or made them hard-core. These were the types of kids coming out of Lyman, your sociopaths and killers.

Flemmi's close personal friend, Joseph "the Animal" Barboza, also passed through Lyman School. Barboza, a fearless thug who committed numerous murders, earned his nickname after tearing off a man's ear with his teeth. In his early years, he was sent to Lyman for various charges of theft and vandalism. Barboza was quick to use his fists, and boys knew he was dangerous. At Lyman, he demonstrated that "might makes right" were words to live by, and his extreme violence achieved legend status while he was still just a teen. He went on to box professionally and became a gangland legbreaker, eventually being promoted to hitman. He later became famous for being the first underworld figure to publicly testify against organized crime, and some of his testimony sent innocents to prison (Barboza's untruthful testimony was actually protecting the true killer, his best friend Jimmy "the Bear" Flemmi). In 1976, Barboza was murdered in San Francisco while hiding in the Witness Protection Program. Barboza's famed attorney, F. Lee Bailey, commented upon his former client's death: "I don't think society has suffered a great loss."

At Lyman, kids could choose from a menu of criminal behavior: learning how to pick a lock, how to fight, how to run scams, how to construct makeshift weapons, were all readily available lessons. They shared information, showing off their knowledge and skill at various crimes, as if part of a professional workshop offering tips to stay ahead of the competition. The older boys taught Bobby how to steal cars, though he was not old enough to drive legally, and had no experience behind the wheel. They instructed him in how to shift a standard transmission, working the clutch and gas pedals, and he soon gained a basic understanding of an automobile's mechanisms and moving parts. Next, they showed him how to properly jimmy a lock and pop an ignition with a screwdriver. Soon after his first release from Lyman Bobby broke into a '48 Hudson. He got the wires crossed, found the right gear, got the engine sputtering and finally roaring. The Hudson surged down Leland Street, weaving from the far left of the road to the far right, zig-zagging all over, sideswiping parked cars all the way down the block. "I knew how to steal a car before I knew how to drive one, thanks to Lyman School," Bobby said.

Bobby learned from Lyman veterans how to craft a crude firearm called a "zip-gun" from a car radio antenna. He was shown that an antenna tube could be affixed to a handle grip, usually a block of hard wood or whatever was available to create the gun. The bullet would be held in place by an end cap which had a small hole to allow the firing pin, usually a nail, to pass through. The hammer was propelled by a rubber band, striking the firing pin, and was able to project a .22 caliber bullet. Though limited in power and accuracy, the velocity of the round was enough cause very real bodily harm.

Bobby was learning new criminal tricks, but the Lyman School for Boys was anything but a summer camp. The stories of reform schools he had heard about morphed from street folklore into painful realities which would now have to be lived. At first, Bobby didn't think Lyman was so bad; not as fun as running around Scollay Square, but also not as horrific as he'd heard. That impression was short-lived. Humiliation, degradation, and fear, though not obvious at first, permeated Lyman's grounds. It wasn't long before Bobby personally experienced the reality of reform school.

Now, these two guards there, this one guy named Ball, and this other big fat guy, obscenely fat. And I misunderstood whose name was who and I called the wrong guy Mr. Ball. Then I'm sitting down and he comes over afterward and he smacks me, hard. Just because I called him the wrong name. You want to cry, you got that little knot in your throat, but I wouldn't let the bastard see me cry. That was the starting process, the tough mindset you get in your head.

At Lyman, kids were made to fight one another at the guards' direction. In an attempt to make the bouts fair, fighters

31

were paired up according to a rough estimate of weight class and age. Interracial pairings were avoided (the black kids tended to be the more skilled fighters), whites usually fought whites and blacks fought blacks. One Saturday, Bobby didn't have a suitable white counterpart, and was matched up with a black kid of similar age, size, and weight. Bobby could fight fairly well despite his young age and small physique, and, although he didn't always win, he had learned a few tricks in the course of his street experience. He knew to never back down, and he surprised everyone when he beat his opponent. But the glory of the victory, and the candy prize, was short-lived. Minutes later, Bobby was told he had to fight another black kid who was slightly bigger than the first. Without time to rest, he stepped back into the makeshift ring, dodging punches and delivering his own. He was feeling winded and fatigue was taking over, but he managed to win again. He still wasn't done. The supervisor sent in another opponent, even bigger than the previous two. To his own surprise, Bobby also beat him. Now the supervisor was angry, and looked for any kid that could knock Bobby down. He found the biggest kid in the pool of fighters, a teen well above Bobby's weight class, and put him in the ring. By now, Bobby was exhausted from his previous fights, but he held on long enough to land a punch which sent the bigger kid tumbling backward over the benches. The other kids went crazy, cheering wildly at the underdog victory. Bobby was proud he was able to show heart, but especially satisfied because his win upset the supervisor.

Now, Ball comes downstairs and he calls the guard out. They're in the corridor and he doesn't realize that what he's saying to him in the corridor, we can hear it all, and he just laid into this guy. He said, 'First of all, you idiot, he called you by my name and you slapped him for using my name. You smack him unjustly and then you get him down here and he beats every one of your niggers.' All the kids were

32

shocked! He says, 'He beat all your niggers. You mess with this kid one more time, I will break your head.' And I was like, 'Wow!' I was immediately removed from there and sent to another cottage. At first I thought he was sticking up for me. But then I realized it was not the fights, the abuse that was the problem. The problem was that they failed to arrange a fight I would lose, to keep me in place. That was the problem.

Some of the earliest advice Bobby was given at Lyman was to stay out of the disciplinary house, Oak Cottage, at all costs. Oak was reserved for boys returning to Lyman after previous stays, escapees, and general discipline problems. While strict order was the general rule at Lyman, Oak operated under intense discipline at all times. The harshest housemasters were assigned there, and they seemed to relish the duty of controlling the boys.

During the week, boys followed the schedule that all Lyman kids did, with typical days spent doing farm work, planting, weeding, and other miscellaneous labor. Each day, boys were brought into the basement, a large barren space with lockers lining the four walls. Every boy was assigned a locker and was directed to sit in front of it on long wooden benches that ran parallel to the lockers. The kids were ordered to sit up straight, hands in lap, keeping eyes forward, often for hours at a time. Minutes passed like years, the restless boys unable to focus on anything but the excruciatingly slow passage of time. Even the toughest kids had trouble handling the rigors of Oak Cottage.

On weekends, the Oak Cottage basement was transformed into the unofficial entertainment area. As in some of the other cottages, weekend guards would have the boys take some low wooden benches and form a large square to create a makeshift boxing ring. The guards made up the fight cards each week by selecting kids who would be pitted against one another for bare knuckle fighting. The events always happened on Saturdays, as the kids didn't have weekday schedule obligations, and more importantly, the head administrators were off campus. Whether or not the chosen kids wanted to participate in the fight was irrelevant; if a boy was chosen he would get in the ring, no exceptions. Just about everyone was picked to fight at some point. The boys generally agreed that there was no shame in losing a fight if the defeated fighter showed heart. But if he took a beating without resistance, or showed any sort of cowardice, he would suffer a devastating loss of reputation. Once a boy was branded a coward the impression was nearly impossible to reverse. He had to live the rest of his time at Lyman with the stigma of weakness, and the disrespect and abuse that came with it. The fighting wasn't about glory; it was for survival.

Now in the units, when you're in there on the weekend, there's no canteen. So you don't get candy and all that good shit. They would come in with a big brown bag full of candy bars, and we would engage in fights. You fight, the winner gets a candy bar. I would fight Godzilla for a candy bar! When it got boring, they would pick a big guy. They'd say, 'Ok Dellelo, you fight him. If you win we'll give you three candy bars, if you lose we'll give you one candy bar.' Then you get up there and you'd beat the hell out of each other. The shower was there to wash the blood off and stuff.

On sunny days, Oak Cottage Supervisor Jackman brought kids out to Lyman's outer borders to work in the vegetable and fruit gardens. Jackman made it very clear to the boys that anyone who violated his strict rule against sampling would quickly regret the decision. Bobby tested the threat one day when he was assigned to pick parsnips. Being a lifelong city kid, he had never seen or even heard of a parsnip. His natural curiosity overwhelming his fear of Jackman's threats, he dusted one off, looked around, and popped it in his mouth. After his stolen sample, he whispered to another boy that the parsnip tasted just like a carrot. Jackman overheard him say this and approached menacingly. He said, "How do you know what they taste like unless you ate one?" It took Bobby a moment to realize he had just unwittingly ratted himself out. The little sample cost him a beating.

Cottages were typically managed by husband and wife teams known as Cottage Master and Matron. The couples permanently resided on site, often more interested in free housing than in helping boys.

In one Lyman Hall they had the Smiths, a husband and wife team. The wife was one real sick woman, she used to walk around in her bathrobe. When she walked by, if a kid looked at her she would go ballistic and scratch his face up with her nails. Really insane behavior. The whole place knew she was unpredictable. A black kid that was scrubbing the floors with me said, 'If she ever scratches at my face like that, I'm hitting her with this brush.' And I said, 'Me too. There's no way that crazy broad is going to do that to me. She's getting it and so is the husband.'

Attached to the same building as Lyman Hall was Chauncy Hall. They had this term called 'Chauncy Meats,' the kids that were sexually abused or sexually abused other kids; they kept them together over there for the most part. They were all throughout Lyman but the really outrageous ones were put in that unit. If you were over there, you were referred to as a 'Chauncy Meat.'

At one point I was in Westview. There's also a husband and wife team running things in there. The husband's in bad health and he's got a urine bag on him. He's called 'Beeky' and she's Edna. They're molesting kids at night; they get kids that they bring into the room. I mean real sick kinds of situations in there.

Periodically kids would push Beeky down the stairs. It was kind of funny, seeing this big fat guy tumbling down the stairs. One time he got pushed down the stairs, he gets to the bottom he says, 'Edna! Edna! They pushed me down the stairs!' She comes running down and her face looks like Ma Barker. I mean you were scared of her, not him. He was big, but she was the dangerous one. She comes in smacking kids in all kinds of directions, yelling, 'What are you doing here standing at the stop of the stairs! Get out of here you little bastards!' These were the people in charge of us.

For years, it was suspected that the couple had molested numerous boys. Beeky was known to summon a boy out of his bed to report to the headmaster's quarters late at night. Boys would never say what happened in there, but nobody doubted the rumors that circulated throughout the dorm rooms.

Bobby was eventually sent to Hillside, a cottage for the older boys at Lyman. One of the fill-in supervisors for weekends and holidays was a man they all called Tomahawk. He liked to read magazines and books at his desk while the boys sat on hard wooden benches for hours. If anyone disturbed him, the wrath was immediate.

The reason they called him Tomahawk, there's a wooden brush, it's about a good three feet long and it's really hard wood. The bristle end of it is thick it's got those big hard bristles on it. He kept it right by his desk. If he heard the smallest sound, he'd yell, 'Silence! No talking!' Now, kids can't be silent. So he would throw that brush hard at anyone who talked. That bastard was so accurate with that thing. He would split more kids' heads open.

He really got my attention one time. There's the big room, a corridor there, and there's another door where the shower room is. He's sitting way over at the desk in the corner there, he hears kids are in the shower room talking. He's in the corner at an angle, so you're only talking a space maybe a foot wide. He threw this wooden brush and that thing went right between those two doors and split the kid's head open in the shower room.

Crazy Dave ran Hillside Cottage full-time during week days. The kids truly believed he was mentally unstable. He looked for reasons to punish and was highly enthusiastic when he discovered one. Bobby gradually realized that most of the administrators silently agreed that Dave was a lunatic by watching the staff members' reactions to his behavior and overhearing subtle comments.

Crazy Dave would take all the kids out. You'd go picking blueberries or whatever. The way Lyman School is constructed, there's this big long rolling hill, and way over in this corner where the blueberries are they have a farm there with cows and things. Way over on the other side was a bunch of trees cut over in a bunch. When it was time to finish up, Crazy Dave would announce 'five minutes.' Now the last guy out has to pick strawberries, which means you gotta bend over, he takes his strap and gives you maybe five or six strappings on the ass for being the last guy. Not that you did anything wrong, just for being the last guy.

So when he called the five minutes, dummy me, I go over the bushes because it's like a short cut, but I fall in between the trees. So now I gotta climb out, and it takes a while before I'm on the back road. Then I hear, 'Alright Dellelo, come on out and pick the strawberries!' So I knew what the hell that meant. I look over there and I look down this road that leads

37

off into nowhere. Boom! I was gone. I'm running down the road.

Now the alarm gets set off. They got these guys, Poole and Jackman, they run the farm program and also run the disciplinary block. I don't know how they got there so fast because they didn't have radios then. They were a huge distance away; somehow they got onto the wire. Now, I heard the truck. I couldn't have gone 200 yards and they're on top of me. I ran into the swamp. And you got those big grass balls growing up out of the water and I was trying to stay on them. I finally trip on one and I go headfirst into all this green slime. It's a swamp. I hit that stuff and there's a big log, and I skid and I hit that. I sit up and turn around and I'm leaning against it. Jackman and Poole, they gotta be thirty feet away from me. But I'm inside the swamp, they're on the road. And then I looked at them, and the way they were looking, I knew they couldn't see me. I got all this slime all over me, I'm camouflaged. I'm against the tree, I'm just sitting there and I'm watching. They're looking over this way and they're looking that way. They walk away, and I was just totally amazed that they couldn't see me. I'm sitting there, right, then all of a sudden they run back again and they start again looking all around. You know it's a trick right? I said, 'Son of a bitch!' Now they go away, I hear them getting in the car, hear the car take off to check some other spot, and they boogie down to the other end of the road. So I go off into the swamp further and I got into clear water. I'm thinking I gotta get all this slime off of me. I was crossing, it was like a crusty surface, and underneath it was water. There was a river over this way, and there were ducks over there. As I was walking on this stuff I couldn't stop or it started caving in. So I said, 'Oh shit.' It was a river, I didn't know how deep it was. I had to keep walking and I was headed to where dry land was. But there's a river over here, if I go in I'm dead. I finally got up onto the dry land, and then there were tracks, so I followed the tracks now. I finally went down on the main road and as I'm walking up on the main road, the cops are waiting there. I'm in country though, in farmland. So I turn and keep running, we run across this big field. I reach a fast moving river, it's a good fifteen or twenty feet across. So that blocks me, I get caught.

I wasn't going to let Crazy Dave hit me again, so I ran. It was just an awesome experience, but that gets me sent to the disciplinary unit again.

At night, after lights out, kids could be heard crying in their beds across the open dormitory-style rooms. One boy would be talking in his sleep, crying out from bad dreams. Others would be crying, from loneliness and frustration, struggling to not be heard by the others. Another would be groaning, forced into sex by an older and stronger boy. Luckier boys were able to let their thoughts take them away from Lyman, imagining a life drastically different from the current situation. Despite bad attitudes and tough-guy posturing that occurred all day long, the dark was always the ultimate equalizer. There, everyone was scared and alone.

Bobby had proven himself during his time in reform school. It became general knowledge that he may be small but he could fight, and was not to be messed with—Lyman School for Boys had turned him hard. Lyman taught Bobby both how to establish himself and how to resist his captors. Later, at Walpole State Prison, those lessons became crucial to his survival.

Lyman School gave me a deep hatred of authority because the authority figures there were very abusive. I hadn't resolved the power concept yet. I mean I knew that they were the authority, they were in control, and they were in power. But they were also

39

very abusive and I didn't know how to fight back. It gets confusing for a kid because there were some people you met there that were nice but most were evil and mean-spirited people. It's real screwed up, mixed messaging. I hated them for that.

When I came out of reform school, I had the most profound hatred for cops. If I saw a cop walking down the street, he was my enemy. I hated that abuse of authority; I was socialized off the scale.

When you went to reform school you were screwed for the rest of your life, pretty much so. When I went to Concord, 35% of the people that I met in Concord I knew from reform schools. When I got into Walpole State Prison, 35-45% of the people there I knew from reform schools. Lyman School wasn't good for much, but it was a great place to get ready for a future at Walpole State Prison.

CHAPTER THREE

Boys came and went through Lyman long after Bobby was released for good. The revolving door of recidivism continued to spin at the state reform schools and abuses continued without raising much public concern. Reform schools lumbered forward, to the disservice of both troubled kids and society at large. The serious issues of juvenile corrections were typically met with public disinterest, and the work which needed to be done was perceived as too daunting to be realistically pursued. Nobody wanted to take on the challenge.

Not until 1969, when Massachusetts Governor Francis Sargent appointed Dr. Jerome Miller to serve as commissioner of the fledgling Department of Youth Services. From the start, Miller was an outsider. He arrived from out of state, unaware of the rampant problems which plagued the state system: nepotism, incompetence, inefficiency, corruption. Not that he would have cared had he known; he made it clear from the beginning that he rejected the status quo and refused to allow its continuation on his watch.

Miller's vision was to move away from the traditional punishment model and transform juvenile corrections into a more humane and genuinely rehabilitative process. He believed troubled kids must be handled with dignity, fairness, and compassion to produce positive results, and he personally went into the schools and spoke with boys one on one, listening carefully to their concerns, and learning much in those conversations. Miller understood that each individual boy was unique, with different issues and needs, and would necessarily require diverse approaches and individualized attention— something enormously challenging, but not impossible. In his view, a simple formula could be applied to create positive change by using patience and perseverance to find good ideas and then apply them.

Almost immediately upon his arrival in Massachusetts, Miller began to alienate many and endear few, and he knew the challenges before him would require difficult decisions which would probably create an even larger pool of enemies. However, Miller was committed to the task. He wanted real reform and was willing to do whatever it took. But he was also fully aware of potential roadblocks, and he did expect some level of resistance— he was not an unrealistic man.

However, Miller's steadfast refusal to play politics would trigger a powerful resistance that even he never could have anticipated. He soon learned his biggest obstacle to reform was the existence of the institution itself. In a state well known for its overly bureaucratic agencies, Miller viewed the Massachusetts juvenile corrections system as the embodiment of institutional problems. From the very beginning, the Lyman School for Boys itself was born of political influence, and quickly became the prototypical state-run institution, an unnecessarily large bureaucracy staffed with under-qualified workers filling patronage positions, attracting employees with political connections but no commitment toward juvenile corrections. In return, the school's allegiance to its political friends created a mutually beneficial situation in which everyone stood to gain— except for the kids sent there.

Alternative programs which threatened the reform school system's stability were never seriously considered for implementation, even when such alternatives were clearly in a child's best interest, and even when the institution had consistently proven to be a failure on so many levels. Occasionally, progressive programs were allowed to develop, mostly at the token level and paying only lip service to the notion of reform. Those programs were typically short-lived due to a lack of funding, resources, and interest. Programs that did manage to launch were never quite adequate to produce significant changes in the system itself. Juvenile initiatives at the time tended to serve the juveniles who were easiest to help, *i.e.*, kids who did not belong in reform schools in the first place. They were not designed to assist the neediest kids and most difficult cases—true delinquents—who would most benefit from services. The failure of these programs allowed for the outdated obedience and punishment model of the reform schools to continue unchallenged. Jerome Miller found this completely unacceptable.

Miller disliked how juvenile punishment applied disproportionately to poor and minority children. Troubled children who were fortunate enough to have parents with money (usually white kids), almost always seemed to be able to avoid reform school. They were sent to anywhere but reform school: to group homes, work programs, private schools, therapeutic counseling, and other unrestrictive programs. Poor minority kids committing similar offenses, always seemed to have a bed ready for them at one of the locked facilities.

In Miller's view, this disparity revealed the unspoken explanation as to why juvenile institutions were so resistant to change. In order for society to distance itself from the difficult work involved in juvenile rehabilitation, the offenders must be viewed as irredeemable, too far gone to turn their lives around. As long as they were consistently perceived as criminals, their punishment could always be justified. To address the real issues of social class and racism would require caring, dedication, time, and funding—all resources the public didn't want to squander on criminals. Reform school superintendents soon realized that the juvenile recidivism rate was extremely high, but instead of analyzing the reasons and looking for meaningful solutions, they began to deflect blame away from the institutions. Reform schools were doing their job, they said; it was the *kids* who were the problem. Bad kids would never change and would fail no matter how much the institution tried to help them. Since they were beyond redemption, it would be foolish to create new programs within juvenile corrections, a grand and expensive exercise in futility. Therefore the best, and cheapest, thing to do was to punish. And that's what exactly the reform schools did.

Miller was disgusted by the traditional reform school's heavy-handed approach to dealing with kids. He believed this counterproductive model thrived because of the institution's complete lack of accountability; there was no oversight, no uniform standards set by the state. Furthermore, the institution operated without transparency, intentionally out of the public eye. Miller believed there would be outrage if people knew what actually occurred in these institutions, and changes would be sure to follow.

Miller considered dozens of new approaches to achieve his vision of "reforming the reform schools." First and foremost, it was essential for reform school staff and administrators to be more compassionate, so he started there. He created a new rule which stated that if a boy was put into isolation, the staff member sending him there would be required to stay with the boy in isolation until the time was over. Implementing this type of accountability effectively ended the use of isolation from that point forward. It did not, however, change the negative attitudes held by many reform school employees. Miller could create new guidelines, but mandating ideals of respect, kindness, and compassion was beyond the reach of any rule or policy. The change would have to be cultural.

Miller's approach did not win him many friends; in fact, it further alienated him from those he sought to lead. He did not hesitate to publicly criticize individuals and specific groups that stood in the way of juvenile reform, thus managing to eventually anger everyone around him. Judges, law enforcement, state employees' unions, and even his own allies and staff all began to view Miller as trouble and wished him gone. He willfully lacked interest in learning the rules of the political game and ignored those who were key players. Completely disregarding the power structure and its inner workings may have freed him to be publicly outspoken, make bold choices, and take extreme action, but it also exposed him to attack from every angle. Miller's style was so blunt that he not only endangered his programs' chances of success but placed himself on track toward professional suicide. He continued forward anyway.

The institution, Miller realized, was so firmly embedded that it would simply continue forward, passively resisting change, and eventually outlasting him. This worried Miller, as he understood that any amount of ideas, money, or resources committed to the changes could only endure as long as his tenure lasted; the next commissioner would likely revert to the political game. Miller became frustrated, and over time, he came to the conclusion that the existing framework was irretrievably broken. Given that fact, he had to consider what was possible, if any plausible solutions were available. While he pondered many ideas, his mind kept returning to a simple but radical idea: abolish each and every reform school in the state.

Miller couldn't find any workable ways to remedy the continuous failures of the institutions, and if they couldn't be made caring and decent, then he saw no purpose in their existence. He reasoned that when something is so fully broken and beyond the ability to be salvaged, it must be discarded and replaced with something entirely new. He knew his abolition idea was extreme, and was certain to be controversial, but the more thought he gave it, the less outlandish it seemed. With the reform schools gone, change would be inevitable. And judging from the current state of affairs, Miller reasoned, things could only get better.

At the center of Miller's vision of authentic reform was the notion of individualized treatment for every child. Miller knew punishment alone didn't work; compassion and humanity must serve as guiding principles if a child was to have a genuine opportunity to change for the better. He believed that in order to truly rehabilitate and help a juvenile, a qualified professional must thoroughly examine a child's background, giving due consideration to any relevant factors when developing a course of treatment for each individual child. He ardently believed kids could not all be treated the same due to their varying backgrounds, emotional states, mental and physical health, intelligence levels, and cultural leanings. He determined the institutional structure could not and would not change toward that end. As Miller deliberated his options for reform, it became clear there was only one choice.

And so, one by one, Miller closed all seven reform schools in the state, with the last of the schools being unceremoniously shuttered one afternoon in the fall of 1972. Even still, Miller was unable to claim victory. To spite him, the legislature refused to divert funds earmarked for juvenile corrections—the funds reserved for reform schools—to Miller's programs. Instead, taxpayer money continued to fund full salaries of reform school employees who reported daily to empty institutions with no work to do.

The closing of the reform schools did not ignite an explosion in the crime rate as many critics had predicted. In

46

time, statistics proved Miller's critics wrong by showing there was no significant impact on the overall crime rate. Miller addressed the "myth of the violent teenager," where he demonstrated how statistics regarding violent juvenile crime were wildly distorted and used to justify the necessity of reform schools. Citing high recidivism, he pointed out that without true reform, locking kids up failed to reduce crime. Though crime statistic data backed his theory, he was ultimately dismayed that his idea of closing reform schools did not spread. Other states continued following the institutional status quo, despite evidence that closing such schools would save money and benefit kids, without leading to a rise in crime.

When the schools closed, Miller saw to it that the kids were placed in any program determined to be worthwhile for that specific child. They were dispersed to specialized schools, group homes, foster family care, and wellness programs: basically anywhere that was not a reform school. Miller believed if he could remove the juvenile from the institution, they could connect with much-needed sources of compassion that alternative programs offered. The institution, as is, Miller believed, was hopeless.

Jerome Miller surprised everyone by not just talking about reform but by actually taking bold action. At its core, Miller's idea was based in common sense; the reform schools, in both concept and practice, were broken beyond repair and needed to be abandoned out of necessity. He acted despite strong opposition and continually refused to succumb to politics as usual, ultimately at the expense of his career in Massachusetts. Though forced out, Miller had left his mark on juvenile corrections, raising the possibility that reform schools were incapable of humane treatment, and that their closure would not jeopardize public safety.

People have no idea the favor Jerome Miller did for the state of Massachusetts when he closed the reform schools. They served no useful purpose, they were abusive. Being sent to reform school was like a bug getting stuck in fly paper. Once you were caught up in it, you were never getting out.

CHAPTER FOUR

Lyman School for Boys may have been behind him, but a teenage Bobby could see few legitimate prospects for his future. Going back to school seemed out of the question. Living at home with his mother was unappealing, and the idea of getting a real job even less so. Instead, he roved the city streets and became a full-time criminal, doing what he did best: breaking and entering. He embraced the lifestyle and enjoyed the challenges of making a living by planning a job, outsmarting the cops, undercutting his competition, and circumventing security systems. He liked to plan his actions carefully, leaving no trace of his presence. Roaming throughout downtown Boston in the early morning hours, he carefully studied the alleyways, fire escapes, rooftops, backdoors, secret entrances, and windows. He spent hours examining buildings for angles of entry, considering possible escape routes, noting connections between the buildings, and assessing valuables located therein. Working alone was his preference, where planning and execution were entirely his own. Nobody else could get in the way, and, even better, he didn't have to share his take.

Over time, he gained greater and greater confidence in his abilities, and was undeterred by the vague notion of getting busted. Even if he were caught, he reasoned, he'd been inside before and knew how to handle himself. His abilities and experience were developing to the point where Bobby had found his comfort zone.

I tried a legitimate job for a couple weeks. Me and my buddy Nicky when we got out of reform school we had a job at Turkleson Machine Co. factory. They made Revlon fingernail polish, the covers. That machine used to burn me. I said, 'That's it, I quit.' I had a check for $24.00, I went up and told my *partner, I said, 'I'll meet you at the Palace.' Went over there, cashed the check with my uncle, he owned the Palace. Cashed my check and drank that thing up. By the time Nicky got there I was shitfaced. I had burn circles with a dot in the middle from that goddamn machine. Then I did some roofing and waterproofing, that was pure labor for like $20.00 a day. That wasn't money. I could make more than that in a night going through the buildings. That was easy money, plus it was my own thing. It was just me and my brain against this building.*

By now, Bobby's internal criminal radar was constantly on, always searching for opportunities. Sometimes he found them in unlikely places. By thinking like a criminal he learned that he could sometimes co-opt legitimate information for criminal purposes. A visit to the local Better Business Bureau office provided a variety of pamphlets informing the public about consumer scams, rip-offs, and fraudulent business practices for citizens to be aware of. Bobby saw a different angle, intently studying the information as detailed how-to instruction manuals for scamming. He would read through the literature until he thoroughly understood how the gig was set up and executed. When he felt he had mastered the information, he'd head to Scollay Square where he'd run bait-and-switch routines, shortchange scams, and other types of fraud. "I got a lot of my ideas reading those things," he said.

Those small time scams were easy, but always resulted in short money. Bobby wanted bigger scores. He set about prowling downtown streets in the middle of the night, finding unsecured fire escapes, unlocked doors and windows, disabled alarm systems, and low police presence. Entering buildings, he found valuables and cash to pocket and slip away into the night. Without signs of forced entry, missing items often went unnoticed for some time; by the time a break was reported, there was very little to connect him to the scene. When coming into contact with new people, Bobby sized them up either as a mark, a potential ally, or maybe a future business partner. In time, his network developed to the point where opportunities had become plentiful, enough so that he enjoyed the luxury of cherry picking when and where he moved. For a time, he hustled and lived well. But when he looked to make even larger scores, he understood a much higher risk factor would be involved.

"My biggest mistake was picking up a gun," Bobby said.

* * *

At eighteen years old, Bobby's criminal life took a new direction. Entering a liquor store in Boston, he pointed a gun at the clerk and demanded the money from the register. But as he was in the middle of the robbery, customers kept entering the store. Each time someone new came in, he took their wallet and directed them at gunpoint inside the walk-in refrigerator. A small crowd was building in there as customers kept coming, watching Bobby trying to resume the robbery. Finally, he was able to get out of the store. Despite the interruptions in the plan, he got away with cash in hand, and he spent the couple hundred bucks quickly. However, it was only a matter of time before one of the many eyewitnesses at the scene identified him from a photo array of mugshots at the police station, and he was arrested a short time later for armed robbery.

Bobby waived his right to a jury trial in the hope of avoiding a long stretch in prison. The state was reluctant to grant any sort of leniency due to his criminal history, but because his prior record was purely juvenile matters, those crimes could not be taken into consideration in his adult armed robbery case. Since there were eyewitnesses available, trial would be far too risky, so Bobby entered a guilty plea and took a five-indefinite sentence to be served in Concord. His lawyer said it was a good deal; after serving six months he'd be eligible for parole and wasn't likely to serve more than a total of one year, maximum.

Bobby knew things would be different this time. He was now a legal adult and was headed for an adult prison. No more judge's warnings, programs, probationary periods. No more Lyman School for Boys. Now, he was going to have to do his time as a man.

Upon arrival at Concord State Prison, Bobby was pleased, and a little surprised, to see so many familiar faces. This was a significant benefit, as many new inmates arrived knowing few, if any, people at all. A fledgling inmate lacking allies or a mentor to guide him through the complicated culture of prison was at a major disadvantage. Having a network of friendships and acquaintances in place from the first day gave Bobby automatic good standing with key individuals, including prison staff. Another advantage was his reputation from Lyman School. In the men's prison where stories about new guys traveled fast, it was helpful that some older inmates who knew him passed on the word that he'd become hard in reform school. *Leave him alone. He will go after you.* Predatory inmates tended to look for weak, unconnected inmates to victimize. Bobby was neither.

Still, he wasn't untouchable, and while he knew that prison had some perks and levels of comfort available, he also knew he'd have to compete for them like everyone else. He was determined not to become one of the men living a daily nightmare while incarcerated, and would use the skills he'd learned to survive. Lyman School taught him how to fight, how to use violence to his advantage, how to manipulate individuals. Those lessons would serve him well as he began serving his first adult prison sentence.

We were in the Industrial School for Boys, in Shirley, MA. I escaped from Shirley in '58, went to Jersey in '58-'59. I stole the deputy superintendent's car when I escaped. I was in Jersey and then I came back here for some stupid reason. The hotel I was working in New Jersey, these people had hotels in Florida. So the season was ending in Jersey, and I was going to go to Florida with them. I was the bell captain in Jersey, and the hotel that they had in Florida, I would have been the bell captain down there, which was awesome. So I came back here to see my mother and family before I went down there and when I came back I got spotted and busted. So that puts me in Shirley, they put me in Cottage Nine.

My good friend Nicky Yasaian's in there too, we knew each other from Lyman, and at this point were pretty tight. We had a plan. There were just two guards for Cottage Nine. These two guards watching over us are punks, and they had the keys to get out of there; they're carrying the keys to the front door. They also got their car keys in their pocket. So we were going to snatch these guys, take their keys, lock them up, take their cars, and get the hell out of Dodge.

We should have done it right away, but we decided we're going to do it at night after supper, after everyone gets some food in their belly. We'd snatch these clowns and we go. Unfortunately, we get ratted out.

It was funny, the superintendent was a guy named Hastings. And they're not happy with me because I had stolen the deputy superintendent's car, put it in the snow bank in Boston. So he calls me, they got us all sitting down in a big room, and they bring me into his office. He slapped me; it was like a little bitch, touching you on the face. He says, 'Now, what was this all about?' And you say something about

53

his mother or some damn thing, and he screams, 'Get him out of here!' So upstairs in this place, there are these cages which were like mesh screens. They had two 100 watt light bulbs that were on 24 hours a day with just a mattress on the floor. I think you might have had a blanket, no pillow. So they had us there, and they transfer us from there because when they got the story of what we're going to do, then there's no way they could have left us. They can't keep us in these rooms forever, so they're going to have to bring us back downstairs. We're not scared of them. The thing is we waited too long. We were going to wait until night because it's really active around there during the day and stuff, and it's not as active at night. That was the only thing that saved them. They would never let the two of us out...there were like three or four of us that were like the leaders of the thing. They had us up in the dens. They would never let any of us out together. They said forget it, transfer them to Bridgewater.

Now Bridgewater, the Institution for Juvenile Guidance, what a hell of a name. It was a ninety-five man joint and it had a twelve-foot wall around it. You were too young for Concord and too dangerous for the open institutions. So they put you there. In there, we were pretty tough kids. You're supposed to do like nine months there, I kept fucking up so I think I did about eighteen. Couple incidents we had there, couple fights and stuff we had there. The reputation that you built there went with you when you went to Concord and whatnot. Reform schools are a pipeline to prison. You land in them, you're at a higher degree of probability that you're hitting the state prison. You're going back to jail, you're going to a nut house, but you're not going to stay in open society. It damages you that bad.

It was a foregone conclusion me and Nicky would partner up when he got out. When I got out of the Institution for Juvenile Guidance, he was there. He didn't really know me. You could send in clothes and cigarettes and stuff. So I asked him what he wanted for clothes. He wanted these snapjack shoes, pointed shoes, the things snapped down, and the pants with the pegs and all that stuff. That was the style in those days, the things that made you super cool in the Institute for Juvenile Guidance. He gave it to me but he wasn't expecting it to come. So I tell him it's going to take me a minute to make a little money, but as soon as I get it I'll send them in to you. I guess other people do that game with you, 'Oh yeah I'll send you some stuff,' but they don't ever do it. So you don't really expect it.

Now I get out, I never went out with the idea of not stealing. That was not part of my reality. So I got out, I did my Boston routine. I hit all my buildings as normal. Then I bought all the stuff Nicky asked for and had it sent in to him. Two cartons of cigarettes and all these clothes in a box. I did what I said I was going to do, that blew him away. When he gets out, I was living on Seaver Street at the time, he hooks up with me.

Like Bobby, Nicky was tough and had a reputation of his own upon arrival at Concord. They both understood this was a men's prison; reputation alone would not be enough, and they'd have to be willing to back it up at any time. Not only did they have to be willing to fight, they had to be willing to fight immediately upon the slightest provocation. Bobby and Nicky agreed, as a rule, to never bully others. But if anyone tried to push them around, their policy was to defend quickly and violently. They wanted to send the message to all potential predators: *Leave us alone.* "We applied the golden rule from Lyman," Bobby said. "Never be a pussy."

Me and my partner Nicky, we used take the prison overalls, you wet them and then you rub them. It's called dry pressing. You just keep rubbing it until it's dry; it puts the crease in there. It's better than ironing the damn things, they stay like that forever. Nicky was on the table ironing and this big black guy was claiming to the other prisoners that this was his table. Nicky's unaware of that. And he's doing the press, and the guy comes over and says, 'Hey motherfucker, that's my table.' That's all he got to say. The pair of pants was over his head and Nicky was beating his ass. Now, it gets broken up, and we all head to the yard. All the black prisoners were saying to him, 'You're not gonna let that honky beat you up,' and things like that. We go out to the yard, me and Nicky are packing, I mean we are sworded up, and they see that. That's not what they're interested in. The guy says, 'Whoa, wait a minute; this does not need to go there. I was disrespectful to you. I should explain the situation to you without acting like that. What you did was the right thing to do. You acted like a man and I can't argue with that.' And it's all set. Men dealing with men and it gets resolved. He was a man and he used that method of dealing. You can't be polite to people in prison, they take advantage of that. So sometimes you've got to be really aggressive. And the guy was aggressive at the wrong time, and Nicky straightened him out. Then it ended up coming to a head, but everyone acted like men and said, 'Hey we don't gotta go this way.'

In the early years of their prison lives, Bobby and Nicky made no special effort to become part of an established group or form any particular alliances. They reasoned that the partnership they had was strong and effective, so expanding beyond that was unnecessary. Recruiting others into the fold wouldn't provide much of a gain, and they definitely didn't want to pay tribute or share a cut of anything they earned or stole. If anything, joining forces with others was more likely to bring on more problems and potential betrayals. Many new inmates joined an existing group for the benefit of protection, but the idea of becoming subservient to someone else held no appeal to them. They didn't want to be followers. Bobby said, "I wasn't going to stab someone I had no beef with because someone told me I had to." From their perspectives, the partner arrangement felt right and there was no compelling reason to change it. They'd leave well enough alone for the time being.

Like everyone else, Bobby and Nicky were placed on the new line when they first arrived. One afternoon Nicky said, "Hey Bobby, look at this," producing a paper bag. Bobby peered in and saw it was loaded with candy. He smiled, knowing Nicky pulled some strings to get the contraband. They had a laugh over it, but then Nicky seemed concerned, abruptly stashing the bag away. He said, "The wiseguys are gonna give us a problem over this."

A core group of wiseguys and some of their fringe tough guys hung around the prison drill shack, a domain they had controlled for years. They were all assigned to work there, supposedly supervising men assigned to groundskeeping duties. Nobody ever did any actual work. Though prison jobs were supposed to be open to any inmate, only certain men were allowed to work there; nobody bothered applying unless invited to do so. The wiseguys there, as on the street, did not appreciate anyone in their territory making money or possessing valuables without paying tribute to them. Failure to do so was a serious offense, a sign of disrespect which carried harsh consequences.

Soon enough, they heard about the candy bag, and sent an underling to the new line to see Bobby about the situation. With his arms crossed, he motioned toward the bag with his chin.

"The guys in the drill shack want some of that."

"Oh yeah...?"

"Well, where's my half? Gimme my end. Now."

The situation turned out just as Nicky had predicted: a shakedown. But on principle, Bobby couldn't simply hand over the bag. This was his beloved candy. In Lyman, he literally fought for it; he certainly wasn't going to let some low-level thug bully him like a frightened school boy. Bobby remained motionless, saying nothing. It was clear the bag would stay with him. After a moment, the thug's expression changed from indifference to contempt, but he left without making a scene. As he exited Bobby's cell, he said over his shoulder, "You have to come by the drill shack by one o'clock, right after chow." Bobby understood the implied ultimatum—bring the candy or else.

This would be a major test, and he had to get it right. Because he was new to prison, he had to be very careful in the way he chose to handle this situation, as the outcome would have serious long-term repercussions. Unlike most new liners though, Bobby did not feel intimidated by the threat. In fact, the threat made him angry. In his mind, there was no decision to make. *Never be a pussy.* "I wanted to show them who they were fucking with," he said.

Bobby found Nicky, quickly informed him of the situation, and instructed him to get two toothbrushes right away. Nicky brought them back to Bobby's cell where they filed the handles down to sharp points, forming lethal picks. One o'clock came and went. They then went to Nicky's cell with their weapons, sat and waited. When neither of them showed up to their scheduled appointment at the drill shack, the annoyed representative came looking for them to summon them to the shack. Then, the meeting would not be about the candy or who owned it. The wiseguys had already decided they would be taking all of the candy, and the only issue left to address was an appropriate punishment for Bobby and Nicky.

We grab the two brushes; we file them down into two picks. I'm standing on the tier, this idiot comes up the stairs. He walks into Nicky's cell, I come in right behind him. Before he can think about it, he's got two picks on each side of his throat. We got him up against the wall. He says, 'Wait a minute! Wait a minute! You don't understand! I don't mean anything by this! I'm just being a good guy! I know you guys are ok guys!' Shit the bed, right? Now, that was our introduction to Concord. Immediately that goes out across the wires. There's this big tough guy, got jacked up by these two young kids. We were kids, but we were tough kids.

Bobby remained vigilant after the incident, never dropping his guard—that was how people got hurt. He assumed there would be repercussions for defying established inmates' orders but, to his surprise, nothing came of the incident. Apparently, the story went around faster and wider than he expected. Word went around that Bobby and Nicky were not good targets. For predators, it made no sense to fight tough kids, as they'd be risking their own reputations, and maybe even getting hurt. There were plenty of other young inmates that, if pressed, would fold without resistance.

A solid reputation in prison not only provided some protection, but brought about business opportunities as well. Before Concord, Bobby and Nicky were partying regularly with a couple of sisters, boozing and dancing all over the city. They weren't serious girlfriends, just a pair of girls with drugs and sex as common interests. The girls had an older brother doing time in Concord, and he sent a message to Bobby that he wanted to meet.   Nicky sensed trouble and insisted on coming along. Without any further discussion, they "suited up," wearing loose, heavy fabric clothes both for protection and to conceal the weapons they carried.   They sought out the older brother and guardedly introduced themselves.   He got straight to the point. He said, "Listen, I know you're going with my sisters.   Don't misunderstand me, you're cool with me.   If there's anything I can do for you, anything you need, I'll get you whatever you need." He had done a background check, and they'd been thoroughly vouched for by reform school acquaintances.   He also heard they jacked up the drill shack tough guy and were unafraid of the possible consequences. The respect had made them feel validated, that they were earning a place in Concord.   Had a background check revealed any vulnerability, they would have been seriously hurt.   But since they now had credibility, the older inmate saw an opportunity for mutual benefit, and used the outside social connection with his sisters as an opening to forge a prison business connection.   Others would soon follow, offering Bobby and Nicky a piece of all different types of prison business: drugs, food, weapons, and whatever else came along.

Bobby and Nicky could never entirely rest upon reputation, as Concord's rotating cast of inmates meant they still would face occasional challenges.   A man named Steve came into the prison and was instantly perceived as a classic psychopath.   He looked the part, never breaking character with his dead-eye stare, aggressive physical posturing, and over-the-top tough talk. Steve only spoke to a few individuals and refused to engage in even basic small talk with most everybody.   He had an aura of mystery and secrecy which seemed to compound his image as a dangerous loner.   Most inmates bought the act.

For a time, Steve worked with Bobby running the looms, with loud bobbins shuttling back and forth to create clothing, blankets, and other textile products. They generally ignored one another, but one day they had a disagreement over some minor issue, and started to exchange words. They stopped working and headed for each other, but the fight was stopped when guards stepped in. They exchanged glares, silently agreeing that the situation was not resolved yet.

So we're in the dining room and your tiers all sit at specific tables. We're sitting down, and I shouldn't have got up. On the table they have both hot water and cold water. The hot pitcher is tea or coffee and the cold one is either milk or ice water. A friend of mine, Pat, is sitting across from me. You call down 'hot water' or 'cold water' and you pass the pitcher down, and another guy will pass it down and then you have the pitcher. But this Steve kid's a real piece of work. The pitcher is between him and his lover on their side of the table. So I mean, you gotta pass it down because the guy across won't be able to reach and get it. Pat asked a couple times to pass the pitcher down, and this kid is just paying no mind. It's on my side of the table, so Pat asks me to get him the pitcher of tea. I should have stayed sitting down. I get up, walk over there. To this day I don't know what he says. I got the pitcher in my hand and I hit him dead in the face and I crown him with the fucking pitcher right there in the dining room. Screws are all over the place. He jumps up, now we're slipping on the tea. We go over on the table behind us and he's on top of me. I grab him by the throat, lift him up and hit him. Now the guards are on top of us. I grab his shirt and twist it. They got his arms behind him and they got his legs. They got me around the waist, and they got one of my legs up. But I got him by the shirt and I got my head down so they can't get my head. And they're holding him like this and I'm just blasting him while they're trying to pull us apart. They finally get us separated, he's all

61

fucked up. I'm hopping down the line on one foot with like eight guards on me; they got my arms, my legs, my head. And just down the end of the dining room there's a corridor and that's what they call the plant, the hole. So they bring us in there.

He's standing over there, I'm standing over here. He's all bloody and I don't have a scratch on me. There's like an army of guards. He mumbles something, looking at me, trying to be menacing. And I don't say a word, I just start heading for him. This big screw steps in and says 'Bobby...don't.' He turns to other guy and says, 'You, shut the fuck up. Get him upstairs.' They bring me downstairs and throw me in a cell. I think I did like three or four months in the plant for that. And then I came out and he's looking for peace. Because now, you're in the dining room, you don't care, all these screws running, I'm still beating the shit out of him, ignoring them. All the guys are watching and saying, 'Look at this kid!' So you get a reputation.

Even guards and administrative staff, who typically disrespected all inmates, gave Bobby his due. He realized this once after a three-day isolation stint for a minor infraction. When his time was up, he was required to attend a hearing before the disciplinary board. He explained to them that the guard assigned to Plant Nine had it out for him. In the past, they had many verbal altercations and disagreements over small matters. He learned from the board that he had received a write-up for defacing prison property, for scratching his initials into the isolation cell door. Now, Bobby knew he was being targeted. He never scratched his initials anywhere. But if a guard wrote up an infraction, it was almost always accepted over the inmates' word, and they were powerless to fight back. A minor offense like defacement of property was very easy for guards to fabricate, and the cost to the inmate was harsh in comparison, usually a few days in isolation. So Bobby finished his three days but was then immediately sent back in for two more days, despite his protests. At the conclusion of his fifth day, he was back in front of the disciplinary board. Now, the same guard claimed that Bobby had removed the identification number tag from the prison issued blanket and had written him up again. Bobby couldn't believe the guard would continue the game for that long. When Bobby entered the room, the deputy looked up and saw him. He pointed at the door and yelled, "Out! Out! Get your ass out of here!" Bobby spun around and left, thinking, *Oh man, I'm never getting out of this place.* He was told to wait out in the hall while the discipline board held a conference. A guard in the hall made small talk with Bobby, and after a long time finally said, "Ok, I'm going to find out what the hell's going on in there." He entered the room and Bobby waited, knowing that another trip to the plant was inevitably coming. He wondered how long it would be this time. The guard returned a few minutes later, grinning widely.

"This is my first time ever seeing this."

"Oh, damn. What now?"

"You just got thrown out of the segregation unit!"

The guard who wrote up Bobby was also thrown out of the segregation unit. The deputy's reputation of "tough but fair" was well known, and Bobby thought he wasn't a bad guy, which basically was the highest accolade an administrator could receive from an inmate. He understood how respect was a two-way street, and acknowledged Bobby's reputation, saying, "Look, stop busting balls. Settle the fuck down or I'm going to bury you in the plant." Bobby didn't take it as a threat, just a simple statement of fact from a no-nonsense deputy. He liked that the deputy held both inmates and guards to the same standard. It

63

was *fair*. That policy struck Bobby as reasonable one, especially in prison where fairness and logic were largely absent.

* * *

After one year in Concord, Bobby was up for parole consideration. Just before his hearing, he received the surprising news that the DA's office was hitting him with a new case, an indictment for armed robbery of the Commodore Hotel in Cambridge. He'd been looking forward to being released, and wasn't happy that the indictment was withheld until his imminent release from Concord. Nicky was also indicted as a co-defendant in the robbery.

Ben Chessky was known as the "fix-it" criminal defense lawyer in town. He'd built a reputation as a capable lawyer in Middlesex County, the man who could be counted on to negotiate a very good deal for his clients. He so often represented underworld figures that he was viewed as a sort of in-house counsel for organized crime. His services were highly sought after, and he was hard to reach. Bobby's mother dated a number of connected men over the years, and her boyfriend at the time was a former Chessky client. He made some calls, and Chessky agreed to represent Bobby in the new case. He reached out to the handling prosecutor and worked out a potential plea bargain. Finally, he was able to secure a decent deal, a three-to-five year sentence. If Bobby insisted on going to trial, Chessky explained, he'd serve at least a decade if convicted. Bobby was happy with the deal and agreed to do the time.

Just one day before the plea was to be finalized before a judge, two inmates escaped from the Middlesex County Jail in Cambridge, shooting and killing a sheriff in the process. Chessky contacted Bobby with the bad news.

"We've had some bad luck. Those guys that killed Sheriff Robertson yesterday, the escapees? That killed our deal. There's no three-to-five anymore."

"Oh shit. What can you get us?"

"The best I can get is six-to-ten."

"Six-to-ten? We'll only do one-third before parole, that's two years and change."

"That's right."

"Yeah, we'll take that."

Bobby couldn't believe that was all the time he was going to get. It wasn't as nice as the original three-to five-deal, but still a very good deal considering both the charges and his prior record. Bobby and Nicky were brought in to court from Concord to finalize the agreement on the record. The judge was businesslike and stern. He asked if they understood they had a right to a jury trial and that they were waiving that right. He asked if they understood that they had the right to have the Commonwealth prove the charges against them beyond a reasonable doubt. He asked if the facts as presented by the prosecutor, if presented to a jury, could result in a guilty finding. He asked if they were under any the influence of any drugs or alcohol. He asked if they were pressured in any way to plead guilty. He asked if they were satisfied with their legal representation in the matter. They answered yes or no at the appropriate times, and the judge was satisfied that both young men were knowingly and willingly pleading guilty. He then announced the sentence by raising his voice and dramatically bellowing across the courtroom, "I sentence you to SIX to TEN YEARS at Walpole State Prison." His declaration caused the courtroom audience to recoil in shock, a wave of whispering in reaction to the sentence. The intonation suggested he had just condemned them to die in the electric chair, but Bobby and Nicky could hardly refrain from laughing at the judge's theatrics. It was a sweet deal, and the two knew it.

With the plea complete, Bobby's new sentence superseded the Concord sentence, and he was immediately transferred to Walpole State Prison, with Nicky soon to follow.

CHAPTER FIVE

Walpole State Prison always had a reputation as a scary place. It was well earned. The prison housed the most hard-core criminals, the most disciplinarian staff, and was notoriously violent. Though Bobby and Nicky felt confident and had gained some prison experience, Walpole was big time. Bobby was still a skinny nineteen-year-old, and Nicky was a baby-faced, handsome kid who risked gaining unwanted attention from older predatory inmates. But with all the contacts from Lyman, and now from Concord, the pair's entry into Walpole amounted to a high school reunion of sorts. They were welcomed by a number of people they already knew, some from reform school, some from jail, others from the street. Their social network already firmly in place, each young man started serving the first of what was to become many years behind prison walls.

* * *

In any prison, most first-time inmates found little respect from the veterans and were forced to accept a lower social status until they built a reputation which justified a promotion. At the very bottom of the prison food chain, lower than anyone, were predatory sex offenders known as "skinners." In the prison world, those who harmed children were viewed as the worst humans on the face of the planet. Those prisoners were always treated with the utmost contempt, disrespect, and even hatred by both guards and inmates alike. The prison code authorized unbridled violence against molesters; no personal beef was required to deliver merciless beatings. Guards, for their part, could be counted on to look the other way as inmate vigilance was meted out. The guards generally offered a grudging respect toward the average prisoner, but not the skinners. When addressing one, a guard would not ask to speak with him. Instead, he'd yell, "You fucking punk! Get the fuck over here!" To Bobby's surprise, skinners played the role—they were treated like punks because they were punks. Bobby felt no sympathy; any man soft enough to *allow* himself to be treated so poorly *deserved* that kind of treatment. The subservience may have stemmed from a sense of self-preservation, but Bobby and the rest of the inmate body viewed it as nothing short of pure weakness, warranting every bit of mistreatment.

A rapist is the top end of the skinner level. A child molester is at the very bottom. He's in trouble. People will spit in his face, fucking beat him up, steal his stuff, burn his cell out, hurt him. People in jail don't like child molesters. There are numerous situations I've seen, guys walking down the corridor. This one child molester, we called them 'baby blasters,' was coming from the hospital with two screws escorting him back to the protective custody block. My friend Al said, 'I wasn't even thinking of nothing, I was just walking to go to the hospital. This piece of shit is walking toward me. I look up at him, and it was the look on his face.' Al's a big guy, dropped him with one punch. Stepped over him and just started blasting him. The screws just stepped out of the way. The screws aren't risking their ass for a skinner. After a while of him blasting this guy they said, 'Hey Al, you know, he got enough, you got him Al, you got him, lighten up.'

My friend Jack was another one, he was in Walpole with me. A dude, him and his wife, they starved their baby then they hid the baby in a grave some place. He's in the joint, coming down the corridor, again with escorts. Jack's walking down the corridor and he sees this guy. As they come to pass each other Jack just drops him. Jack's a big guy, solid as a rock, always working out. You love children, you protect children, you don't hurt children. This guy is a piece of shit, he's against everything you stand for. There's no problem dropping this guy right there in the corridor. Give me the ticket, take the good time, don't ever let a piece of shit like that walk in the same area that I walk in. That's the attitude.

The two guys that sexually molested and killed the kid, Jeffrey Curley. One of those guys, the fat one, this guy got serious beatings in the prison. They were holding him in protective custody, cannot put him in general population. And this is one of the things with Curley, the father, he pushed for the death penalty...people were really pissed off. People had sent him letters and stuff saying 'What are you doing?' We're in here, first shot we get we will kill that son of a bitch that killed your kid. What are you pushing the death penalty for? He did a turnaround, he's now anti-death penalty because he realized how the prosecution had played him. They didn't give a shit about his kid, they played him because they wanted him to testify for the death penalty. They were selling his kid's death, but they didn't care about the kid, they cared about getting the death penalty back. But those guys get beat up on a regular basis. You can't put them in a prison where guys are in there for murder. Gangbangers? They're not going to tolerate pieces of shit like that next to them. I don't want that guy in a cell next to me.

Classic example from years ago. We were all in Seven Block, and they moved us from Seven Block to Two Block. They did a three month study as to whether they could move Seven Block to Two Block without having a major riot. They finally came to the conclusion that they could move us without having a riot. When they come in about the moving and stuff, everybody's going to go into the Two Block, the same cells they were in here. So we want to take everything that we got here over there. Because to get TV reception you had to use a piece of wire, attach it to the antenna and throw it on toilet paper up on the window to have a connection. They told us to take all your wire, they didn't care, they just wanted a smooth transition. We took all the wire out of the regular line circuit. Unscrew the thing, pulled all the wires out, just stripped the block. When the next group came, the skinners, came into that block nothing worked. They had to rewire the entire block. When they complained about it they said, 'Shut the fuck up, that's your cell. We'll fix it when we get around to it.' They were in cells that were dark and no electricity.

You learn stuff, you learn behavior patterns. Like an individual that's always saying, 'I hate stool pigeons, I hate rats.' Ok, fine, there's nothing else to say after that. If you're beating that to death, what you're telling me is you're a stool pigeon. It's called reaction formation. You're overacting the part. Same with child molesters. There's a point where you can say that and it's normal, but when you carry it to an extreme, the first thing that kicks in is reaction formation. Turn it around, that's more likely what the truth is. This guy is a child molester and he's trying to cover his tracks. A lot of times when you see people wearing rosary beads and carrying the bible and stuff, this is usually a skinner, child molester. Guy's in on a rape case and he's running to God to get away from it.

One of the things the old school guys taught me was prison code is bullshit. I said, 'What do you mean it's bullshit?' You don't trust this guy because you don't trust him. You don't mistrust him or trust him because the code says that you trust him. If you're incapable of thinking for yourself then you're a robot. It was like with child molesters, you automatically all hate baby-blasters, they're at the bottom of the list. But you also understand that some of them are interesting, some of them were molested as children throughout their life and they were just passing on what they were taught. That doesn't make it ok, but you gotta have an understanding of what happened. And who are you? In for murder and for this and that, to be judging other people. It doesn't matter if this guy is a stool pigeon. The thing is all stool pigeons don't rat on everybody. You operate on a need to know basis. If you don't need to know, you don't know. Listen, don't tell me something that I don't need to know. Because if something goes wrong, you're gonna put me on the list of who could have possibly have ratted it out; and that's going to make me kill you for calling me a rat. So you learned how to categorize and put people into blocks. It was part of the survival technique you learned.

* * *

In Walpole, a simple misunderstanding in prison could lead to a racial war. Two Block housed a diverse body of dangerous inmates, from gang members to bikers to lone psychopaths. Inmate groups tended to split along racial lines, with each adopting their own cultural norms, manners of habit, and patterns of speech. They usually stayed out of each other's business, following the unwritten but critical rules of prison culture. At times, however, the segregated nature of the blocks, and the failure to understand one another, created dangerous problems.

Over in Two Block, you had your hard-core white, hard-core black, hard-core Spanish. It almost exploded. White guys had a phrase, 'Black and Deckers.' When we said, 'Get the Black & Deckers,' that meant suit up, get your weapons, without a long conversation. Soon as someone said, "Let's get the Black and Deckers," you knew something's coming

71

down, you don't ask questions you just suit up and get ready for whatever is about to go down.

Now, unbeknown to us, black guys heard this in a different context. They thought it was a racial slur. They didn't hear 'get the Black and Deckers'... 'Get the niggers' is what they were hearing. We didn't know that.

Now some shit starts to jump off. Because you got the hard-core white, black, and Spanish so you can rub each other's elbows. These types of individuals go for their weapons right away, there's no pussy here. We end up all down on the flats, with coats on. Which means you're packing. We're all coming head to head. This one black kid, named Bobby Thompson, who isn't a bad guy, he said, 'I'm sick and tired of all that racial bullshit.' Usually the hard-core doesn't play racial bullshit, doesn't play pussy. If I don't like you, I'm not going to call you a nigger; I'm just going to take your head off. There's no name calling nonsense, we're going to get down, go get your weapons and we'll resolve this right now. There's no bullshit, you don't play that racial card. Usually the guy that's playing the racial card is some weak dude who's trying to impress people, looking for somebody to get around him, he can't step up to the plate and take care of business for himself. So when Bobby said that, the white guys said, 'What are you talking about?' Because these guys don't play that. They're for real. These guys are killers, there's no bullshit game playing. Bobby said, 'Oh yeah that Black and Decker shit!' When he said that, the white guys busted out laughing. The other black guys now for the first time are like, 'Whoa, what is this?' Richie Devlin says, 'Bobby, do you know what a Black and Decker is?' He says, 'Yeah, I know what a Black and Decker is.' Richie said, 'No, you don't. Bobby, this is a Black and Decker...' and he had this knife right there. 'That's a Black and Decker.' So we laughed. The other black guy said, 'Oh wow man, we always thought that was a racial thing.' I said, 'Listen, we had no clue that's what you thought.' Nobody ever said a word, but we were always using that phrase. You see when shit's about to go down it's 'get the Black and Decker's…' everybody comes out with weapons…I mean what do you think we're talking about? They thought it was a racial thing, you were using it against the black guys.

The white hard-core took exception to a common practice of the blacks, the use of the term "brother." All blacks referred to each other as such, both in person and by reference, to promote unity amongst their race. The practice extended to all black inmates, regardless of social status within the prison, including stool pigeons and child molesters. The white hard-core brought the problem to the black leadership:

It's simple. We don't want those scumbags living with us in the block. Here's the rule: if a stool pigeon comes into the block, and he's black, we will tell you about it. And it will be your responsibility to clean your house, or we will do it for you. We don't want to hear any bullshit. White dude comes in the block and he's a stool pigeon, and we don't clean our house, you clean our house and nobody's going to say shit to you. But you're not cleaning our house; we will clean our own house.

While just about anyone in Walpole could be violent at any time, it was the white population which was most predisposed toward using swift and brutal violence. When a black stool pigeon or skinner came on the block, black leadership would normally approach and inform him he was not welcome to live amongst them. He would be invited to get his things and leave immediately; it was clear that declining the offer was not an

73

option. If he didn't, the stool pigeon would be beaten severely and ultimately forced to leave anyway, but at the very least was given the basic respect of a fair warning. By contrast, the whites didn't bother with the formality of issuing warnings or ultimatums. When a stool pigeon or child molester came into their Two Block, he was guaranteed to be stabbed. The zero-tolerance policy was strictly enforced and well-known throughout the prison.

Even guards knew. To the inmates' dismay, the fear and intimidation of such a hardline policy was co-opted by the guards as a control tool. Without actually intending to do so, a simple threat to throw someone in Two Block would scare the hell out of most guys. Knowing very well they could be killed, many inmates were forced into cooperation.

And unfortunately the institution used that. It was not unusual to see a guy being brought to the block, his arms would be wrapped into the grill door, his feet would be up on the wall. Would not come into the block, he'd be yelling, 'No, no, I am not going in there!' They had no intention of putting him in there because they knew he would have got killed and they would have been in trouble. But they used it to intimidate him. They'd say ok you bastard, if you aren't gonna do what we tell you you're going to do, you're going in that block with those lunatics. He'd say, 'Oh no, I'll do anything you want!'

* * *

Now with Walpole, when I went in there it was the last part of the old-school. There were burglar alarm schools, safe cracking schools, lock picking schools. The old school taught the new school. This was the college of crime.

At Walpole, Bobby's criminal education switched into high gear. He soared through numerous electives from the criminal program of studies offered by veteran inmates. Because he had burglary experience, he was interested in learning everything he could about the art of lock picking. Some old school inmates were locksmiths by trade on the street, and for the right candidate, would serve as a mentor to pass the skill on to a new generation. Bobby came into prison at the tail end of the golden age of old school criminals, and he understood that culture. Because he showed due respect to those men, he was welcomed as a lock picking intern, and he took the opportunity very seriously. He figured if he were to learn, he should learn from the best.

One of the things that we did in Walpole, you'd have like maybe fifteen or twenty locks that were stolen from around the prison that would be on the bed. Say you got a six man crew, I pick a lock, show you that the lock is picked, lock the lock and give it to you. So the pile is mine, and as I'm picking the locks I'm giving them to you; you're picking the locks and giving it to the next guy. Now, let's say I get shook down and they find five locks in my cell. I'm getting locked up in isolation for up to fifteen days. When I come out, I have to steal five locks somewhere in the institution to replace the ones that I lost. So you learn to pick locks fast. Get them out of my possession, get them to you as quick as I can. And if you got more than six guys it's neat, because as soon as I get them out of my possession by the time they start coming back to me, I'm banging them out and passing them right along. So there's no pile of locks in there. That's how you learn to pick locks.

* * *

Bobby was paroled after serving two years and eight months of the six-to-ten year sentence, under the old "one-third" rule in Massachusetts. He was scheduled for release from Walpole on a Friday afternoon. His mother had been driving him crazy, calling the prison every fifteen minutes to check on his status, to see how he was doing, whether he had lined up a job, if he'd taken care of the paperwork. Everything finally cleared and he was given civilian clothes or "state clothes" as they were known. He was given his small bag of personal effects and an indifferent administrator directed him to walk out the front entrance. Nobody was there to pick him up. A guard came out and explained that his mother had just called and said she was still in Revere, about forty miles away. At best, she could arrive in Walpole in an hour. Impatient to go home, Bobby went back inside to call a cab, figuring he'd pay for it with the two hundred bucks he had just emptied out of his prison account. The staff told him that if he wanted a ride to Boston, a state truck would be leaving shortly and was willing to take him along. He agreed immediately, not caring who was driving, as long as he could get off the prison grounds as quickly as possible.

On the trip north, Bobby tried to relax and begin enjoying his newly granted freedom. As they reached town, not far from his old neighborhood, he asked to be let out at Egleston Square near the MBTA station. He jumped out and made like he was heading into the station to catch the in-town train. As the truck pulled away, Bobby hailed a cab instead. He told the driver his destination was Revere, but he first wanted to head up Seaver Street past his old house, then down Columbia Road through Uphams Corner. The driver looked suspiciously at Bobby in his rearview mirror, knowing that Bobby just got out of jail, but uncertain as to whether he was legitimately released or escaped. Bobby sensed his discomfort and explained, "I just got out today. I'm looking to go by my old neighborhood, and then I'm going to my mother's house to stay." The cabbie eased up a bit after that, but remained somewhat guarded. As they passed by Uphams

Corner, the cabbie was unaware that in the backseat Bobby was looking, very intently, at the Boston Gas Company.

Bobby's re-entry plan into society was to make a fast score. While serving time, he didn't acquire any legitimate jobs skills. None were available. The only thing he had learned in the past few years was how to be a better criminal. For the moment though, he was free, and he didn't have time to waste wondering if counseling, job training programs, or school would have helped. He knew that the Boston Gas Company had cash on the premises, and that it would be an easy job that he could pull off alone. When he made the decision to rob the gas company in his cell days earlier, his thought process had been simple; he needed money, they had it. He arrived at his mother's house that Friday evening, and by Saturday morning he had a single action .22 pistol in his pocket. It wasn't his weapon of choice for this kind of job, but he didn't have the time or money to be picky. The gun had been readily available to him, conveniently found hidden under his brother's mattress.

Within twenty-four hours of his release, Bobby was on his way to committing an armed robbery. In a stolen car, he drove close to Boston Gas and jockeyed into a parking space within walking distance. Bobby gave a last minute check of his gear before heading in to take the place down. The nylon mask perched on his forehead, creased twice so that only a quick flip of the finger could bring it down under the chin to distort his facial features, was ready. A wool night cap hid the nylon from view as he approached. In his hands was a tri-folded Boston Globe newspaper, concealing his gun on the inside. He made the short walk to the building. He pretended to mill about with the large group of people waiting at the bus stop located near the front door, hanging back as everyone boarded. He looked left down the road, then right, and thought, *"Coast is clear. Deep breath, go.*" He brought the mask down, drew the gun, and sprinted for the door, planning to burst through and demand the cash. As he went to push the door open, he slammed face first into the glass. Stunned, he tugged the door hard. It didn't budge. It was only then he noticed a sign, in large red letters: "CLOSED ON SATURDAYS."

Monday morning, Bobby returned to carry out the stick up. This time he succeeded, and netted almost $4,800. Later that day, Nicky was released from Walpole and showed up at Bobby's mother's doorstep. They were talking, and Bobby nodded at a bag resting on the counter and said, "Hey Nicky, take a look." Nicky opened the bag, saw the wads of cash packed inside. "Oh shit! Already?" They both laughed.

Bobby's friend, Billy, ran into a veteran Boston cop named Lynch a couple days after the robbery. Lynch said, "Billy, when you see Bobby, you tell him that Field's Corner and Uphams Corner is my district." Billy didn't know what he meant, but passed the message on to Bobby.

"What was he saying that for?" Billy asked.

Bobby laughed. "Because he knows I robbed the place."

Lynch had been around for years, and knew certain individuals preferred to pull solo jobs. He also knew Bobby had just been released from prison, so it wasn't hard for him to make the connection. He relayed a warning through Billy.

"Hey, Billy, you just tell Bobby that this is my area. Tell him don't be robbing in my goddamn area."

Despite his suspicions, Lynch didn't go after Bobby. His family and Bobby's were from the same block, and had been close. Both Bobby and Lynch knew that if they came across one another in the street one day, it would be a bad situation if they were shooting at each other. Bobby later admitted that had he known it was Lynch's domain, he never would have hit Boston Gas. Though he hated cops, Lynch had been straight with him and he appreciated the fair warning. Out of respect, he would steer clear of his area in the future.

Neighborhood loyalties and family connections sometimes blurred the distinction between cop and criminal. When living with his mother, Bobby would start walking at the northern end of Revere Beach and head south along the water. He'd have a bottle of Smirnoff 100-proof vodka for the trip, and he'd rip the bottom strip from his t-shirt, tie it around the bottle, and through his belt loop. Then he'd casually walk the length of the beach, taking long pulls from the bottle while enjoying the weather. Though illegal, nobody on the beach ever got hassled for public drinking unless they got out of control. Returning from a beach walk one day, Bobby spotted a waiting cop car at the end of his street. Naturally, he was suspicious. As he walked slowly by, he eyed the two cops inside. The officer sitting on the passenger side cranked down his window.

"Excuse me. You're Bobby Dellelo, ain't ya?"

"Oh man, here we go again," he thought.

"Look, I ain't trying to harass you or anything, not saying that you're doing anything or planning on doing anything. But if you *do* plan to do shit, if you don't do it in Revere, we'll let you know if anything comes out on you."

He realized the cops weren't harassing him, but they were actually trying to help him out. If he didn't make their jobs harder, he'd get something in return. Not only would he receive tip offs, but they'd pretty much leave him alone. *"Fair enough,"* thought Bobby. *"I can do that."*

With cash in his pocket and his brother's pistol safely back under the mattress, Bobby felt restless. He wanted to bypass the transition process from prison to free society and go directly out on his own; no living with his mother, no borrowing weapons. His first order of business was a road trip up to Portland, Maine, to get some guns. After shopping around at several sporting goods stores, Bobby found what he needed in a hunting shop and placed a half-dozen handguns of various sizes on the counter. The sales clerk looked at him strangely, but also seemed excited about the pending commission for the sale. "I'll take all of these," Bobby said. The clerk was a bit nervous and asked Bobby for identification. "Don't have any, but I got this," he said as pulled out a large wad of cash and laid it out on the counter. The clerk scanned the store for any witnesses, and quickly told Bobby to write his signature and address in the store's log book. Bobby made up some bogus information, and a few minutes later, walked out with a brown paper bag filled with guns. When he got home he was careful to destroy the serial numbers by drilling each gun, filling the divot with plastic seal, then allowing it to dry. By the next day, he had a small arsenal of completely untraceable guns. He called Nicky and let him know he was ready to go to work.

Over there by the New England Medical Center they had a hardware store, a big one. We got into that place, and they got the safe. There's a T handle and a drop handle on the safe. The T handle, if you knock the dial off and you put a punch, you could punch where the dial was, and push that piece through and open the safe. The drop handle was a different mechanism, you couldn't punch it, and you'd have to peel the safe. This place had a T handle. Now, we punch it, the thing isn't working. So now we're going to heat it up. I got two blow torches, the butane kind. Nicky's got the two of them on the safe and I'm getting the punches ready. They had a big smokestack in the middle, right where the safe was, where you could throw shit and burn it and the smoke would go up.

I smell wood burning. Nicky's used to sleeping at a certain time, waking up at a certain time. And we're deep into his sleep time. When you do B&E's you don't have that problem because you're up all hours, you cat nap here and there during the day. He had the butanes on the safe, and he's hitting the wooden floor. The floor's burning and I can smell that smoke. I said, 'What is that smoke? Nicky! Wake up!' It's bright red. Not so much flames but there are burning embers. So we tried punching it again, but it was just such a crazy situation that we said let's get the hell out of here, without realizing that I hadn't made the last try.

In the newspaper, it said they couldn't figure out why the thieves had left $40,000 in the safe, when it was open! So that ended B&E jobs with Nicky.

PART II

CHAPTER SIX

Late one night in October 1963, Bobby was out looking to steal in downtown Boston. He roamed the streets dressed in his work clothes, wearing gloves, his tools in a small bag. As usual, he pretended to window shop, slowly walking up and down the street perusing the stores, seeking a target. By pure chance, he ran into Nicky on Broad Street He asked Bobby what he was doing there—as if he didn't already know. Bobby reluctantly acknowledged his business, knowing Nicky would want to come along, and knowing that he definitely did not want his help. But Nicky was very enthusiastic, and without waiting for an invitation declared, "Alright, I'm in!" Nicky needed money badly, and Bobby eventually allowed their friendship to trump his better judgment. To limit the liability of having his friend along, Bobby thought they'd hit something quick and easy— something hard for Nicky to screw up—so the pair walked toward Washington Street to see what they could find.

At the time, Washington Street was one of the sleaziest streets in Boston, the main artery of the Combat Zone, packed with movie houses, night clubs, bars, arcades, and shops. It was the jewelry stores there which attracted Bobby the most, and they soon picked a store situated on a corner block to hit. He explained to Nicky that the job wasn't going to be a simple smash-and-grab. Bobby insisted that if a job were to be done properly, it could not be rushed. That, he explained, made for sloppy amateur work, and that was how people got caught. He liked to take his time, pay attention to detail, maximize the take, and make his exit. This was not Nicky's style, and it worried Bobby.

Bobby took him on a convoluted route to the point of entry to avoid raising suspicion of anyone in the area. They went around the side of the building, and slipped into the alley. A six-foot gate stood in the way until Bobby wedged his hand through, reached up inside, pulled the latch, and quietly swung the gate open. Once inside, he cut the latch. Moving further down the alley, they scaled up a vertical pipe to an I-beam which connected to the adjacent building. Reaching that building's roof, Bobby jimmied the door lock, and they took the freight elevator down to the basement. They were now beneath a clothing store, next door to the targeted jewelry store. The two men went into a small alcove where the electrical box was located, punched through the thin plywood wall, and entered the clothing store. Emerging from the basement to the first floor, they took a minute to survey the goods, but moved on without taking anything. On one side, a series of dressing rooms lined the wall. Bobby determined that if they could get through the wall behind the booths they'd be able to make a clean entry into the jewelry store. Inside one of the booths, they went to work opening up the wall with small hand-held tools. Once through, though, they ran into a problem; a large glass display case with locked sliding doors sat immediately in front of them, preventing a direct path into the store. They considered looting the case only, but Bobby insisted they get into the store where much more valuable items were located. He set to work on the case doors and was able to jimmy the lock, carefully sliding the glass panel over and pop it out without breaking it. They were in.

> *They had alarms, no video cameras. They left the product out because they felt secure because they had an alarm. I'm up by the window and it's about waist high, then the window's there. So I'm right up under there, the front window facing the street and the door's right there. I can see people walking by and I'm laying down there. I would peek up, see nobody, reach up and grab the diamonds, the rings, and anything else. But then I see there's a cop standing*

right there, his back is to me. I look over and see Nicky's head; he's got his whole head inside the glass case, looking at everything. He's looking at nonsense stuff, you're not gonna lug all that out of there. But he doesn't see the cop. I'm taking diamond rings and throwing them, trying to get his attention. I had to throw a couple before he looked up. His jaw dropped when he saw the cop is standing right there! But he's looking at the traffic, he's not looking inside the store. So he said, 'Oh shit!' and he pulls out of the way. When the cop goes, he says, 'Now! Now! Now!' So I grab a bunch more of the diamonds and boogie down the end. We got a whole pile of jewelry and boxes. When we were in the clothes store, he filled boxes up with clothes. And we had piles of them, you can't take all these boxes. So when we finally get down to the nitty gritty at least two boxes full of good jewelry, we got clothes. He just couldn't differentiate. We sell the jewelry, you can get a thousand times more than the clothes you got in these stupid boxes. You got these shirts, shorts, socks, all this other shit. So he fucked that score up too!

We ended up with one box of jewelry. At the time, we fenced it through my father, Sal Cesario, a made guy. I didn't know he was my father until I got out of jail. I brought it to him and he got me $650. So we split that.

Bobby was young and his sense of adventure high. It was around this time he was beginning to feel that he wanted something new in his life, a change of scenery. He had a good amount of cash stockpiled from various scores, and with this nest egg, he was thinking seriously of moving far away from Boston. The city itself was small, a town where everyone seemed to know everyone else's business. In his line of work, that was not a good thing. Cops in town knew his name and were watching him very closely. He also had to avoid being forced to pay organized crime tribute for operating in their self-proclaimed turf. It was getting very risky to do anything unnoticed. Moreover, he'd never been very far from Boston. Bobby thought it would be interesting to check out some other places, visit other parts of the country, somewhere he'd be able to start over again.

I never really thought about going straight, it was never much of a consideration. I was a thief, so wherever I go, I'm going to be able to steal money. I'm a good second story man, so if I use my forte it's going to be hard to catch me. With that kind of money, a distance away, I'd be all set. Of course I would have changed my name and all that. I probably would have gone to school to be a locksmith at some point. Because there you get all your material that you need to know. If you took a locksmith course, once you get done with it, they offer you advanced courses. They're not going to teach you safe cracking if you don't know how to pick locks. So a lot of the advanced stuff comes only after you learn the basics. It gets you more money. You get these trade magazines, so all these tools you need you could get.

I had $2,500.00. You're talking early 1960s when that was a lot of money. So if I hit California, I got a hell of a nest egg. In those days, an apartment was like ten bucks a week. If it was a little bigger with a little extra stuff, maybe twenty bucks. I got $2,500.00 so I can really lock into something nice, scope the area out, and pick my targets.

It was an appealing vision to Bobby. He'd be comfortable living in a warm, sunny area, able to make a living and enjoy life. Scollay Square, Lyman School for Boys, Concord, and Walpole would become memories he'd leave behind, and just as soon forget. After kicking the idea around for a while, he finally made a decision: *I'm outta here.* He could hardly wait to wrap up his affairs and prepare to make the move. He was excited for his new life ahead and it was all going to happen soon.

Then Nicky called him with a plan.

Nicky had also been thinking about his future. He was planning to marry his girlfriend, and had thoughts of settling into a more domesticated lifestyle. But having been recently released from prison, he was broke. With no money for basics, much less to buy a ring or finance a wedding, he kept complaining to Bobby that he needed money fast. "We gotta hit something, we gotta hit something," he kept repeating. Bobby wasn't interested. Nicky always found a way to botch a job, and besides, Bobby already had more than enough cash to launch his own plan. But Nicky persisted. He didn't want to strike out alone, as he didn't quite have the skills to pull it off, and he knew that Bobby could fence anything they stole. Partially out of loyalty, partly to shut him up, Bobby said he'd think about it. He wasn't going to loan Nicky part of his nest egg, knowing he'd never see it again. But, he thought, if they did do a job and they scored well, Nicky would have what he needed and his own nest egg would be even bigger. Maybe now, instead of an apartment, he could buy a house, a car, and still have cash left over. Moreover, Bobby had done so many jobs at this point that he was confident he could train Nicky well enough to pull off something successfully. He didn't bother fretting over the possibility of getting caught. For him, the biggest, and only, concern was how much they could steal. Concluding that it would be a move beneficial for both of them, Bobby called Nicky. "Okay, let's do it," he told him.

Nicky had already selected a location. He had his sights set on robbing I. Kopelman & Sons Jewelry, Inc., a second floor jewelry shop at 453 Washington Street in downtown Boston. While out looking for an engagement ring for his girlfriend a couple weeks earlier, he'd strolled down Washington Street checking out all of the watch shops, furriers, diamond shops, and jewelry stores. When he noticed the huge inventory and assortment of diamonds at Kopelman's, he got excited. His first thought was that it was a good place to buy a ring. His second thought was that it would be a better place to rob.

Bobby had never personally been inside this particular jewelry store, but this was Nicky's gig, so he deferred. Nicky was antsy about moving fast. If this was Bobby's job, he'd be patient and wait for the best possible time to do it. But this time was different; Bobby also had motivation to get this done quickly. His mind was made up to leave town for good, and he wanted to do it as soon as possible. Nicky assured him that he had cased the place and it would be easy. Bobby asked about the alarm system, and Nicky gave his thoughts. Somewhat satisfied, Bobby asked about possible exit strategies. Nicky's selling point was that the MBTA station was very close by, and they'd be down inside the bowels of Boston's subway system and long gone before the cops arrived. The plan seemed reasonable.

Bobby always did his homework before he made a move. Normally, he would have gone to the location once or twice prior to the robbery and pretended to be a customer. Had he done so for Kopelman's, he would have instantly spotted the elaborate alarm system including kick pads, silent alarm buttons, and controlled doors. He also would have determined that there would be no way to hit the place without sounding the alarms. A thirty-second review would have made it clear he should decline. Instead, he took Nicky's word for it.

On Wednesday, November 6, 1963, the pair met at diner on Charles Street to go over last minute arrangements. With guns concealed in their waistbands, they walked a few blocks and arrived at Kopelman's just before noon. As they ascended the staircase to the second floor, they pulled nylon masks over their faces. Bursting through the door, Nicky headed straight toward the jewel cases. Bobby came in beside him and turned right, entering the large diamond room, full of adrenaline, gun drawn. Customers were startled at the sight of the weapon; some froze in place and put their hands up. Against the far wall he saw a manager tending to a few customers, with exposed diamonds on the counter. Beyond the display was an open wall safe with dozens of large diamonds in plain view. Bobby's eyes widened.

These jewels could be dropped in a bag by the handful. The diamonds were not just tiny earring-sized jewels, but large showy pieces worth thousands. For a fraction of a moment, I thought, 'Wow, we're going to be super rich.'

I no sooner got into that room when the alarm went. I said, 'Whoops.' Now, you're in in-town Boston, you can't fool around with a burglar alarm, everyone and their mother's now looking. This is the corner of Winter Street and Washington Street, across from Gilchrist's, across from Jordan Marsh. It's high noon and there are people everywhere. We boogied out of there fast.

Neither of them had touched a single jewel. Witnesses later said that the two backed out of the store with guns drawn to keep the customers at bay while they escaped. Bobby reached the door first, stepping into the corridor, with Nicky coming out beside him. They paused for a brief moment to figure out what to do next. To the left of the entrance there was a stairway heading to the upper floors, just off the landing. They considered heading up, until they saw several Kopelman employees, who were working in a company owned room upstairs, looking down at them to see what the alarm was about. Instead, they turned and bolted down two flights of stairs to the ground floor. There,

Nicky made a hairpin right turn and ran toward the back of the building, frantically looking for a back exit to escape into the alley. Bobby decided against that route, and headed straight for the main entrance back onto Washington Street.

Patrolman Myles McGrail and Sergeant John Chennette were only steps from the entrance leading upstairs to Kopelman's when the alarm sounded. Both had been conducting a traffic detail at the intersection of Washington and Winter. McGrail responded first, heading straight toward Kopelman's. As he opened the door, he came face to face with a fleeing Bobby Dellelo. McGrail was unaware that he had walked right into an aborted robbery attempt and was looking at one of the suspects. When he saw the mask and gun he reacted, reaching for his own weapon. Before he could unholster, Bobby slammed a knee into his groin and struck him in the head with the butt of his pistol, dropping him in the doorway. He leapt over McGrail and took off running. The moment he hit the sidewalk, he banked left and immediately saw Sergeant Chennette over the top of a parked car about twenty feet away, moving toward him. Without breaking stride, Bobby pointed his gun at him, and the cop ducked behind a parked vehicle for cover. Chennette was not showing a gun; Bobby had room to run, and no reason to shoot, so he kept moving. His original intent was to head straight up Washington, but Chennette was too close. Instead, he banked left at Gilchrist's department store and ran up Winter Street toward Tremont. With gun in hand, he sprinted past the retail stores, pointing the weapon at scores of pedestrians to clear his getaway path.

Halfway up the block, Bobby looked back over his shoulder to assess his situation. His mind raced. *Did he need to shoot? Were any cops chasing him? Where was Nicky?* He saw nothing and kept sprinting forward. Then he heard a series of loud banging noises coming from behind him.

Blam.

Blam.

Blam.

The blasts were consecutive, measured shots, spaced out over one-second intervals, as if the shooter was taking careful aim. He saw an old woman walking in the opposite direction, next to an 18-foot box truck, parked half on the curb, half on the street. For a moment he swore he saw bullets piercing the side of the truck. The woman lost her balance, and stumbled up against the truck, throwing her hands against its side in a panic.

He turned his head as he ran, looking for the source of the gunshots, and suddenly went crashing to the brick walkway. A shipping clerk unloading a truck for Gilchrist's department store had heard the alarm, and saw Bobby running toward him. He saw the gun, and could see that Bobby wasn't looking, so he stuck out his foot to slow him down. Bobby tried to avoid the trip at the last second, but couldn't clear the obstacle. He jumped right back to his feet but had lost precious seconds. In that instant he had to abandon his original getaway plan, which was to run down the alley behind Gilchrist's, break right into a movie theater, emerge from the other side, cut back across Washington, duck into Filene's, and escape out the back door to Devonshire Street. But now Chennette was closing in and his options were running out. Had he not fallen, he'd have made it to the end of the block and Chennette wouldn't know if he had turned left or right. But now, he'd be a clear target in the alley. Bobby got to his feet, gun still in hand, and resumed the race. He ran hard, trying to create as much distance as possible between himself and the pursuing officer. "If I reached the Common, I'd have options," he said.

But until he did, his exposure in the narrow way with heavy foot traffic was high. He needed to outrun the cops.

Bobby spun to face the officer and threw down on him. To his surprise, Chennette was chasing him with his gun in hand, but the weapon was pointed down. Again, he considered shooting, but instead turned and continued running up Winter Street

> *At first, I thought he was shooting, trying to take me out. But when I saw no gun, there was no reason to shoot at a cop who was not shooting at me, not immediately threatening my life. There were lots of people around, someone could get hit.*

The shots he heard had come from around the corner on Washington Street, out of Bobby's view. *"Was that Nicky?"* he wondered.

Bobby made it to the crossroad at Tremont Street, directly across from Boston Common. Cars, taxis, and delivery trucks jammed the street. He ran across the street to the cab stand in front of Park Street Station and jumped into the back seat of an idling cab, breathing heavily.

"Go across the Common," Bobby said.

"I can't drive across the Common, there are hundreds of people," the cabbie said.

Bobby pointed the gun at his face. "Go across the fucking Common."

The driver hesitated for a moment, until the gun's barrel touched the back of his head. The cab edged forward, but was immediately boxed in by a delivery truck. Traffic clogged Tremont Street as far as he could see. Bobby realized that despite his threats, they weren't going anywhere. It was enough time for the cops to catch up.

McGrail approached with his gun drawn but not leveled. As he got closer, Bobby had a very simple choice to make: shoot or go to jail. Before he could decide, Chennette appeared on his side of the cab. As if he could read the exact thoughts going through Bobby's mind, he said through the open window, "You shoot him, you're a dead man." Bobby now had two guns drawn on him. He considered making a move, but quickly realized it would be suicide. Instead, he froze, thinking, *This is it, I'm dead.*" If he gave them a reason, any reason, he knew they would open fire on him.

"That's cool," Bobby said, casually letting the gun loose in his hand. Chennette quickly reached in and snatched it. Seconds later he was yanked from the cab, cuffed, and slammed up against the wall of Park Street Station. Bobby's demeanor was nonchalant, almost friendly. "You got me," he said. They didn't know about the .32 caliber pistol hidden in his waistband.

After Bobby had run up Winter Street, Nicky had exited the building and taken off in the opposite direction, banking to the right down Washington. In seconds, he encountered George Holmes, an off-duty officer in plain clothes, who had been chatting with Chennette and McGrail at the time the alarm sounded. Holmes faced Nicky, with one hand empty and a shopping bag in the other, holding up both hands in front of his chest while commanding him to stop. Perhaps he was going to try to grab Nicky, or may have been signaling to the armed man that he was unarmed. Maybe Nicky thought he saw a gun. Maybe he actually did see a gun. Maybe a lot of things.

Nicky raised his .32 automatic at Holmes and fired at point blank range.

The first round struck the butt of Holmes's holstered gun, ricocheting into his side and causing him to double over. As he pitched forward, a second shot caught him in the upper left shoulder, traveled down his bicep, and split after connecting with bone. Two bullet fragments caused exit wounds near the elbow. Holmes then twisted to the side, where the third shot entered on the left, piercing both lungs. The bullet came to rest on the other side, barely prevented from exiting by the officer's skin. Holmes may have survived but for the final shot, as it had caused irreparable damage to his vital organs.

George Holmes was forty-one years old and a married father of four. That afternoon, he died on the sidewalk in downtown Boston, shopping bag still in hand.

See, that's what we don't know. I went over the scenario lots of times. The bullets didn't hit all in one spot, they're all over the place. Just hits there, hits here, hits back here. He was just firing wildly, he wasn't firing accurately. They say he was six to ten feet away, which is close. At the kind of range he was from the guy, he could have fired one shot, hit him in the head, and dropped him and been gone, and get away. Because he did get away...after he shot him there was no one to chase him, and nobody was trying to stop somebody with a gun.

Now there's a street between Washington Street and Tremont, a little partial street down toward Boylston. A woman saw him throw the gun underneath a car once he got over toward Boylston. He gets away, she gets a cop. Cop comes over, gets the gun out from under the car. This saved my ass because this is the murder weapon. So there's no question about it, I didn't shoot the cop.

My argument, through all the time, has been that the joint enterprise ended. I am guilty of attempted

*armed robbery but I'm not guilty of murder. The
game the prosecutor plays, as you see in the records,
is the gig upstairs, we both go out side by side, guns
pointed. Well that isn't what the evidence was. The
core issue of the case is that the joint enterprise had
ended. So he purposely misstated the record relative
to a core issue of the case. Downstairs he says that I
had kicked a cop with a shod foot. I got a not guilty
on this one, because I kneed him, it wasn't done with
a shod foot. That I had kicked him twice so that
Nicky could jump by him, although the cop says he
never saw him. As soon as I run by him, he comes
after me. Well he's following me. Nicky comes out
and goes somewhere else. We don't know what
Nicky's doing. Nicky could have left before I did, he
wouldn't have any knowledge of that.*

*Now, as I come out the door, Chennette is on the
other side of a car that's right here. I could have shot
McGrail; I could have shot this guy, Chennette. I
bank to the left, I'm going up Winter Street. Now,
this is the second time the prosecutor purposely
misstates the record on a core issue in the case, the
joint enterprise. Being distanced was important.
That you know you're not right there, that it happens
right there...there's nothing you can argue. Upstairs
a cop says I ran out and left him there. Downstairs a
cop says he never saw him. I'm up on Winter Street.
But that was the core thing; somebody had to go
down for the dead cop. So I ended up with a first-
degree murder charge.*

*When McGrail opens the door, I got him. I mean I
can cap him. Why that's important is that I could
have shot McGrail at the door. I could have shot
Chennette over the car. Going up the street when I
thought the shots were fired and I turned around, I
had a dead shot at taking Chennette out. But he
didn't have his gun up. Then in the cab, I could have*

killed McGrail again. McGrail said this, Chennette said the same thing. The lawyer asked, 'Could he have shot you?' He said, 'Oh yeah. He could have very well taken me out.'

McGrail comes to the other side of the cab, now I got dead on him. He's on me, but they weren't about shooting me. When I realized that, I just gave him the gun...because I had another gun on me. It wasn't like I was completely captured. I was going to use the other gun to get away later with. But that scenario there, the prosecutor in charging the jury had said if they hadn't put their gun down for one second I would have killed them, and it was totally contrary to the record. I mean both cops said I could have killed them. They were really thankful that I didn't shoot them when I had the opportunity to shoot them. So that was like the life saver with the jury. See, at the time they had the death penalty. So they found me guilty of first-degree murder with the recommendation that the death penalty not be imposed.

Bobby was brought down to Station Two on Atlantic Avenue, in the heart of Boston's meat packing district, a decrepit old brick building surrounded by factories and run down commercial buildings. He was barely inside the lobby when the beatings began. He remembered being spun around in the elevator and kneed in the groin and fists striking him from every angle. "I remember being afraid the .32 tucked in my waistband was going to go off while they were hitting me," he said. From there, he was in and out of consciousness. He later woke up in Boston City Hospital, his body bruised and cut all over. The .32 caliber was long gone.

Bobby's lawyer, Helen Mejean, publicly accused the Boston Police Department of police brutality. At first, they indifferently claimed to know nothing of his injuries; he must have fallen and injured himself during the arrest. However, they became more defensive when the case caught the attention of the Department of Justice, who dispatched two F.B.I. agents to interview Bobby and photograph his injuries. The Boston Police Commissioner publicly fired back at Mejean and the Massachusetts A.C.L.U., strongly defending his officers' actions, and even calling for an ethics investigation of Mejean. She was undeterred though, and continued to push, demanding the MA Attorney General launch an investigation; his office declined on the grounds that a state level investigation would be duplicative of the ongoing federal probe. More public accusations flew against the police (for which Mejean received threats, and required 24-hour protection) and there was confusion as to who ordered the investigation. Finally, the AG's office in Washington issued a statement saying that any allegations of civil rights violations are routinely given a preliminary investigation by their office. The investigation stalled out and none of the officers who beat Bobby were ever charged or disciplined within the department.

After a few days in the hospital, he was transferred to Charles Street Jail, where he was held without bail. There, he heard stunning news on the radio: Nicky was dead. At first, he figured he had died in a shootout with the cops. But when he got word that Nicky had committed suicide by overdosing on sleeping pills, he was in a state of disbelief.

Nicky had gotten away, was supposed to get married. It didn't make any sense. He always said that he wasn't going to do time again. Everybody always used to say we were going to die with our boots on. Everything between him and me was this joke; 'Make sure you take your shoes off.' That's what he did, he took his shoes off, had them beside him and took the pills. It broke my heart. Why kill yourself? We could have escaped. We'll go over the wall later, no big deal.

It was a fucked up situation. I was pulling a type of crime I had no business in doing. You know, the fickle finger of fate. If he did not bust my balls to help him get money to buy furniture, I would have been gone. I wanted to go to California, and I wanted to see Hawaii. And I think once I hit Hawaii there's no way I would have come back. I would have found something out there to do; I don't think it would have been legitimate, but I would have settled in out there.

Bobby was handcuffed to a hospital bed. Nicky was gone. There would be no California, no Hawaii. He was facing life in prison, perhaps even the death penalty. Barring some kind of miracle, Bobby's life as he knew it was effectively over. He was a few days shy of his twenty-first birthday.

*   *   *

Bobby was charged by indictment with the crimes of First Degree Murder, Conspiracy, Unlawful Possession of a Firearm, two counts of Assault by Means of a Dangerous Weapon, and four counts of Assault with Intent to Commit an Armed Robbery. Because he was facing charges involving murder during the commission of a crime punishable by life imprisonment, a guilty finding would allow the jury to consider the death penalty. Unlike his previous crimes, his attorney would not be able to negotiate a plea. The Suffolk County District Attorney's office refused to offer Bobby any deals, especially since a police officer had died.

In early 1964, after a month of psychiatric evaluation at Bridgewater State Hospital, doctors determined that despite his "anti-social behavior" Bobby was psychologically healthy and was capable of meaningful participation in his legal defense. With this ruling, his trial was scheduled for April.

Judge August Taveira presided over the ten-day trial at Suffolk Superior Courthouse beginning April 6, 1964. Bobby took the witness stand in his own defense. His attorney guided him through a history of his juvenile criminal behavior, and asked him to provide details of his harrowing experiences at the Lyman School. He was also directed to give details of the robbery, which he did openly. Finally, he was questioned regarding the events following his arrest where he described the lengthy questioning by police, and the severe beating he received. Bobby was surprised he was asked to testify; it wasn't part of the defense plan and he felt unprepared to take the stand. Though he tried his best, his testimony was aggressively cross-examined by the prosecutor, and it hurt his case.

> *Helen Mejean was appointed to represent me by the court. She did the case pro bono because of the publicity. It was a three-ring circus. She was kind of a strange lady, an ambulance chaser, she came into court each day wearing unmatched, fucked-up clothes.*

> *She initially didn't want me to testify. I was happy with that. In the eleventh hour she changed her mind, I went on the stand without any preparation. I had just turned twenty-one, I had no legal understanding. At first, she said under no condition can you take the stand, and then she said at the last minute you gotta take the stand. I got up there and got slaughtered. She was thoroughly incompetent as my lawyer.*

While Bobby readily admitted to his attempt at an armed robbery, he vehemently denied the murder charge. Under the Massachusetts felony murder statute, the fact that he did not pull the trigger was irrelevant. As long as the state proved that he participated in a felony, and someone died during the commission of that crime, he would be equally guilty of murder as

99

the actual shooter. The heart of Bobby's defense was simple, that the joint enterprise had ended before the shooting. He wasn't even present at the scene of the shooting: Nicky ran one way, he ran the other. They weren't acting as partners when the murder happened, rather Nicky acting on his own. Therefore, he reasoned, he was not guilty of felony murder.

At trial, Assistant District Attorney Angelo Morello emphasized the joint venture theory. He told the jury that Bobby and Nicky left the jewelry store side by side, with guns drawn; suggesting that each man aided the other's escape and the joint venture was still intact. He also told the jury that Bobby kicked Officer McGrail twice so that Nicky could jump over him and escape, that they were still aiding and abetting each other during the getaway. On direct examination, McGrail himself contradicted this statement:

"How long were you down on the ground?"

"I jumped right up."

"How fast?"

"I was down there just seconds."

"Where was Yasaian?"

"I never saw Yasaian."

Bobby maintained he was not assisting Nicky's escape at all; he was merely getting past McGrail to make his own escape. When Nicky came to the front door after finding no exit at the back of the building, he burst through the door to the sidewalk and ran to the right. Bobby and McGrail were already gone.

To put Bobby in close proximity to the murder and strengthen the case for a joint enterprise, the prosecution told the jury that Bobby was on the corner of Washington Street and Winter Street at the time Holmes was killed. This was beyond exaggeration; it was factually incorrect. Bobby was already long gone up Winter Street when the shots were fired. On cross exam, Bobby's attorney queried Sgt. Chennette:

"Did you hear the shots?"

"Yes I did."

"Where did you hear them?"

"I was on Washington Street, just turning onto Winter."

According to the prosecution, Chennette should have been standing next to Bobby at the moment the shots were fired.

"Where was Dellelo?"

"He was up on Winter Street."

"He was moving pretty fast?"

"Oh yeah, he was moving."

Bobby's defense counsel offered a meek defense in closing. Instead of hammering away at the joint venture theory, she focused on the attacks against Bobby's character. To counter the prosecution's assertion that Bobby was a hard-core criminal, she told the jury that Bobby was a small time hood, using his prior record as support.

> The Commonwealth presented his background to you yesterday. And what was it? On January 6, 1960 it appears that he held up a store and he had a knife. Now, you are supposed to believe he is vicious. Now we got him, not only a diamond thief, but a vicious kid. And how old is he, 17 or 18? He got a little knife and he marches into this little

store, and what does he steal? Forty dollars from one man in the store. This great big diamond thief! And four dollars from another man—that is on the record. So they went into another store. Well, forty dollars, that is not enough. Here, I am referring to the record. So he had forty-four dollars, and, evidently—I don't know what he figured—it wasn't presented in evidence, use your own logic. So he went into another store, and what did he get, this great big diamond thief? Eight dollars. Now, the next hit was better. The same day, two other people in another store, ninety-five dollars. So this great big diamond thief, what did he steal with his vicious, bad, horrible record? One hundred and forty-seven dollars.

The prosecutor didn't bother arguing about Bobby's past and instead used his closing argument as an opportunity to deliver a dramatic speech.

Now, Mr. Foreman and Gentlemen of the jury, there have been men in our society who devote their lives to the aid and advancement of their fellow men in the field of science or in the field of medicine. They dedicate their lives for good. Those who work in our laboratories, doing medical research, work, working far into the night to find a cure to ameliorate human suffering. Yet, on the other hand, we have individuals, on the state of the evidence, the believable evidence, such as this man who, like the vultures of the desert, swoop down upon them and pick their bones through exploitation, through stealing and through acts of robbery.

You have a solemn responsibility to perform. In time of war, brave men rally to their nation's flag and don their uniforms and go to foreign soil and lay down their lives, if necessary, for the preservation of democracy; for the preservation of the principles which we believe in; for the preservation of our system of government, as symbolized by this edifice of justice in which you are now sitting.

Now, in times of peace, the struggle for the preservation of our democracy is transferred from the battlefield to the jury box. And it is this jury rail that protects the citizens of our country, protects the women and children of our families, protects the man who is operating his place of business, and who protects those who work in their places of business—protects them against the acts of plunderers, marauders and robbers such as this defendant is, on the state of the evidence, the believable evidence.

Attorney Mejean made no objections or request for curative jury instructions to any part of the closing argument. On April 16, 1964, the all-male jury returned with a verdict after several hours of deliberation. Bobby Dellelo was guilty on all counts.

While Bobby was not surprised by the verdict, he now had to worry about the very real possibility of the death penalty. Once convicted, the jury was allowed to consider both aggravating and mitigating circumstances in deciding whether or not to impose the ultimate penalty; but if they unanimously agreed, he would die. Because he passed on the opportunity to kill the two officers, and did not in fact not shoot Holmes, the jury recommended that he not receive the death penalty. With the possibility of execution now gone, the judge handed down the only punishment available under the law, a natural life sentence without the possibility of parole.

There was no reaction to being found guilty. There was no surprise there. It wasn't like I was innocent or had a shot; I knew I was dead meat. I knew I was going to be found guilty. Somebody had to go down for the cop. That was a foregone conclusion. Nicky was gone and it was just me left.

The life sentence didn't even register at the time. I was more concerned about how I was going to get out. The life sentence, even the possibility of the death penalty, it wasn't in my reality. It didn't dawn on me what 'natural life' meant at that time.

CHAPTER SEVEN

At age twenty-one, Bobby returned to state prison to begin serving out the rest of his life behind bars. Life in the notorious Walpole State Prison, he knew, would not be comfortable or easy. The primary goal for any man serving time there was simple: survival. Any prisoner lacking the proper allies was fair game to be shaken down, and anyone without physical capability or willingness to defend himself was quickly identified as prey. Attitude and image were essential tools for self-preservation, with reputation and perception being more important than reality. A man didn't need to actually be a killer, being *perceived* as one was what really mattered

A very small group of men within the population at Walpole State Prison was considered to be "hard-core." They were the leaders and decision-makers within the prison, a small group wielding power and influence over the wider majority of inmates. Members of the hard-core had diverse criminal records, an assortment of bank robbers, thieves, rapists, and murderers. Most were serving very long terms, usually life sentences; a convict passing through Walpole on a short bid would be disqualified from membership. These were men whose crimes on the street often involved resisting the police, and their incarcerated behavior was especially defiant of authority. The hard-core men were equally feared and respected; anyone who disrespected them could expect a swift and violent response. If their power was challenged, they would respond violently. Hard-core inmates had nothing to lose but their dignity, and they would rather die fighting for it. They let everyone, including the guards, know who was in control, and were ruthless in preserving it. But as long as they were left alone and allowed to do what they wanted, they could guarantee the prison would remain calm.

In Walpole at this time, about five percent of the population is hard-core. If you can control that five percent, you control the entire prison. If you get in a clique, you know, people clique together inside of a prison for security reasons. You don't get in a clique but you're knowledgeable of people in all these cliques, and thereby if you know how to play the game you know how to control people in these cliques. And you can't be a pussy. Nobody respects a pussy. You gotta be able to step up to the plate and when you say something you mean it. If the shit's gonna get down, you gotta get your weapon. People know he'll hurt you. Step out of line, this guy will kill you. If that impression is out there, then people will listen to you, as long as you have a brain and you're not talking irrational stupidity.

Now I knew people in various groups from reform school. When I hit Walpole, thirty-five percent of the people there I knew from reform school. My reform school reputation carried into the prison. Nicky and I were young guys. Eighteen or nineteen years old when we stepped into Walpole for the first time. People knew these kids would get down with you. We both knew how to fight and we would fight in the blink of an eye. Certain situations, we went for our weaponry. It was other older school cons stepped in between and said, 'Take it easy guys, you don't need this.' But that told them these kids will go, they'll get down. So you get the respect, so that grew with me. I had the reputation and the tentacles into all the other groups.

In the prison world, as in society, influence and control are held by few and imposed upon many. Bobby saw that in Walpole, just as in Lyman and Concord, privileges and favors were granted and restricted based on personal relationships, reputation, influence, and positions of power. Consequently,

106

some select inmates experienced confinement in a less brutal way. Thus, control over other convicts and guards became very important. It was the way they preserved prestige, established business relations, minimized risk, and increased protection.

Like every prison across the country, a series of cliques and subgroups existed throughout Walpole, ebbing and flowing with the ongoing population shifts. Some men merely sought to align themselves with others for companionship and a sense of camaraderie, but most knew the real reason was not a robust social life, but rather a necessity for security and safety. Cliques typically formed along racial and ethnic lines; interaction with outsiders was strongly discouraged. If an inmate did associate with an individual from another group, it was mostly for business purposes.

Bobby rejected the ethnic-based gang concept from the beginning, but also paid careful attention to the group dynamic. His interest in psychology and sociology prompted him to closely observe each of the various groups, how they operated, who made the decisions, and who carried out orders. In Walpole, racial divisions had perpetuated years of distrust and animosity between groups. Wielding influence within one's own clique was challenging, but to extend that power to outside groups was a much more difficult task. To the extent that an individual could do so, however, the dividends would be substantial. Watching inmate leaders operate over time, Bobby learned that it would be impossible for a single man to influence the population as a whole. But he did recognize that it was possible to create alliances with key members of certain groups, thereby indirectly influencing those groups. And if those groups could be influenced by the small core of men he associated with, the entire prison could be controlled as well. Thus, Bobby endeavored to create relationships with each major group existing within the prison.

Some groups he used for information, others as business associates, some for friendship, and some for favors. In time, he used his reputation and personality to build solid relationships and gain trust throughout the prison, which in turn enabled him to do something most others wouldn't dare: cross racial lines.

As policy, Bobby never judged a man on his crime. He took each individual on a case-by-case basis. The idea of ignoring a man because he committed an unpopular crime, or was of a certain race, seemed silly to him. "If you dismissed him right away, you would never know, he could be of value in some way," he said. Like every other prisoner, Bobby hated child molesters and was not fond of rapists, but he could put those feelings aside if the man was a potential ally, source of information, or provider of goods.

He also thought the rampant racism within the prison was ridiculous. To him, the "nigger" and "spic" name-calling he heard many whites using was weak, it was playground-style bravado used to mask fear. Bobby didn't see race as a separating force. He said, "Why should I hate a guy just because he's not white? That makes no sense." But while race was an irrelevant factor to him, he did closely scrutinize individual behavior. A man's actions and reactions in various situations, particularly stressful ones, revealed character. If an inmate consistently acted with integrity, he was considered a stand-up guy regardless of color, age, or crime. Same for Walpole's so-called "pieces of shit"—color didn't matter if you were a rat or a pedophile.

I was not a racist and never had any black/white issues. But I was stubborn. I never broke my word to people, regardless of race. That means we go all the way. As far as you want to bring it, I will not shit the bed and run on you. I don't play that nigger and spic game, I don't get involved in that kind of nonsense. So I had the respect of the Spanish and black prisoners.

So when we had the organization going, this is how I controlled the whites. The five percent, if you know how to control the five percent, you know how to control the prison. I knew how to control the five percent. I was a master of my environment and I learned how to manipulate it.

Any time I gave my word, you knew I would keep it. So if I told you, ok we're going to get into this, you want to go that way, I'm behind you. You could count on that. You also could count on if I warned you not do something, you took that to the bank. You didn't want to open that door because in your mind you knew that I would cut your head off. I didn't beat people up, I didn't stab people. I didn't have to because I knew how to manipulate the game.

The white guys, they probably had resentment, but they didn't have the balls to bring it to me. I'm with the hard-core. So when you look at me, you look behind me, you think, it's not just that I take him on, I take his friends on too. These are his friends, the hard-core. All my friends are killers.

In his previous stay in Walpole, during a stretch in isolation, Bobby was celled-up next to a new inmate, a young black man. Though he was still in his teens and inexperienced in the ways of the prison system, Bobby immediately recognized him as a potential leader within the black population. Bobby could see in him that he had heart and was fearless, but that he also had a level of intelligence which greatly surpassed his peers. From his very first day, he had significant ongoing problems with the guards. As an African American serving time for a crime involving a white victim—assault with intent to rape—he was not received well by the mostly white and often openly racist guards.

109

He never backed down, though, taking his beatings but always going down swinging.

Bobby saw in that young man, Ralph Hamm, many of the qualities the old timers had seen in him when he himself was new to the state prison. This young man was a natural leader, and Bobby knew that one day he would be part of the hard-core. He decided to take him under his wing, guiding and educating him in the ways of prison life. Despite the racial difference, a genuine and mutual respect emerged.

> *Ralph was about seventeen, eighteen years old. And because he had the thing with a white woman and he's a black guy with the two other partners, he had beefs with the screws. He comes down the corridor, his head was bleeding badly. I mean he came down with an army around him. You exercise two at a time and there was a little yard, the corridor that we were in. So I got out with him, we're walking up and down, we get to talking. He's not a bad guy; very intelligent kid, got heart, got the balls. I'm educating him because I knew what his situation was. Now we got close in there. Ralph was a physically big guy; he could take care of himself. Ralph controlled the blacks. So if I'm in with Ralph, I'm in with blacks.*

"Bobby D. and I have a high regard for each other," Hamm said. "It is a mutual kinship forged by the fire of struggle and survival in 1970s Walpole State Prison. Bobby was my most important mentor during those early years in Walpole Prison, and without his tutelage and protection I would have been murdered in prison decades ago. He is solely responsible for saving my life. He probably won't admit it, but he knows that it is so."

Inmates questioned Bobby for paying respect to a man of another race, but he wasn't really concerned with others' advice or opinions in that regard. He decided early in his prison career to give respect to anyone who deserved it, and expect the same in return. Because Bobby was established as a member of the hard-core, he was able to bend the rules.

But his reputation didn't make him untouchable, as he learned when "Jimmy the Bear" Flemmi, the notorious reform school alumni, came into Walpole as a convicted killer. His street reputation and family name carried enormous influence, and he carried himself with a fearless swagger. Bobby didn't know him well and rarely spoke to him, but somehow the Bear became angry with him over a trivial matter. Bobby was unaware of any problem between them when the Bear approached him in the yard one afternoon and, without a word, launched a sucker punch. As he was on the ground, Bobby knew he had to respond immediately; there were dozens of witnesses and his reputation was very much at stake. He jumped up and they went at each other, exchanging blows. The Bear seemed surprised that Bobby dared to challenge him. The crowd cheered them on, and as Bobby landed a few good shots, the Bear started to drop his defense. He finally knocked the Bear to the ground, the crowd wildly cheering. But with such a big audience watching, Bobby knew it wouldn't be good enough to quit after gaining the upper hand. He continued pounding away even after he'd clearly won, only stopping when he was pulled off.

News of the fight spread quickly, and when word of the incident came back around to Bobby, he was pleased with what he heard: he had given the Bear a sound beating, and successfully defended his reputation. Ralph Hamm later cited this incident as a main reason why Bobby was trusted by the prisoners as a leader. He was the only person who ever stood up to the Bear and walked away.

Bobby recognized that a delicate balance was necessary to maintain his influence. He needed to be credible and accessible to provide leadership to the inmates, but low key and invisible as possible to the prison staff. During one organized work stoppage, Bobby had the ability and control to direct over half the inmate population into the prison yard to stage a massive protest. Naturally, the numbers began to dwindle over time, as prisoners often found it difficult to sustain the energy for long term protest. Once the numbers dropped to about 150 men in the yard, Bobby pulled the plug to ensure that the numbers never got sparse enough to identify exactly who comprised the leadership. If they could be identified as a group, the administration would use any means necessary to strip them of power. So he ended the situation simply by declaring victory and ordering a halt to the work stoppage.

The method of controlling is quite simple if you understand. But you'd have a problem for a period of time until you learned how to identify. If you're right-brained and you can see things holistically, then you can see the pattern that makes up the prison and who's real and unreal. In the prison system, you don't just come into the system and become part of our crew. It may take you years to prove your mud. Words don't mean a goddamn thing. You watch how someone behaves, you watch when he gets in a condition how he reacts to that, how he stands up, how he holds his mud. Sometimes you see somebody, you say that's a good kid. You learn how to quickly spot people and you pull him into the fold. That's what I did with Ralph Hamm.

The hard-core made their nest in the notorious Two Block. Guards weren't interested in trying to wrest control away and, to the extent possible, stayed out of their block. They knew that challenging the hard-core would be the same as initiating a war;

it was easier to leave them alone and look the other way when it came to minor infractions. The Two Block men were happy with the arrangement, and for their part, behaved relatively well in order to preserve their comfortable situation. They had all the food they wanted, plenty of drugs, and dozens of small amenities which were officially considered contraband. "As long as we stayed in our block, and nobody got killed, the guards did not mess with us, and vice versa," Bobby said.

Bobby and his crew in Two Block often gathered up on the second tier. Up to ten guys would pack into a single cell and sit around smoking weed, telling jokes, playing cards, and hanging out. From the tier, they could see directly across to the observation window where guards would be watching them. As they toked oversized joints, they'd laugh at the guards shooting daggers their way, knowing they weren't going to do anything about it.

"We got some good shit over here, come get some!" some inmate would shout.

"Fuck you!" they yelled back. The inmates loved it, bursting into laughter.

While they generally left each other alone, occasionally the hard-core and the guards were forced into confrontation by circumstance. On one occasion, an electrical problem shorted out the circuits, leaving the entire block in darkness and disabling the electronically locked doors. Immediately, the guards saw the enormous potential for trouble and ordered everyone in their respective blocks to lock in. The lights were fixed and operable a short time later, but for reasons unknown to the inmates the lock-in order still remained in effect. While the rest of the population cooperated, Two Block inmates ignored the

113

increasingly stern orders to lock in. Tensions escalated very quickly on both sides.

They were having problems with the lights, doors were not working. Now they're locking everybody in their cell blocks. Finally the lights come back on and they want to lock our block in. Our block refuses to go in. They get everyone else to lock in and they come into our cell block with forty guards, two twelve gauge shotguns and everyone's got clubs. They come into the block, they fire. Now we didn't know it was plastic rounds, but a 12-gauge shotgun in a cell block is like a Howitzer going off. The pellets hit up on the top of the building down the end, so you know something fired out of the gun. So this one guard says, 'Lock and load.' You hear both shotguns lock and load. 'Fire one for effect!' BOOM! I said, 'You bastard!' He fired a shotgun! He panics and tells the other guy 'fire' and again a huge 'BOOM!'

When they come in, guys climb over the tiers down to the flats. Guys come down the stairs, push their way through all the guards so that we're all down on the flats. All forty-five of us are down on the flats. And they do that shooting. Phil Harding, a Devil's Disciples member, yells, 'Fuck these punks! Let's go get those guns!' Everybody moves toward the guards. They ran so fast out of the damn block! You got forty guards with clubs, two twelve-gauge shotguns, and they turned and ran out of the block!

So now they gotta recruit, they're going have to bring in state police and everything. I had to grab everyone and said, 'Listen, lock in.' 'Oh man, fuck that,' they said. I said, 'No, no, no, no. Listen to me. We won. We just chased all of these screws out of the block. They're going to come back with more weapons and state police and they're going to win in the next run. We won. Get the fuck in the cells. We got a victory, get in the cells.' And I got everybody back in the cells, everybody locks in. We got the victory. They didn't come in there and force us into the cells, we voluntarily went into the cells after we chased them out of the block.

Now, the screw that had our block, this guy Glen, he's making the rounds, we're all locked in for the morning of course. He's making the round with two rookies. He was so proud! Walking down the tier talking about us, calling us 'my men.' Like it's his cellblock, right. 'My fucking men.' Forty guards with shotguns chased those punks out of the block, these are my men!

A former Walpole guard who served a stint as the union president, spoke of the hard-core control dynamic in his memoir published some years later. He acknowledged the existence of the inmate/guard power struggle, and that it was an open question as to who was really running the prison. He said, "One of the most cold-blooded individuals I met during my time at Walpole was Connie Mancuso [Bobby Dellelo]. Another bank robber/killer who ran a formidable gang, Connie's record included an escape from Walpole, in which he had disarmed two officers escorting him to a court hearing. Mercifully he handcuffed them to a tree and left, instead of blowing their brains out. After a short time he was recaptured and returned to Walpole. He immediately reassumed leadership of his gang. Mancuso was the kingpin of his block and proud to let everyone know it. He himself did not dirty his hands, but he seldom tried to hide the fact he controlled what went on."

As years passed, an influx of new correctional officer recruits gradually replaced a generation of retirees, and new faces at the administrative level brought about renewed interest in challenging the Two Block inmates' power. Almost overnight,

Walpole saw a new hyper-enforcement of rules. The previous laissez-faire policy was gone, and inmates were now written up and being thrown into segregation for small infractions which, up until that time, had been customarily overlooked. The hard-core found this unacceptable. They needed to demonstrate that trying to control them was futile, and that they were not going to be stopped from doing business as usual.

They fucked with us one time, so I said here's what we're going to do. You take a towel and you put two knots in it, stick it in the toilet, and jam the thing up. You put a sheet over it, you flush. Initially there's a noise, until the water hits the sheet. Then as it pours over the side there is no sound. You don't know this thing is flushing. Forty-five cells, I write out this instruction and have it passed all down the line, and have everybody agree, vote on it. So nobody got a copy of it, it's just one piece of paper. So that makes the rounds, comes back, everybody agrees to it. When the guy makes the last round, the eleven o'clock shift, the key's gotta go in, so nobody can get back to us for at least an hour, when anything goes off. So I told them as soon as he makes his round, once he walks out that door, everybody flushes at the same time. We have at least forty-five cells flooding for at least an hour. That's a lot of water. So everybody gets on board, guy makes the round, sssshhhtttt, everybody starts flushing. It was the funniest thing in the world. Mice were floating down the tier on cardboard, holding on for dear life. I mean there were waves of water going down, the sound of it going over the tier was like a waterfall, like Niagara Falls down there. And it's all flooding out to the corridor.

Now, the stupid bastards turn the water off, but they gotta get behind the blocks. To get behind the blocks, they gotta get a key. So it takes time to get a key

116

because of the shift change. Now they run into the back of the block, they open up the block, they go in and they don't turn off each one separately. They take the main flood valve and shut off all cells at one time. The water coming from the water tank has an open-ended pump. As long as there's a requirement this pump will pump pressure. So the greater the need, the higher up the pump is pumping. It's open-ended, it has no limit. So when all of these forty-five cells are dumping water out, this sucker is pumping like nobody's business, and some idiot shuts it off instantly. You can't have big pipes in prison, people can climb out, so there are ten pipes coming in. All ten explode from the back up pressure. Eight hundred and fifty toilets in the system, all the diaphragms explode. They had over $100,000 in damage, that they knew we did, and that we could do again at any time. They said, if you can, just leave them alone. Whatever they want to do in that block, they can, just as long as they keep it contained in Block Two.

They got these metal chairs, you turn them sideways on the ground. And that little square piece with the bottom rudder and the chair level. You get these aluminum foil trays from the kitchen, and it fits perfectly in there. You put your cheeses and your rice, and all the shit you want to eat from the canteen. You take toilet paper, and you roll it up and make a circle, it's called 'making a donut.' Then you cut the sides in and you light it in the middle. You put it down and you get a steady flame. And that's how you cook your food on the block when you don't have hotplates.

Now the guard is coming down with a fire extinguisher along the wall. And the guys that are cooking spot him and say, 'What the fuck are you going to do with that?' He says, 'Umm, I gotta put that fire out.' 'If you put water on this fire, I will run that fucking fire extinguisher up your ass. Get the fuck out of here!' He runs out of the block now, because he's been threatened. Nothing happens, nobody comes in the block, everything is ignored. He just left. Now the next night, guys are coming down the stairs, this same guy is sitting at the desk. A guy says, 'We're going to be cooking tonight, you gonna be coming down with your fire extinguisher?' He says, 'Oh no, you guys can do whatever you want in this block.' Now we know that it's a hands-off policy.

What they eventually did, they shipped two hundred of us out, and caught more than half of the hard-core. They threw guys in segregation which pretty much caught the rest of the hard-core. They brought all the PC's the two hundred of them in the federal system back to the state prison system. They just bitch slapped them and they gave everything up. All the gains that we had made, they ended up giving it up. They didn't have the intestinal fortitude to step up to the plate and demand that they be treated like human beings. They accepted being treated like scum, and everything got fucked up.

CHAPTER EIGHT

By 1968, I had been in several different prisons, from Walpole to Norfolk, to federal prison, and back to Norfolk. Because I was in Norfolk before and got shipped out, and I knew what basically had to be done to get out of there, to escape.

The prison wall at the time had twelve strands of wire going into the wall, it's a capacitance fence. If you got within a certain distance you would alter the electrical field and it would set the alarm off. Fog coming in, that would set it off. Birds flying over, that would set it off. I was in industries, and sitting on a bench looking out the window and the sun got in the right position, I could see the twelve wires were pulled together and tied around the pole. That's an automatic short circuit, so that tells me it doesn't work anymore. So that's not a problem. It's only a problem if I try to climb up, it sets off an alarm, and you got me.

I was in 7-2. You come up a stairway in the middle of the building, the corridor goes left and right, I'm on the left side. At the time I was working in the hospital. I'm in my cell getting ready to go out, and a guard comes up. He tells this guy, Bernie Epps, 'Pack your stuff, you're going back to Walpole.' What this means is the paper work is already done. He's going to get his property, get put in the truck, and they drive him away. Picard was the deputy. Epps was saying to the guard, 'No, no, no, please just call Mr. Picard, please.' This guard was not too smart, a doorknob, but he finally gets it and says you stay here, don't move. He goes and talks on the phone and comes back and says go ahead. Now his footlocker is in the corridor. So I sat down on my bed and I'm thinking I gotta see how this plays out. Twenty minutes later he comes back, and without saying anything he starts to push the footlocker back into his cell. Guard comes up and tells him to leave it right there in the corridor. Epps says, 'No, it's ok, talk to Mr. Picard.' The guard says, 'Leave that right there, don't move.' He goes back to the phone, talks to Picard. Then he comes back and helps him push the footlocker into the room. What do I have here? A stool pigeon. I see him as an advantage. This is someone I need to connect with, someone who's going to give me a direct line into the deputy's office.

Bernie works in the paint shop. Which is what I want, I need to get into the paint shop; this gives me access to the entire prison. So he and I become bosom buddies. We spend time together, pick locks together. I show him this and that trick. After a while he gets me into the paint shop with him, I'm in.

In the paint shop downstairs there's a maintenance room down there, lots of junk there, and I find a 36-foot rubber buffer cord, half-inch thick, under the desk. Everyone forgot about it, it wasn't even listed. We were going to paint my cell, so I put the buffer cord inside the drop cloth. We walked around with the paint buckets and our other gear, so there's no attention given to me walking around, a drop cloth is nothing unusual. We get to the unit, I say, 'I'm gonna throw this in my cell, wait down there, I'll be right back.' Inside the cell, above the door is a little vent. I had loosened the screws up already. Pulled the desk over, jumped up on it and pulled it off and stuck the cord right in there and screwed it down.

Now we're painting the cell, and I have control of the color of the paint. That's what I needed. I put a hole in the wall, and there's about a three-inch space between the two walls to the next cell. I take the cord and put it in to the left until it stops, then to the right until it stops, back and forth zig-zag inside between the two columns. Then I put a nail inside, tied the end of the cord to it. Then I put newspaper in, took plaster of Paris, covered it over, and I had the paint to cover over that. I had to put a nail above it and hang a shirt over it so I knew where the hole was later.

So now I got that set up, and I picked the lock into the supply room. Now this kid, he comes in with me but he's stealing brushes and stuff, but he's not stealing stuff for personal use. He's stealing stuff so he can do better work for the state! I had opened all the locks on the cabinets and there were four boxes of vertical wire cutters. So I took the bottom one out, slipped it down my pants, put everything else back. He doesn't see anything.

Now I take advantage of this stool pigeon. I make up a story and explained to him, I got a screw who is going to bring in drugs for me. I tell him I got a connection that we're going to get five thousand black beauties. It's going to cost $2,500 but we don't have to pay for it up front. We can take it off the top when we sell them. I tell him this and now he's bringing that info back to the administration. A screw with drugs, this is a huge score. There are eighteen units in Norfolk and they're doing a major shakedown, but they're staying away from 7-2, our unit. They don't want to move. I grab him and say, 'The guy on the street got sick, it's going to be two or three more weeks. I guarantee the screw can't wait to bring the stuff in.' He turns around that information around back to the institution, so now they don't want to shake down my unit!

Now I have the cutters and I'm letting another guy use them because he did avocation work in his cells. I have the radio that's got the weather channel and they are saying dense fog is coming. So I say to the *guy I need the cutters back. I met him again in Walpole years later, he said, 'When you took the cutters from me, you had no idea how mad I was. When that fucking alarm when off I knew it was you! That's why you took the cutters!'*

But now, to make an escape I need a key to the grill. At the end of each corridor where the stairwell is, there is a grill door. I'm on the open side, which means I didn't have a toilet in my cell. So there's a community bathroom down the end, two sinks, two toilets, two showers. The lock on my cell door is the same lock on the gate. So now I take the lock out of the door, put the knobs back, put a shirt over it so you can have the door open with a shirt on top of the door knob so you can't see it is missing. I slip it in a towel and head for the bathroom and unscrew the thing, open it up, and I got the piece of aluminum to make a key. The guard is making his round and he's coming toward the shitter. I pretend to be in the stall having stomach problems, moaning and groaning, making fake fart noises. He's not sticking around for that! So he takes off and I can now make a key out of the aluminum. So now the key works in my cell door, I try the corridor door, the key works.

I take plaster of Paris and put Vaseline all over my head. I'm trying to get a half a face to put on the pillow, to make a dummy for my cell bed, to make it look like somebody. But when plaster of Paris is hardening, it gets really hot, which melts the Vaseline. It hardened so much that I couldn't get this thing off my head. It was caught in my ear, behind my ear, in my hair, it was really stuck in there. I had to get a hammer, and beat this thing with a hammer to get it off. I had a headache you wouldn't fucking believe!

So now I just take newspaper, put the plaster of Paris on it, make it the shape of a head. I put the mask on the pillow, then went to the door with a flashlight. I went back and forth, and kept adjusting to the point where you could look at it and it looked just like a person. But if you looked at it in daylight, it was the most hideous thing you ever saw! In the paper it said I made 'an image of myself.' It didn't look anything like me or anyone else! But it was passable in the dark.

I took all my clothes, put them on the dummy, and then I put pepper all over it. On my chair I had somebody else's shoes, socks, dirty underwear, dirty pants, dirty shirt. We were watching this on TV later we were laughing our asses off. The dogs were looking for people in the jail! They held the boxer trunks up to the dog's nose, but all my underwear were BVD's. They didn't add it up, it was kind of funny.

That night before the fog looked like it was fully rolling in, you could see the tongues of fog floating down. It was time to go. I punched the wall, pulled the line out. I had a plastic mat, a rubber mat for offset press. That was on top of the desk, and you could see it had cut marks on it. I also got two handles from the metal shop, handles to the metal buckets. I fold it in half, fold it again. Two of them together make a four-way hook, a grappling hook which I attach to the line.

A friend of mine was an artist, and he knew that I was going to make an escape. He has an art easel; it had two rods to hold the canvas, so you didn't really pay attention to that. There's a picture of two horses on a cliff, that's what he's painting. I had it, pretending to be painting this thing. The screw would be making his rounds and I'm sitting there like I'm some great artist painting this thing. He'd compliment what I was doing, saying, 'I like that, looks good.' So at night time, he'd stop and put his flashlight on the painting to look at it. So now I take the rods off, put them together.

Every thirty minutes the guards made a round, so I had to operate quickly. The screens on the windows, they slide out. I undid the screen at the bottom and I could slide down feet first. The thing where the latch locks onto was on my chin. So I'm hanging out the window, I drop everything, and I'm hanging by my chin. I turn my head and as I'm falling down I hit the screen and pushed it back in. It was a good ten-foot drop, hit the ground and rolled. Grabbed my shit right away and looked around...there's no fog! I said, 'Oh shit!' They later said in the paper that the fog provided cover for me to go over the wall, that wasn't true at all. The fog came later.

I take the rubber mat, it's two feet by two feet. I rolled it up because I was going to put it over the wire and go under it. I'd use that to shield me between me and the wall. The space is almost a foot. Out in the yard with the vertical cutters, I sat against the fence. The little brads at the bottom of the fence, snip snip. Along the two poles, snip snip. So all I have to do is pull the fence and roll underneath, won't have to climb over and deal with barbed wire.

When you look out your cell, there was a dark spot, light spot, dark spot, light spot. And it looked like it was light on the other side of this dark spot, but that was an illusion. It's only on the fence. When I went under the fence and started to crawl, the grass was yellow it was so bright up there, it made no sense to be crawling. I got up and ran to the wall!

Now I knew that three or four panels to the right were where the fences opened up. I can't delay, I gotta move. So now I'm running low and I see a screw in the tower. There are four towers in Norfolk, one in each corner. So this guy is walking up and down and obviously I can't have him see me. I get underneath the electrified fence and I get to the outer wall. Now once I'm against the wall the towers can't see me. They didn't have the angle to see down. But I'm still exposed, because screws looking down or prisoners looking out their windows could see me and tell the cops I'm going over the wall.

So I throw the hook up over the wall and it hits a metal bar at the top. It makes a loud metallic bang. The vehicle trap tower light comes on, and he's scanning along the fence. I hit the ground and snuggled against the wall. He can't see me but the light is running along the fence. When he gets to almost where I was, there was a noise over in the industry area. He swings his light over there, and sees two guards making their rounds. Now he knows what the noise was, he turns the light off. But now I've got two towers awake and two screws walking around. Shit! This time I throw the hook and it goes through the wires and down the other side without hitting the stanchion. Then as I pulled it up, it hooks perfectly. Now going up the thing, this cord is stretching. I'd go up a little, hear it creaking, a little more, keeps creaking. I got to where the stanchion is, at the top. When I grabbed that thing, a nuclear bomb could have gone off and my hand still would have been holding that fucking stanchion!

I get up on top of the fence. The vertical angle is carrying the hot wire. The horizontal one has got the capacitance fence wires that don't work. The stanchion to the twelve wires is between the vertical stanchion with the wire. So when I'm standing there

125

I'm between the two stanchions, I'm right in the middle of the wire. There was this this really loud buzzing sound I could hear in my head. I thought it was the pressure, under the stress of the situation. I took the rubber mat, it was rolled up. I tried to put it on the wire, and the electricity came right through that rubber and nailed me. I dropped that thing to the ground, it was no good to me. I had squirrel fur gloves, which I had cut open and put latex gloves inside them. I had boots that were rubberized inside and outside, with black shoe polish so you couldn't tell. The wires were 4,300 volts. I had to build up the balls to touch that! I took the vertical cutters, cut the wire, I had to rock the cutters back and forth to get through. When it snapped there was a barely visible arc, and then absolute silence. The fucking thing was on! In Walpole, you'd have to touch two and ground yourself. In Norfolk, all four wires are on. That's the buzz noise I was hearing, the electricity running through them. I went through and slid down the line on the other side.

I hit the ground outside the wall, I rolled. I never thought about the other side of the wall. When I got up, I patted the wall. I wouldn't care if you shot me right then, I beat the motherfucker! So I turned around and it's like daylight it's so bright. I said to myself, 'You've got to get the fuck out of here right now.'

I went over to the tree line, went in. I came back over toward the road. I had a big legal-sized envelope filled with pepper. I ripped it in half, put each half in my back pockets then dusted myself with the pepper. Also, I put holes in my back pockets so the pepper would trickle out as I ran, it would throw off the dogs looking for my scent. Then I crossed the road.

Going up the street, there's a split, there's a white house there. To the right it goes to Walpole, to the left is the Old Post Road. So I'm on the other side of the street and I see the car coming around making the rounds. So I slowed down to see if he saw the line hanging down from the fence. But when I hit the ground, there was a little pillar sticking out, and when I snapped the line it went right into the crease and he couldn't see it. I watched him drive right by. Great!

I went up the Old Post Road. When a car comes I'd run off the side of the road and hit the ground. Every time I did that I seemed to land on a rock. I finally said, 'Fuck this.' There was a driveway, it went up and around. A car came by so I ran across the little lawn. The next thing I knew I was flat on my back. There was a fucking wire! It was waist high and I hit it running and flipped right over. I'm on my back looking up at the night sky.

Now there are train tracks below the road. There's a protective fence I have to get over to get down there, but I find a part that's bent over. I climb over and there was a beam sticking out over the tracks, so I looked over and I was just going to jump off it to down below. But something in me said not to jump. So I got down on the beam and hung from it, then let go. I had time to think, 'Where the fuck is the ground?' I hit the ground, it was an embankment that was at an angle, so I slid down to the tracks. It was a secondary track, a cargo track. When you get to the town of Walpole, the main line crosses it. I follow the track and pass under at least four bridges, kept going. It seemed like I was following the tracks for a million years. I never heard an alarm. I was trying to get distance between myself and Norfolk. So I'm going in the direction I want, and as soon as I see a prospective car, I'm going to steal it.

127

I'm chugging along the tracks, trying to distance myself from Norfolk, and five minutes seems like an hour. After a while I see this big water tower and it says Dedham Sand Company. I'm in Dedham, I didn't realize I went that far. Now I come up to the station and there's a parking lot behind it. There's a station guy there, he watches me come across the tracks and walk down to the parking lot. But now I can't do anything because he's watching me. So I go down to the main drag, which is Route 1A and there's a big sign that says 'Boston.' I cross the street and there's a utility company and behind it there's cars parked there. One of them was a '53 Chevy. The ignition on it, when you pull the key out you can grab the lip, turn it and start it up with no key. The window was cracked, so I opened up the door, I got in the thing and started it up. I'm headed for Boston.

Now the fog comes in. You can't see anything. I'm on Route 1, and there's a car in front of me. I'm watching his red lights to follow which way to turn. He's going 80 miles per hour in pea soup fog. I can't even see the side of the road. I got scared and started to slow down, but then realized somebody behind me could now crash into me. I've got no choice, I have to stay with this guy at his speed. If he crashes I'd see his lights and could step on the brakes. We're driving for what seemed like forever. But then just like that we're in the Fenway, the fog was gone.

I drive all around the Fenway in Boston looking for a cop. I want a gun. Can't find any cop in the city of Boston. It's getting light out now. There's a pond there near the Fenway, a marsh with gardens, here in the morning I see five or six cop cars coming out. They were in there sleeping!

Now I head over to Beacon Street. I was waiting for nine o'clock then go find a friend of mine who was working in a bar. I see the meter maid coming down the street checking cars so that made me pull out. I went over to where he was working. He's coming out of the bar with a guy. They're going to go to New York. He sees me coming, he looks surprised, wasn't expecting to see me. He says to the other guy, 'I'll explain it to you later on.'

We get over to his place. I get a suitcase full of clothes. I get a sawed-off shotgun, star automatic 9mm, .32 revolver, and over $600. So I'm off and running!

It was fifteen years before that when someone last went over the wall in Norfolk, but they didn't get away. On the outside of the wall there's some concrete blocks coming out from the wall. This guy jumped down off the wall. One foot hit the solid and the other in between, and he breaks his back. Prior to that, nobody's gone over that wall that I know of. To this day nobody else besides me has gone over that wall.

I was out for twenty-four days. I went to New York, and from there I went to New Jersey and stayed in the East Park Street Hotel, it was like a business hotel. I came down one time and there were cops everywhere. Nixon was doing a campaign stop there. Now I'm armed to the teeth, so I turned right around and boogied out of there. But down the street was the PATH trains, and I could get over there and get over to the Village. So I was playing in the Village and sleeping in Newark. I had set up a jewelry store and a credit union as targets. If my friend didn't show up, one of them was getting hit. Probably the credit union, it had a back door where I could have totally taken them by surprise. He shows up. The

129

better thing that would have worked for me is he didn't show up, I took down the credit union, and I would have been off to California for who knows what. But I came back to Massachusetts with him to hit a bank, to do a bank score with some other people.

I end up in a place in the South End, Boston. One of the guys that lived at the house was weird about me being there. He didn't shut up and that's what drew the cops. One of the guys, J.J.—who was also wanted—went outside and the cops snatch him. 'Where the fuck is Dellelo?' they're asking him, they've got machine guns. He says, 'He's upstairs.' Had he simply told them I'd left five minutes ago, they couldn't have justified going into the building.

I look out the window and I see cops walking across the roof of the building across the street. There are all these cops with guns, Boston police, state troopers, FBI agents. The roof is covered with them. I can see they're on the roof above me, I can see their shadows on the building across the street. In the kitchen, there's a window, a transom. I got out through it and climbed the wall and got into the apartment on the floor above, the fourth floor. You heard them kicking the doors in below, boom boom. There was no place to go to hide so I went under the couch. I'm under the couch with the pistol resting across my chest.

The guy downstairs where I had been, also a wanted man, the cops could see him by looking under the door. They tell him to open the door but he won't do it, he's panicking. But they're about ready to shoot up the door because they think it's me in there. They're saying, 'Bobby don't shoot. Come on out, don't shoot Bobby.' I'm lying there hoping they shoot this guy, they would have lugged him away thinking

130

it's me. He finally opens the door. He has his hands up, he's totally confused, they realize it's not me and snatch him, take him away. But because J.J. said I was upstairs, now they're kicking in the doors on all the apartments. They kick in the door where I am. Being coward motherfuckers, instead of just looking behind the couch, they kick it against the window so if I'm back there it hits me. My hand went up over the springs and got caught, I couldn't pull the gun out. They lifted up the couch and said, 'Don't move, Dellelo.'

They get me downstairs in the cruiser. They were talking about another kid who had shot a cop, and they were getting angry at me. 'This is the same thing, this motherfucker got one of us too.' One of the cops put the machine gun right to my head. I'm thinking, 'I'm going to get shot for a cop I didn't even shoot!'

We get into the police station. The old school detective, Cunningham, he's as much as a thief as I was. We're in the little interrogation room. He asks J.J. a question, says, 'You told us where he was didn't you?' He was letting me know J.J. ratted me out.

Later in court, Cunningham was on the stand. I got this lawyer, ex-DA, Thomas Heating. It didn't occur to me that the reason he was an ex-DA is because he was an incompetent idiot and they got rid of him. He's talking to Cunningham in the courtroom. 'Mr. Cunningham in your professional opinion, do you think my client would have shot you?' He looks at me and then back at the lawyer and says, 'I don't know what was in his mind.' The lawyer asks him the same question again. If Cunningham said yes I would have jumped over that bannister and beat him to death in front of all those witnesses. I called the

131

prosecutor over and he comes over. I said, 'I'm done with this idiot. What do you want to do?' He asked me what I was looking for and I said 3-5 years concurrent. There was a shotgun used in the bank robbery, he wanted to hold that back and suspend it. I said no let's put it all together, three 3-5 year sentences concurrent to each other on-and-after the life sentence. He says, 'Mr. Heating, I think your client wants to talk to you.' He comes over to me and I was so fucking mad. I said, 'You idiot. Stand right there and shut the fuck up. Don't say a word.' He didn't know what to say. The judge had a thick folder on me. In those days, anything that I did they listed it, if it was a probability I did it they listed it, and if it was possible I did it they listed it. It was a couple inches thick. I don't know what they had in there. I pled guilty to three 3-5 year sentences.

Now I go to Norfolk on the escape, and I have the same idiot lawyer. He says they're offering you 9-10 years, and I told him that was crazy, the most I can get is ten years. For a year, I said let's go to trial. He goes back and talks to them and comes back with a final offer of 5 to 7. I said tell them to fuck off.

Denny, the transportation guard, he said, 'What's the matter, Bobby?' I told him my idiot lawyer is talking 5-7 years. He asked me what would I accept and I told him 3-5 years. He tells me he'll see what he can do and that he'll be right back. He comes back with the prosecutor and the deputy of Norfolk, Picard. He asks if I'd take 3-5 on each charge, concurrent, on and after the life sentence and I said yes. He looked at Picard and asked, 'Alright with you?' He agrees and the prosecutor says let's do it. My lawyer had nothing to do with it! He was trying to get me to plea to 9-10 years.

After it's a done deal Picard says, 'Bobby I have a question. I'm not looking for any information but I just have to know. When you escaped did you go anywhere near the oval, over by the area where the maintenance guys live?' He said the dogs kept running to the oval. He asked, 'Did you go out that way?' I smiled and told him I didn't. He said, 'I knew those fucking dogs didn't know what they were doing!'

It's funny, in those days everyone was corrupt, you used to be able to buy parole boards and stuff. I was one of the good old boys, and nobody got hurt. They gave me credit, that's the way they evaluated it. The funny thing is they almost appreciate that kind of thing. If you were slick enough to outsmart them, they gave you credit for it.

After a few years inside, though, you see other individuals that are doing natural life bids or large sentences, and the insanity of their lives. You realize that's you, and that starts to register. And the danger of the wall becomes less and less. I'd rather get shot on top of the wall than die in here on my knees. That's the attitude that I started to adopt. I wasn't going to accept my chains. I think that's probably what really saved me mentally, is that I didn't accept my chains in the prison system, and I fought back. I didn't surrender myself. You see guys that totally compromise all their principles and they became like empty souls. And I wasn't going there. That's why I was always trying to escape.

CHAPTER NINE

Years behind bars passed by and Bobby evolved into a veteran convict. And as he did, the younger inmates coming inside represented a new generation with a different set of principles. Old school cons like Bobby operated within a different cultural code than the inmates of the later years. "If a man said certain things to you, those words were intended disrespect and a fight was on," he said. The younger guys, or "kids" as they were collectively known, were accustomed to hollow threats and insults. They took it for what it was—pure talk—understanding that words did not necessarily require them to deliver. Bobby grew up knowing that if he said something, he had, with no exceptions, to back it up. What he didn't realize was that the younger generation was all about words, with very little action. Bobby mistakenly thought that if they said something, they actually meant it. He also noticed a lack of respect for elders, no reverence for the experienced older men. The generational divide in the prison population often caused communication failures, and occasionally gave rise to problems.

Working in the law library, Bobby's high profile job caused him to interact with everyone at some point or another. A new kid, whose father was a Boston cop, was particularly arrogant and disrespectful during his frequent library visits. One day he asked Bobby for the daily newspaper, which was kept behind the circulation counter. Bobby told him it had already been promised it to someone else, and the kid started to protest. He slammed his fist on the counter and snatched the paper away from Bobby, retreating to a table to read it. Bobby was furious. He waited for the right moment, creating a ruse by sliding some papers off the counter, and then emerged from behind to retrieve them. The kid was confidently leaning back in his chair reading the paper and hadn't noticed a thing. Bobby appeared next to him, propping the chair with his own leg so it stayed off balance. He grabbed a fistful of the kid's long beard and yanked him to within an inch of his own face.

"Motherfucker, if you ever in your life talk to me like that again I'll kill you, you fucking punk."

The kid was stunned. "No, no, no, Bobby, I didn't mean it like that, you misunderstood."

Bobby glared at him, letting the message sink in, and slowly removed his leg from the chair. With a fresh perspective of the situation, the kid hurriedly gathered up his papers and retreated back to his cell while Bobby repositioned himself behind the counter. The civilian librarian approached him with a smirk. Bobby, thinking the transaction had gone unnoticed, realized he actually had a bit of an audience. "Thank you for not killing that kid," the librarian said. "The last thing I need in here is a body."

Sometimes retaining control meant establishing a quid pro quo, especially when it came to dealing with prison staff. Bobby discovered that finding a way to make someone's job easier was always a good bartering chip. If presented properly, it could be traded in for the allowance and protection of certain privileges. Bobby utilized this technique by running a tight ship in the library. He kept the room neat and clean, and strictly enforced the rules for all patrons. He also ordered books and supplies, and provided maintenance and service for computers as necessary. Furthermore, he was knowledgeable about the library's resources and was helpful to those researching their cases. Because he made life easier for the administrators when it came to running the library, he gained their trust. In turn, he was essentially left alone manage as he saw fit. As long as he kept the computers working properly and the book inventory straight, he and his crew could use the library for whatever purposes they wanted. This meant they had a place to hang out, had consistent computer access, and other perks such as outside coffee and doughnuts. They always made sure the administration was happy with the library operations, and inmates well understood that no trouble was to happen in there. When it did, they delivered a very clear message.

*　*　*

While many prisons allowed inmates to have physical contact with visitors, Walpole's security policy strictly prohibited any and all touching. Visitors and inmates viewed each other through Plexiglas windows in one of the sixteen booths available for visits, and conversation happened indirectly through recorded phone lines on either side. The no contact policy supposedly prevented drugs from coming into the institution from outside sources. However, everyone knew that drugs of all types were available almost as readily as on the street.

Over time, it became obvious that the quantities of drugs moving around Walpole were far too great to have been introduced by visitors, especially in light of the no contact policy. When inmates were overdosing in prison, the media and public became curious as to exactly how the drugs were reaching the inside. The DOC, however, officially insisted that the drugs came in through the visitors only.

If the inmates and families couldn't have contact, how did the DOC think drugs were getting in? Holidays are a financially vulnerable time for families existing on a guard's salary. Inmates know it and move in. Guys would offer a certain guard $3,000 to bring in a Marlboro box packed with pure heroin. Getting it in was always tricky, but the cash offer could buy off just about anyone. Once inside,

136

the prison value of the drugs would be astronomical. So long as nobody got busted, everybody wins.

All the time I was in jail, I never once got drugs through a visit. My supplier was guards, always guards. That's where the quantities came from.

Bobby learned the game of the drug trade in prison. Being a dealer meant power, but not the guns, girls, cars, and clothes type of power the street players often flashed. It was a dangerous and very competitive business, and he knew his success depended on building and maintaining important contacts, which included both guards and inmates. It was a calculated risk, but if he played his hand well, Bobby knew that he could minimize the problems while reaping the benefits. With his network of influence, he decided it was something he could be successful with. For the first time in his life, Bobby entered the drug dealing business.

A benefit of having available product wasn't so much its cash value (there was only so much one could purchase inside the prison) but its demand could be used to create layers of protection around oneself. Bobby correctly reasoned that if he acted as a supplier to a wide base of clients, they were going to make certain no one bothered him. If Bobby was attacked, shaken down, or thrown in the hole, there would be a lot of unhappy prisoners without their drugs. To be sure, the protection was not out of friendship or personal loyalty, but rather a customer base who wanted to ensure their supply flow. Still, protection was protection, and that was always a good thing.

Along with a few trusted friends, Bobby built a sizeable drug clientele. He took extreme caution when dealing with the guards who were involved in supplying drugs, as they were also some of the meanest, toughest officers in the institution. Military in demeanor, they were hardnosed, no-nonsense guards who strictly enforced every infraction and never expressed any compassion toward inmates. The authoritarian reputation provided good cover; nobody suspected by-the-book guards of breaking institutional rules much less dealing drugs to prisoners.

The guards who supplied, they reminded me of the violently anti-gay inmates who lashed out to cover the shame of their own homosexual behavior. I didn't like or trust them, but had little choice. If they wanted in on the drug game, there was nothing you could do to stop them. It was easier to work with them.

Dealing was dangerous, and not just because of the typical problems stemming from drug debt. One veteran guard/supplier Bobby worked with saw an opportunity to leverage the situation for his own professional gain. Knowing exactly who was buying and selling, he began reporting to the control room, advising shakedowns of certain inmates returning from Two Block. For cover, he cited bogus suspicions of drug activity, while never revealing his firsthand knowledge as the actual source. A shakedown would reveal contraband drugs, the inmate would be punished, and the guard reveled in the credit given for his watchful eye. As he pursued the accolades of his superiors, he created a very dangerous situation for Bobby and his crew. They quickly distanced themselves from him and severed all business ties. If anyone even suspected that they were a part of the set ups, they'd be dead.

The risk of dealing carried benefits in addition to protection. When Bobby was dealing in Talwin (a synthetic narcotic popular amongst prisoners), he and his associates acquired them for about thirty cents apiece. At the time, the prison value was roughly ten times that amount. The profit margin was exorbitant, but not in the same way it would have been on the street. Cash flow within the prison was low. A large

138

majority of the inmate population had no money; they didn't have prison jobs or other means to earn, mostly relying on outside friends and relatives to deposit money into their accounts. Employed prisoners didn't fare much better, as they were exempted from the state minimum wage law and thus made extremely low wages. Bobby's dealing netted small amounts, where a street dealer would have made hundreds or thousands. However, a few bucks in prison could be far more valuable than a few bucks on the street. In Walpole, Bobby never lacked canteen money and always had cash to offer as a bribe. Even better, he could afford to purchase stolen maintenance equipment like hacksaw blades, hammers, and chisels—useful items to aid an escape.

Dealing drugs was a competitive venture, and sometimes force was necessary to preserve the business. Bobby and a couple friends stole keys to the utility closets in their cell block, and turned one of them into a homebrew manufacturing and storage facility. Since they controlled the block, they had free access to the gallon jugs located there to make booze whenever they wanted. Everyone knew about it, but nobody said a word. Some they shared around the block, but most they drank themselves. Sometimes, when he got drunk, Bobby would shake down other dealers. He'd grab a couple drinking buddies and they'd jack up the first dealer they saw. On one such occasion, a guard from the block called into the control center to report what was going on.

"Hey, Dellelo and his buddy here, they got a guy against the wall with knives on him."

"Are they drunk?"

"Yeah, they are."

"Then mind your business."

They felt justified in ripping off other dealers, telling themselves that they were righteously protecting their customers from the dealers' unconscionable prices, taking some of his product and threatening him to make it clear who, exactly, was in control. *We sell the drugs in here, not you.* The guards were indifferent; they weren't enthusiastic about getting stabbed while trying to intervene in a drug beef.

Guards would announce '6-5, guard on the flats, 6-5, guard on Tier 2,' before making their round. They didn't want to see anything, didn't want to rock the boat, so they clearly announced their presence. Prisoners were like, 'Do what you need to do, get your paycheck. But do not fuck with us or one of us will have to leave—and we wish it could be us. But it can't be us, so you do the math.'

While Bobby's interest in drugs was primarily selling, he did begin using. He was serving a life sentence, and enjoyed the temporary escape the high brought with it. Drugs provided a calmness rarely found in Walpole, though he knew it was a false comfort. When he used, he experienced the feeling of incapacitation, the state of helplessness, and the vulnerability that came along with zoning out. It was something Bobby loved, letting go of prison's stresses and anxieties, even if for just a short time. But in a place like Walpole, he could hardly afford to let his guard down.

Bobby's cousin, Louie, came into Walpole to serve a sentence and talked Bobby into popping some downers with him one night. Bobby was still primarily a pot smoker at the time and was inexperienced with most pills. Louie talked up the high, so Bobby shrugged his shoulders and without much thought, popped four downers at once. Sitting back on his cell bed, he felt a warm numbness wash over his body.

"Hey Louie, is this how it's supposed to feel?" he asked, slurring his words.

"Yeah man, it's nice, right?"

"You bastard. As soon as I come out of this I'm going to kill you!"

Bobby refused to accept any more pills from him after that episode.

You have to learn how to use heroin, you don't just 'use heroin.' The first time, you throw up, you get sick as a dog. To stop people who are interested in it, you give him heroin the first time but don't teach him how to use it. They are going to throw up and get sick. How was that? Are you crazy, that shit was terrible! But when you learn how to do it, ok you're going to throw up now, just kick back and relax, rinse your mouth out, lay back and enjoy the high. You have to learn how to use the drug. You get up and move around on heroin, you throw up. You get dizzy and disoriented.

I did speed for a while, but the paranoia was intense. I had one funny experience. When you do speed you get into this profound writing with all this philosophical shit coming out of your brain and you start writing like crazy. I was writing all night, and at this time lights went out around 10 p.m. At the end of the bed is the light from the security lights. Your eyes are all crimped up. And this guard comes by, he's being a nice guy, he says, 'You've been up all night. You have about forty-five minutes until count time. You should try to get some sleep.' He knows I'm going to be wiped out for the rest of the day. Now he goes by, I don't see that he's being a decent person. I'm paranoid, I think he wants my writings. I stash them all over my cell. The next day or so, the day

141

after that, I run into one of the pieces of paper. You read this, oh my God, this is pure insanity! This makes absolutely no sense whatsoever. A lunatic wrote this. I had to search the entire cell to find all this shit. The bedposts, underneath it, the back of the drawer. I mean this stuff was everywhere, I had written a stack of madness. So I did that, and then had the hallucinations.

Eventually I realized I can't do that anymore. You end up losing your mind. Guys go running down the corridor naked, screaming and hollering, and end up in the nuthouse. So I wrote that off. I wrote the heroin off, the speed off, and I kind of settled on weed. I liked that because I could smoke some grass, lay back, listen to music, and go to sleep if I wanted.

When Bobby was serving time as a state prisoner in the federal prison in Lewisburg, he made about $75.00 per month working in the shops. Every cent was invested in the purchase of marijuana. As in Walpole, he created relationships with various importers, so quantities were not difficult to get. He'd sell the surplus to a small but trusted clientele, make his money back, and have plenty to smoke for himself. When he was subjected to urine tests, he'd hand them over and laugh, "Here you go, pure cannabis!" A social worker tried to warn him, delivering a stern lecture about the dangers of drug use. Bobby interrupted him. "What are they going to do, throw me out of prison? As long as there's grass in this prison, I'm going to find it, I'm going to buy it, and I'm going to smoke it!" The social worker sighed in defeat.

Sometimes, dealing drugs led to strange friendships. For a time, his best connection for weed in Walpole was Wayne, a high-ranking member of the Devil's Disciples motorcycle club. Wayne had access to everything, including heroin, speed, and coke, but his weed was the most popular. He supplied Bobby, who would take a little for himself but resell most of it. Around the prison,

Wayne was known as a serious individual. His personality was direct and businesslike, and he could be extremely dangerous if crossed. Bobby and Wayne developed a good working relationship, having built trust over time and through a mutual interest in martial arts. But Wayne expected people to be on guard, and liked to challenge Bobby at times when he was vulnerable. He had a knack for showing up at Bobby's cell just after he'd smoked a load of pot.

"Let's work out."

"Now? Are you serious? I don't wanna fucking work out right now."

"We're going to work out, right now."

He pulled Bobby onto his feet and forced him to work out while high. He started in with punches, making Bobby defend, and gradually moved up to throwing full kicks, giving Bobby no choice but to sink or swim. He took some good shots, and knew if he was too high he'd be in for a serious beating. But he found that he was still able to fight while high and effectively protect himself. By forcing Bobby to fight, Wayne taught him a valuable lesson; if drugs impaired his ability to protect himself, get rid of them. For Bobby, it was settled. From that time forward, he would use nothing stronger than marijuana.

Eventually, even the marijuana habit began to have serious drawbacks. Years later, when Bobby was serving in solitary, the long term effects began to reveal themselves. He'd always been able to read and function while high, and that was the main reason he believed marijuana was mostly harmless. But in isolation, where he had no access to marijuana, he began to recognize a difference in his memory capacity. While working on his appeal in his tiny cell, he'd have dozens of photocopied cases strewn across his bed, desk, and floor. It hit him that he knew exactly where everything was at all times, something he'd never been able to do with marijuana. He never fully realized what he had lost, but now that his memory capability was restored he understood the implications of long-term drug abuse. It had been years since his mind had been in such sharp focus, and he preferred it that way. He loved pot and loved getting high, but his memory recall and ability for sharp thinking were crucial for crafting a successful legal appeal, and ultimately, his survival. He gave up his favorite pastime without looking back.

I tried every drug there was. And that wasn't for me. You start to see guys that do drugs and what the consequences of that behavior are. They had what was called a rinse. Which is you take a piece of cotton, when you cook the heroin on the spoon, you soak it through that. That piece of cotton, if you put it in water again, you can re-shoot whatever's left in there. And they referred to that as a rinse. I've seen guys that were hard-core, solid guys that would perform tricks to get the rinse they were so addicted and strung out by the drugs. It was unbelievable. A guy that makes a conscious decision to be with another guy, I don't have a problem with that. It's when you see someone that's driven that way by drugs or an emotional disorder, it's not a choice.

A guy that's addicted to a drug has no control on the decision process. You see that, and that kind of scares me. That happens to everybody. Everybody that uses speed and coke becomes paranoid, there are no exceptions to that rule. It kept you in prison, this stuff traps you in prison. Ultimately, the drugs for me became boring. It began to feel like part of the prison system. At one point in time the institution really used drugs to control the population, and I didn't want to be controlled by that.

* * *

In the early 1970s, Walpole State Prison's population hovered at approximately 580 inmates. Most were using drugs. During this period of rampant drug use, unprecedented violence consumed the prison, with vicious assaults and murder becoming commonplace. Due to deep rooted conflicts between the administration and the guards, the operation of the institution increasingly fell under inmate control. With a staff of mostly disgruntled correctional officers, the inmates took advantage, feeling emboldened and pushing the boundaries of security. Traditional methods of control such as throwing men in the hole, searching cells, and excessive physical force, were no longer working. The guards were not about to risk personal safety for an administration which allowed prisoners to run rampant. Walpole was falling apart, and drugs were pouring in through the cracks.

A drug-ravaged institution, though, was by no means a secure one, and the drug abuse and violence went hand-in-hand. Drug-induced paranoia often drove men to impulsively lash out at other inmates, guards, and even themselves. But instead of channeling resources toward drug programs and rehabilitation efforts, the administration turned the problem into the solution.

Nearly half of the prison population was prescribed the narcotic Talwin, a highly addictive drug combining Naloxone and Pentazocine, while scores of others used the drug without any kind of prescription. Originally prescribed to inmates suffering from chronic pain, Talwin prescriptions were doled out liberally. If an inmate complained of a sore tooth, he'd get Talwin. If he claimed a migraine headache, Talwin. It became the solution to everything, and soon everyone, it seemed, was on it. The benefits of having a large segment of the inmate population on Talwin were apparent; men who were physically dependent on the drugs became easy to manipulate and control. A previously violent inmate turned docile under the influence of Talwin, a tremendous benefit from an institutional perspective. When a difficult individual acted out, the deputy could simply send him to the hospital under a pretextual justification and direct the medical staff to prescribe him enough Talwin for several days and the problem would be solved. Eventually, even the routine medical assessments used to determine appropriate prescriptions were abandoned, and Talwin was virtually given out upon request.

Inmates turned into drug addicts—and snitches—in droves. The administration knew that even the strictest loyalist to the prisoners' code against informants would be no match against the weight of addiction withdrawal. If an inmate wanted Talwin, he simply needed to provide information about other prisoners that would be useful to the administration and staff. Such easy dispensation of Talwin provided inmates with a strong motive to talk, offering up anything they thought might be useful. Under this arrangement, the institution was able to heighten surveillance, gain actionable information, and gradually re-establish a level of control over the population. Walpole had essentially manufactured a massive pool of drug addicts, which for them, was a cheap and effective security policy.

Talwin's full potency was revealed when the prison's entire supply went missing. Just outside the prison hospital, dozens of men lined up each morning for their daily dosage of medication. Lines were long because of high demand, but the medication was not necessarily for personal use. Many sought to obtain Talwin because it was as good as cash in Walpole, and could be traded for just about anything. Others lined up under orders from a more powerful inmate. Some even needed medication for legitimate medical purposes. Whatever the motivation, everyone wanted a share.

Because he was part of the National Prisoners Reform Association (NPRA) leadership, Bobby was immediately notified of the Talwin theft. A crowd was growing down at the infirmary and tempers starting to flare. Violence was certain if the problem wasn't sorted out immediately, so he made his way down to the hospital to assess the situation. Upon his arrival it was clear that an explosion was imminent. Inmates were acting agitated and aggressive, shouting angrily. Anxious looking men milled about, breathing heavily with fists balled up, looking to find an outlet for their building frustration. The men seemed to feed off of each other's energy, and Bobby knew what that could lead to. Someone yelled, "We're going to tear this place apart!"

"What happened here?" asked Bobby. An acquaintance stepped forward and explained the problem. Inside the hospital area where medications were kept, Talwin dosages were stored in a locked glass cabinet. Earlier that morning, staff members had discovered someone had busted into the cabinet and swiped the brown paper bag containing the entire stash. Everyone was suspicious of each other, and one inmate suggested that the hospital medics possibly stole the Talwin, as they had access to the medical storage room.

The medics, who ranged in age from late-teens to early-twenties, were well-liked by the inmates, even the hard-core. A group of them had learned emergency response techniques in the military and were outstanding at their jobs. As violent as Walpole was, these men had seen every sort of horrific injury while serving in Vietnam, and there was nothing they couldn't handle. Unlike the guards and administration, the medics didn't appear to pass judgment on the men they treated. They simply knew their jobs and did them well, regardless of who needed help. They saved dozens of lives and treated innumerable injuries, always responding quickly and professionally. For this, they

147

managed to impress a population of men who were rarely impressed by anyone.

Bobby and his friends liked the medics, and sometimes called them over to offer up some weed to smoke. The amused medics usually politely declined, but occasionally accepted. Once, Bobby offered a joint, "This is some good shit, try this." The medic took a puff, then handed it back. "Not bad," he said, pulling out a huge stash of his own and holding it up to Bobby's face, "But try this shit!"

They could treat a guy who had been stabbed straight in the heart and save his life without breaking a sweat. As long as the stab wound did not interrupt the heartbeat, they'd always get the job done. They'd be on the scene quickly, apply a towel, wrap another one around the body, belt it up tight, and off to the hospital. They were good guys, they knew their stuff.

As a dealer himself, Bobby knew he'd eventually be accused if the culprit wasn't identified quickly. He pulled one of the medics aside to gather more information. "Look, Bobby," he said, "The only people who know about the bag are us and Remick. I don't know what happened." Bobby had his answer. Remick was a prisoner working in the hospital, and also served on the hospital committee. Most importantly, he was the only inmate who had any direct access to the medicine cabinet. By reputation, he was not a trustworthy individual. He'd been caught in many lies over the years, and was known to have a serious drug problem. Even worse, he was known to be a snitch.

Bobby grabbed a couple younger inmates and said, "Get Remick down here to the hospital." Minutes later, he arrived at the scene. Bobby yanked him by the shirt front into a side room and demanded some answers, but Remick was in no shape to respond coherently. Nervous and sweating, he sputtered some nonsense, his drug-induced paranoia at full tilt.

"Oh Bobby, you gotta understand," Remick pleaded. "They hate me, they're the ones that stole it, they're blaming me to cover up."

"Why would they steal the medication? It makes absolutely no sense. They can get all the fucking drugs they want, they don't need prison drugs. These medics did not steal the medication."

Remick continued to protest but Bobby stopped him cold, he'd heard enough. He knew Remick was responsible for creating the whole mess, but would have to deal with him later. "You shut the fuck up. Go directly back to your cell, speak to nobody. Leave now."

It turned out Bobby did Remick a favor. He wasn't the only one upset with him, as word spread fast who was behind the theft. His half-hearted denials were proof to most men that Remick was in fact responsible. A number of men already disliked him, but now some of his enemies talked openly of taking him out. Wisely, Remick wasted no time transferring to protective custody for his own safety.

Bobby needed to focus on how to fix the situation. As an inmate leader, he couldn't let a riot happen. He knew the response would be heavy, as the guards would be authorized to use extreme force. Bobby had been through previous riots, and while he wasn't opposed to them, he wanted them to be for a just cause. Prisoners' rights were worth sacrificing safety and fighting for, but not drugs. Besides, he ran a drug trade he wanted to preserve and a riot would certainly interrupt his business. But tensions were quickly escalating, men were beginning to boil over, and the situation was heading for a full-scale riot. Bobby pictured inmates attacking guards and each other, any property in sight being destroyed, then the onslaught of tear gas and night sticks. There was, of course, an easy answer—more Talwin—but they had none. The nearest prison, in Norfolk County, was likely to have a quantity on hand. The best plan was to send someone over right away to borrow enough Talwin to tide the Walpole inmates over until the stolen supply was replaced.

At the time, Walpole operated under the leadership of acting Superintendent Walter Waitkevitch, a man widely hated by both guards and inmates. Most felt he was neither fair nor competent, and he was highly vindictive toward anyone challenging his authority. He was disrespected enough to be given the nickname "Wacky Walter," but he was still in charge. Bobby asked to see him, and Waitkevitch came down to the hospital immediately. The escorting guards who fulfilled his request did so not out of sympathy for the inmates, but because they too feared a riot was imminent. They were also anxious about how their boss would handle the situation.

Bobby got straight to the point. "Mr. Waitkevitch, we need Talwin right now."

"Absolutely not. They're not getting anything. It's the weekend anyway, we can't get anything," he said.

"Mr. Waitkevitch, this place is going to explode."

Waitkevich stared for a moment, and then gave a dismissive shrug. He wanted everyone to know he was the boss.

Invoking his NPRA leadership privileges, Bobby grabbed the hospital phone and dialed an outside number. A few connections later, he had someone on the line and began to lay out the details of the situation. As Bobby listened intently to the voice on the other end of the receiver, Waitkevitch watched carefully.

"Where's Walter right now?" the voice said.

"He's standing right here, sir," Bobby answered.

"Put that fucking moron on the phone now."

"Yes sir." Turning to Waitkevich, Bobby held out the receiver.

"Who the fuck is that?"

"The Commissioner of Corrections. He'd like to speak with you," Bobby said, grinning broadly. Waitkevitch looked like was about to vomit. He slowly took the phone and held it up to his ear. Bobby could hear everything.

"Waitkevitch, get the fuck over to Norfolk, pick up the medication. Enough to make it through the weekend. On Monday when you re-up with your medication, you give Norfolk back their medication you took. Do it now!"

"Yes yes, ok ok, sir. Right away, yes. Uh huh, yeah, ok."

Waitkevitch himself personally bolted for Norfolk seconds after the call. Within the hour, Walpole was back in the Talwin business. Doses were quickly handed out, tempers subsided, and calm restored. A major incident had been only narrowly avoided.

Talwin was distributed like candy. But why? To create drug addicts in order to achieve and maintain control. The prison doled out massive quantities of Talwin, and to say that it was with the inmates' best interests in mind would be completely untrue.

In an eighteen month period, twenty people were murdered in Walpole State Prison all because of the drugs. They made drug addicts out of people. Talwin was extremely addictive. And that was the only drug. And even the medics after this incident said, 'It doesn't make any sense, the kind of medication. These guys are walking right into this, Bobby. They're being made drug addicts, and this institution owns them.' I mean this is what they did, is they put very powerful drugs out there. Guys want to escape the harsh reality of prisons. You're going to say no? Of course you're not going to say no in a prison. And here are drugs that cost a ton of money. Now, some guys that don't use drugs, I can go down there, fake medical problems, they put me on Talwin, I get the Talwin and sell it to you. Now I get canteen, I don't have family. So guys learned how to hustle the medication situation. If they had proper control on it, it wouldn't be a problem.

Now, they've gone completely to the other extreme. I got broken bones sticking out, I can't get pain medication. I've got to go into the hospital and stay in a room that's more like an isolation chamber. I don't have a TV, no radio. Because they don't want me to get used to going down there and being treated like a human being. So they went to the other extreme. They don't give you the medications that you need. But on the other extreme, they flooded you with all kinds of serious narcotic drugs. It was 265 guys on Talwin out of a 580 man population, that was the count. I know what it was.

There's an element of individuals that are acute, hard-core drug addicts, and they will be until they die. Don't throw them in isolation, you get them in the drug block. Then you have an ability to deal with them. By dealing with them, you're dealing with the drug problem in the prison. You're keeping it restricted. There are people in the prison system, which isn't really a large number, but there are *people in the prison system if they couldn't find any drugs, I'd go find them for them. Because without the drugs they're total lunatics. They have to be on drugs, they are self-medicating. When they try to self-medicate, when they medicate individuals with psychological problems they're using psychotropics; you don't get high off of psychotropics, you get crazy on psychotropics, drooling. They don't want that, they want to get high. Without the drug, this guy's a raving lunatic and a dangerous person. With the drug, he's over there, quiet, passive, not hassling anyone, not causing problems. That guy is an acute drug addict and I have no problem with giving him drugs.*

Two hundred and sixty-five people on Talwin, I have a big problem with that because you're talking about people that are not drug addicts that are about to become drug addicts. That's a different ballgame. When the administration is giving drugs to prisoners for the purpose of creating stool pigeons, I'm against that. The institution giving drugs to a prisoner that's a lunatic, that without the drug is dangerous to himself, to guards, to other prisoners, yeah I have no problem with them giving him a drug. But they won't do that unless it's a psychotropic and he has to go through all this psychological crap.

A game that they play, they still play it now in Walpole. Adderall, it's dexamphetamine, it's in the same family as methamphetamine. Someone who has ADD or ADHD and you put him on Adderall, it slows him down. If you put him on Adderall and he's getting high, he doesn't have ADD. It doesn't happen, he's getting high off the drug, and it's not slowing him down. They have guys in Walpole that are on eighty milligrams a day! How long do you think you can be on that before you get paranoid and all that other crazy shit. That's what happens in the prison. These guys get paranoid and end up stabbing someone over nonsense. Who's to blame? Alright, you are responsible because you stabbed someone. But so is the institution that got you addicted to Adderall, that got you into that frame of mind. Eighty milligrams a day? That's insanity! That's the kind of medication they're still giving out in the prison system.

Psych services, they don't have enough staff to deal with guys' emotional problems, so they saturate them with drugs. Now, you're not going to get away with Talwin, you're not going to get away with a big narcotic. The only way you can get drugs for pain relief is to go to the hospital and stay in the hospital. Now, you can't have your radio, you can't have your TV. You're in isolation. So what they're doing is saying if you want pain medication, you're going to get punished; but if you want goofball medication you can have that.

But that didn't end the Talwin epidemic. Walpole still had to deal with the high number of addicts populating the institution. Drugs continued to come into the institution and were more valuable than ever because of the restricted supply. There was still lots of violence, overdoses were still occurring. The institution was creating drug addicts and releasing them to the streets, where they'd quickly be arrested and returned to Walpole. The institution publicly claimed to know nothing about the Talwin epidemic, and assumed no responsibility for its role in the problem. Look, I was a drug dealer in prison. I had to survive. It was something I did out of necessity. But the institution was the worst drug dealer of all. I sold to guys who wanted to a get a little high and cope with prison; they created addict after addict and released them to the public. They are supposed to be protecting the public and rehabilitating prisoners, but they were the dealers. It was what they did when it became clear they were failures in controlling the prison population. They turned men into drooling vegetables for control purposes.

* * *

Before the late 1960s, drug addicts represented a very small percentage of Walpole's population. As the decade turned, however, a new breed of convict, the drug addict, dramatically swelled in population, eventually eclipsing traditional criminals as the majority population. Drugs were linked, directly or indirectly, to just about every crime out on the street. Assaults, robberies, burglaries, thefts, extortion, and murders were all committed over drugs, by someone under the influence of drugs, or both.

Older inmates, for the most part, had never been involved in the street drug business. Their crimes were from a different era, and they prided themselves on the skills that their respective crafts required. They feared lock picking, safe cracking, and bank robberies were an art form of days past, inevitably headed toward extinction. The newer guys tended to employ violence over skill to get a job done. Old-school cons separated themselves from the typical new breed of drug-offender convicts; they had skills, talent, and ingenuity while the newer gun-toting thugs required nothing more than bravado.

For generations, the old school taught the new school. In the prison culture, people look at prison as on the same continuum. It's not. There are time frames in it. People leave the system, new people come in, new offenses are created, new drug laws are passed. 'Get tough on crime' brings in people that aren't really criminals, they're addicts, addicted to alcohol and drugs. Yes, they rob banks, but look at what they robbed. They gave them a note, got short

155

money, that money went immediately to the drug dealer, and they immediately ended up the cops' arms. Yes, they robbed a bank but they're not 'bank robbers.' A bank robber is someone who plans to go into the bank, he knows where the money is located. You know that in the bank that if you can find out who the head teller is and where the head teller's booth is, guess what's in there? When the bank opens up in the morning, as a standard rule, they'll take a couple hundred thousand out and put it into their drawer. That way they don't go in and out of the vault. One of the tellers would send a note down saying, 'I need X amount of money.' They take money out, pass it down to the teller. So that's what a professional bank robber does. He locates where the money is in the bank, they come in, take it down, in and out fast, up over the counter. They know how to take a pack of $100 bills and hold it at a certain angle. Guess what pops out? Dye pack. To be sure, what they would end up doing too is throwing the bag through the window. Where's the trigger to the dye bomb? It's in the door frame, not the window frame. So they throw it through the window, they break a thousand dollar window.

But that's the difference, a bank robber is motivated by money, there's professionalism in how they take the bank down. People, like friends of ours that were professional bank robbers, like one friend of mine now. He goes and robs a bank, he's on heroin. This guy's a professional bank robber. He robs a bank. He's got $96,000, no bag, no getaway car, in Chelsea, with cameras all over the fucking city. Drugs drove him to rob the bank. Yeah, he's a professional bank robber, but he wasn't robbing the bank as a professional. He was robbing the bank as a drug addict.

Another friend of mine that got busted, he used his girl's SUV to rob a bank. Robbed the bank, the cops are chasing him, he pulls off the road and gets off. What's the motivation? Money? No, the motivation is drugs. Drug addiction is a bitch, and the jails got filled with people like that, that were pushed into that direction because of drugs.

I got in there in early '60, and when I first got in there, there were lock picking schools, safe cracking schools, burglar alarm schools, short change artists, teaching you the trade and stuff. Guys took pride in their expertise. All of a sudden you start seeing a lot of drug addicts coming into the prison, and you're seeing less and less professional people. It was easier for law enforcement to catch these addicted individuals, I mean it was easy to sting them. But catching a professional bank robber, safe cracker, B&E man, it took finesse, it took police work. And when you chase down these poor bastards in the ghetto, you lost your ability to act as police officers, an ability to intelligently and rationally investigate. They didn't do it that way, they just went down and nailed some poor bastard. You get this one to rat on that one, that one to rat on this one. That's not really CSI shit, and that isn't how they function. And what happens is a lot of people end up in jail that don't belong there. But the bottom line is the old timers stop teaching these types of individuals. It's like I'm not going to give you something that I hold dear to me as a profession. I'm a safe cracker, that's a skill. That isn't something that you just pick up a book, read it, and you got it. This is something you have to train at to become good at, you have to understand all these mechanisms of safes and how to get them open. I'm not going to give that to some junkie that's just going to go out there and abuse it. It's my life skill.

157

We had a guy in there, Louie the Lug. I mean this guy could do anything with any lock. He backed up to the locks in the canteen and picked them behind his back, in the area just in front of the control room, which wasn't even fifteen feet away. In between the control room is the deputy's office. He backed up to the door, he picked two heavy duty locks and a Yale lock and walked away. Other guys came in and robbed the canteen, right in front of the control room. But this is what this guy's profession was.

He was down in Norfolk Prison, they couldn't open one of the safes in the accounting room. They asked him if he would open the safe for them. He said he'd open the safe but didn't want anyone there to see what technique he was using. They said no problem. He went in, he opened the safe so fast, he got bored. So he opened a second safe and that's what they locked him up for, is opening the second one! There's all kinds of stories, but this guy wouldn't teach a drug addict, how to steal money to go buy drugs. Wouldn't do that.

The older generation of inmates was not against the younger generation per se; they were always scouting for new talent. But the valuable criminal knowledge they had spent years acquiring was beginning to die out, as they were unable to find worthy apprentices. In the old days, it was a universal principle to never trust a man who allowed himself to be controlled by a bag of dope. Everyone knew once cold turkey withdrawal kicked in, all addicts, without exception, would become extremely cooperative with the authorities. Addiction was not viewed as a chemical dependency or a disease. It was simply a character flaw; and thus, no sympathy was given. As criminals, they were nothing more than fools destined to be caught.

Old schoolers operated on a theory that it was better to pass on a job than to go forward with inadequate help. Greed and impatience in such situations were foolish, but choosing to work with an addict was plain stupidity. Teamwork amongst criminal partners was critical to successfully complete a job. Each individual cooperated with one another, paid attention to timing and detail, and contributed his personal expertise to the overall scheme. The team could be no better than its least disciplined member, and a cokehead, even if talented, was always the weak link. Experience had shown that trusting an addict exponentially increased the chances of getting killed or busted.

> *They had their frantic coke-babble, a nonstop stream of nonsense and total lack of self-control. Most of the older guys were used to working in teams—who would want to partner up for a robbery, using fully automatic weapons, with such an unreliable person? You work with those guys, you're going to jail.*

The proliferation of drugs and the new breed of inmates it created in the 1970s eroded the old school core of the prisons, generated widespread conflict, and introduced a new layer of challenges for the Department of Correction. Prior to this time, the DOC traditionally ignored cultural shifts within the prisons, advancing through decades with outdated methods of control, and applying old solutions to new problems. Viewing prisoners and prison culture on the same continuum became a highly negligent, even dangerous, position. For years, the longstanding policy of treating all inmates alike projected an initial impression of logic and fairness. But when the drug addicted population shifted from a negligible percentage to roughly 85% of the entire population, the "one size fits all" philosophy became both untenable and unworkable, as it ignored the population shifts across eras. The punishment model system was extremely resistant to change, despite being clearly broken, inefficient, and in dire need of reform. The old way of doing things was a clear failure.

That notion that you treat everybody equally is absolute crap. You can't treat everybody equal because everybody is not equal. Every prisoner in and of himself is unique and different, and you got to deal with each person individually. You can't have a program that fits all for that very reason. That's what causes the problem.

Today, the old school is no longer an influential presence in the prisons. The relatively few old timers, serving lengthy terms or life without parole, have quietly faded into the background. They are marked by their low-key presence, actively ignoring those around them with an equal desire to be ignored themselves. They've outlived their heyday, and a new culture has emerged to replace them. Understandably, they wanted no role in the new era. Rather than passing on what had become their livelihood, their life skill, to newer and unworthy convicts, they prefer to see their own eventual extinction.

CHAPTER TEN

The old Massachusetts State Prison was built in Boston's Charlestown neighborhood in 1805, on the site where Bunker Hill Community College sits today, serving as the state's first maximum security penal institution. By the 1950s, the building had deteriorated into complete disrepair, yet continued to house inmates though deemed to be a "verminous pesthole, unfit for human habitation." Squalid living conditions and the constant threat of violence evolved into the norm, and prisoner complaints about the conditions were ignored. In time, the prisoners reached their collective breaking point, and a series of riots erupted.

In January of 1955, four convicts launched an escape attempt. After sawing through cell bars, they used smuggled guns to take a pair of prison guards hostage. They attempted to create a makeshift ladder to climb the outer wall to freedom, but did not have the materials to build one. To try to increase negotiation power they seized more hostages, including both guards and prisoners.

News of the hostage situation attracted media attention from all over, and the prison was soon surrounded by cameras, reporters, and helicopters. Both local and Massachusetts State Police had secured the area. Even the National Guard was called in, bringing with them a Walker Bulldog military tank to secure the prison entrance. The police did not negotiate, but did issue threats of lethal force. Demands to release the hostages were ignored, and the angry inmates issued threats of their own: *If any force is used against us, we will kill the hostages.*

As the standoff wore on, the men demanded a getaway car but were denied. They became increasingly desperate with a successful escape looking less and less possible. Some of the hostages were forced to begin digging a tunnel under the wall, but the concrete was too tough and the tools inadequate. Finally, they agreed to negotiate with a citizens' panel. There, they listed their demands but refused any concessions, such as releasing some of the hostages. After several hours, the men realized their situation was hopeless. In the end, they handed over their guns and surrendered.

Though they didn't escape, their attempt brought about a public airing of their concerns about horrible living conditions and harsh punishments. If they couldn't be free, they at least wanted someone to listen. Although the poor conditions had existed in American prisons for decades, the average citizen was largely indifferent. But the incident drew massive attention and thrust the prisoners' viewpoint into the public eye for the first time, provoking concern from civic organizations, politicians, and the public in general. In response, the governor created a commission to investigate the Department of Correction's practices, later called the Wessel Commission. When it released its findings to the public, the final report surprised many. It presented a sharp criticism of the prison system, finding that the DOC systematically failed on many fronts: allowing poor prisoner treatment, lacking rehabilitative programs, following no regulations, and operating without consistent policies. According to the report, the primary source of these problems stemmed from a complete lack of oversight, as the DOC functioned for decades without accountability to either a higher authority or to the public. The commission concluded by making a number of recommendations, including improving the effectiveness of parole and probation, increased training for staff and administration, drafting and publishing clear department rules, implementing educational and vocational programs, and increasing both institutional transparency and accountability. However, the Wessel Commission held no authority over the DOC, and its findings carried the force of mere suggestion. Predictably, the DOC was disinterested in sweeping institutional changes, and cited funding issues as justification to avoid taking action.

A year later, in 1956, Charlestown State Prison was closed permanently, and the new Walpole State Prison opened as the state's main maximum security facility. There, some of the commission's ideas were launched. Walpole implemented a prison-industry program, in which men could gain work experience in print shops, foundries, and other labor maintained by the prison. The program was beneficial to inmates, helping to combat boredom, providing the opportunity to learn a valuable skill, and giving men a chance to earn wages. However, the prevailing hourly wage at the time was approximately twenty-five cents per day, as state law allowed inmate pay to be set at a rate far lower than the minimum wage standard for citizens. While the program had its benefits, the low pay and unsafe working conditions upset the inmates. If they worked, they wanted to have the same rights and privileges of other working men. Inmate organization around these labor issues eventually led to creation of the Walpole chapter of the National Prisoners Reform Association.

The NPRA was originally established by a group of inmates incarcerated in the Rhode Island state prison system in the early 1970s. Prior to that time, there had been ideas of uniting prisoners under a labor theory, but without true leadership and organization, nothing ever materialized. The Massachusetts inmates carefully watched the NPRA's movements in Rhode Island, and soon decided to launch their own chapter. They seized the NPRA's central idea of prisoners as laborers, but tailored it to specific needs of Massachusetts inmates, understanding which ideas were needed and could work and which ideas were likely to fail in their state. They had a vision of improving the lives of all inmates.

First and foremost, the NPRA declared that all laboring prisoners must be defined as "workers" and entitled to the same rights and protections as any civilian working under current state and federal labor law. For Bobby and other working inmates at Walpole, they held a common belief that they were employees of the state. After all, they manufactured state-issued license plates, used printing presses to service the entire state, and manufactured steel manhole covers for statewide use. They worked under the custody and control of a state-run institution while directly producing goods and services for the state. They believed their incarceration did not negate their rights as state employees, and therefore they should be recognized as legitimate workers entitled to all the same benefits and rights. This way, not only could they earn legitimate wages, but would find an increase in morale, would be more productive, could pay taxes, and earn money toward their release date. Further, they would no longer be subjected to poor conditions, unfair practices, and other worker exploitation.

This was a new approach. For years, inmates were unable to find wide support for issues framed as "prisoners' rights" concerns. But those issues, such as education and job-skills training now had a new model for promotion. Workers, as a defined group, already had in place well-recognized legal rights, as well as a legitimate framework to address the same issues concerning inmates. Recasting themselves as primarily workers and aligning their interests with those of labor, the inmates were excited and invigorated to pursue their causes.

The Massachusetts NPRA chapter, however, understood that their ideas, like so many others, were likely to die at the conceptual phase. Most programs were acknowledged as decent ideas, but never implemented due to lack of funding. Thus, the NPRA sought to avoid the same mistake, and made it a priority to offer realistic and workable solutions as to how the programs could be financed. The primary idea was to pay the state minimum wage to all working inmates and have inmate employment tax dollars directly contribute to defraying costs of prisons. Next, they proposed the creation and management of a canteen-style shop inside the prison, which could sell basic food, coffee, snacks, and personal items to generate profits. Any profits derived would be earmarked for the establishment of halfway houses, which they would also staff and operate. They offered cost efficient and practical ideas; one suggestion was to establish a savings account for all inmates into which half of his total earnings would be diverted into. The money would be held for his release date (an exception would be made for inmates serving a natural life sentence), while the other half would be accessible for discretionary spending. The idea would create a sense of financial responsibility and autonomy, as well as a nest egg for every man which would increase his chances of success once released. At the time, an inmate received about fifty dollars to return to the street, barely enough to cover bus fare to reach home or a shelter. The NPRA also advanced the concept of having inmates and former inmates fully involved in re-entry and rehabilitative programs. By hiring "non-professionals" the state stood to save the cost of much higher salaries demanded by degreed professionals. More importantly, inmates utilizing the services would benefit from an untapped reservoir of highly qualified and experienced individuals able to understand and respond to inmate needs. The NPRA was unified in the belief that these ideas were realistic, workable, and practical.

Bobby understood that the successful unionization of the prisoners was critical to making any real change, and was necessary to fight the powerful institutional forces of the DOC and the guards' union. For generations, prisoners lacked both a common voice and organizational ability, and were unprepared to sit at a negotiation table to demand changes.

> *There are three pillars in the corrections system. There's the administration, the guards, and the prisoners. Any one of the three that doesn't want to cooperate, nothing can work. All three have to agree on a concept in order for it to work in a prison system. So all three gotta get into bed together.*

> *Now the problem was how to balance the power with the guards union. If we could have gotten certified as a legitimate union, the National Prisoners Reform Association, we could have challenged the guards union. If they acted the way they acted against us as a union, we could have their certification pulled as a union. That would have leveled the playing field. So unionizing was very important, it would force the state to pay us for our labor.*

Bobby, a veteran inmate with over a decade of prison time behind him, would play a central role in leading the NPRA forward into battle. The younger Bobby Dellelo, the boy who went to reform school, was a very different person. At that time in his life he was not much interested in the larger concepts necessary to understand and advocate for the unionization of prisoners. During his early prison days, he was young and angry, and long-term philosophical pursuits were not part of his thinking process. For the most part, he was only interested in maintaining his reputation or figuring out how to escape. But by this time, his years behind bars had provided him with a depth of experience and cumulative knowledge; he was ready to see things in a different way now.

> *Let's go back to the young Bobby in reform school. At that time I could have never formulated that kind of*

concept, the idea of a prisoners union. The Bobby in Concord could never formulate that kind of concept. The Bobby on the 6-10 year sentence in Walpole could never formulate those kinds of concepts. It was only once I had the life bid in Walpole, once I became educated and earned my college degree, then I had the ability to formulate that kind of world view. It now allowed me to look beyond the small world I lived in. I saw things as they were.

Judges, I had a misconception of what judges were. These were men of honor in a high, prestigious position. I didn't see them as the political scumbags that they could be. Same thing with attorneys, prosecutors. Once you saw this, you could now evaluate that. Now you saw what was the right thing and the wrong thing to do.

Things that we did, we did them because that was the right thing to do. You're going to get locked up, you're going to get shipped out, but that comes with the territory. Maintain your principles. I'll die like a man, not on my knees in a corner. That attitude comes into your mind. You were able to put yourself on the line on principle. Getting killed for principle for the sake of getting killed for principle, I'm not talking about that. But there's a certain line you do not allow anyone to cross.

In segregation, we tore the block apart. Ripped the sinks out, all the toilets, the corridors covered in feathers from the mattresses. A guard walking by, seeing this was totally illegal. You had this new sense of freedom. There was nothing you could do to me. Nothing. The only thing you could do to me is to cut my head off. And you wouldn't do that because you'd be scared of doing me a favor. You got that new sense of freedom. You transcended all the crap of the institution, all the crap of the whole prison

system and its concept, their whole misguided sense
of justice, which was more like persecution, and
feathering their own nest. Then you started seeing
the world in a different way. Now I was capable of
developing concepts of unionization.

The NPRA would not only fight for worker's rights, but the basic human rights of all prisoners. Bobby himself knew what it was like to hit rock bottom. He'd suffered beatings, been thrown in isolation, had his dignity stripped away. The typical response was violence, lashing out in frustration at every opportunity. But he came to understand that such behavior was self-defeating, it did not bring about positive change and only resulted in further punishment. Unionization, he felt, was the only mechanism by which he could stand up for what was right and ever have a chance at success. Given the harsh conditions he lived under, and abuses he had experienced firsthand, he wanted to establish a legitimate way to force the guards and administrators to treat prisoners humanely. Bobby was not interested in fighting the good fight for show, as his reputation was already securely in place. He was willing to make sacrifices and suffer for the cause, but only in the pursuit of real, tangible changes. Reflecting on his NPRA commitment, he said:

To be a principled man, one must acknowledge and
embrace that suffering must be endured to achieve
his cause. He will be tested, and will meet full
resistance and must persevere.

Prior to the existence of the NPRA, prisoners' rights issues were handled by the Inmate Advisory Council (IAC). A chairman headed the council, backed by a vice-chairman and an executive board, while each individual cell block was allowed to nominate representatives. Veteran inmate Eddie Mello, serving a life sentence for murder, was asked to assume the chairmanship. Eddie was a reluctant leader, as he'd been thrown in isolation any time he had put himself forward. Bobby strongly encouraged him, attempting to smooth over his apprehension. He pointed out the reason Eddie got in trouble was because he was a known straight shooter, and was not into manipulation or game playing. Further, it was his loyalty to the population that made him well-suited for the position; he was trusted to always represent everyone's interests. Eddie relented, and agreed to accept the chairmanship, but on the condition that Bobby be his vice-chairman. "If I'm going to segregation, you're coming with me," he told Bobby.

Much of Bobby's education in prison politics came through his time working with Eddie. Up until that time, he gave little attention to problems impacting the inmate body as a whole; he was mostly concerned about his own individual issues. But now, he paid close attention to Eddie's decision-making processes and negotiation skills, absorbing the effective tactics he used. Working alongside him, Bobby gradually learned when to push and when to relent. He learned to read situations, to see through facades and understand people for who they really were. Soon, Bobby was able to recognize that many of the inmates' unwritten rules, the so-called "prison code," were often irrational and counter-intuitive, and thus, counterproductive. Eddie showed him that he needed to see those around him in a different light. Bobby took those lessons to heart. As a rule, he began questioning people's motives behind their words, and unspoken rationales for their actions. Through this scrutiny, he began to fully understand how inmates could manipulate and control situations, and internalized those methods. This was all part of his education to survive in prison—understanding how to control his environment, and recognizing others' attempts to control him. In time, he applied those techniques to advance the NPRA agenda.

Bobby stepped into his leadership role with energy and enthusiasm. The inmates trusted his judgment, and tended to be amused by his tenacious optimism. More importantly, he had a strong reputation for keeping his word. It was that reputation which allowed him to be one of the very few men with the ability to communicate across racial lines. He took advantage of his status to relentlessly promote prison-wide unity, regardless of race. The institution took notice, and prison administrators became nervous at Bobby's IAC activities, feeling increasingly threatened by the growing unity. As he had anticipated, Bobby was sent to the Departmental Segregation Unit (DSU) at Bridgewater for his activity. There, he suffered conditions as deplorable as Walpole's. During later negotiations with prison officials he pointed a finger at them and exclaimed, "Your system is sick. You put me in there again and I'll pull out the toilets and burn mattresses again. Any time you treat me like an animal, I'll act like an animal!" His simple articulation of inmate frustration solidified his leadership position. The prisoners respected him, and, when he spoke, the administration was forced to listen.

Fr. Russ Carmichael, a former Walpole inmate, was part of the NPRA External Board during this time period. "When I was organizing on the outside, I had Bobby on the inside," he said. "This was a great relationship. He's the power guy, the strongest guy in there that you could have asked for. Maybe difficult in some other ways...but he's an organizer. He's power and he's total respect. Nobody is going to give him any shit in there. No guys. Walpole went from the most violent prison in the country to the most tranquil overnight when the guards went out of there. You needed that weight and only a guy like him could have done it. Most people couldn't have done what he did, they would have gotten their head broken. They weren't going to do that to him, he'd kick the shit out of anybody. He was too respected for that. That situation needed to have a leader like Bobby.

170

Nobody could have pulled together Walpole like he did. He was a steamroller, he didn't need anybody to back him up and that's the absolute truth. He dropped Jimmy the Bear in the yard, beat the shit out of him. His reputation always followed him, you heard stories about him whether you knew him or not. You heard about the escapes, the fighting for candy in juvie, he was the candy king. And he has brains, he's not a dummy. You have someone who is smart and can organize, and understood the dynamics of what was going on in the prisons better than anybody. "

In Bridgewater, Bobby met his African-American counterpart in Ralph Hamm. Ralph was a charismatic young man who was naturally cast into a leadership role amongst his peers, much like Bobby in his younger years. The two men quickly discovered that their racial differences were irrelevant; they were prisoners together and shared common goals. As Bobby and Ralph's trust for one another deepened and their relationship developed, both men wholly agreed that unless racism was addressed, all inmates would continue to be oppressed. Divisions amongst the inmate population based on racial lines would always serve as a natural divide if inmates did not strive to overcome it. But the administration had a vested interested in preserving racial discord, following a "divide and conquer" strategy which had been successful for so many years. Bobby and Ralph knew that they must each utilize their respective influences over men to make the case for racial unity, to show men that they must put aside racial prejudices for the greater good of all inmates. They had to convince everyone that there must be no hierarchy in prison. Nobody was above anyone else; they were all prisoners and workers, and they were all subjected to the same conditions. Thus it was imperative for them to unite and pursue their common goals together as incarcerated men. The task was a daunting one, but both men knew that if carried out properly, it could produce real change for their collective benefit.

"I became a so-called leader in the prison reform movement back in the 1970s," Hamm said. "At the age of 21 I helped to found Black African's Nation Toward Unity (B.A.N.T.U.) in Walpole prison prior to aligning myself and B.A.N.T.U. to the cause of the N.P.R.A. My joining the N.P.R.A. came as a direct result of a request from Bobby, talks with Arnie Coles, Ed Rodman, and the B.A.N.T.U. Board of Directors (both internal and external). I was skeptical of the N.P.R.A. cause but I believed in Bobby, which sentiment I relayed to the B.A.N.T.U. membership body. I was also a black militant in the extreme, which made me suitable to the role I was to play as Vice President of the N.P.R.A. in the future. Although I did not possess a true working knowledge or understanding of the machinations of the D.O.C. and its minions as Bobby did, we determined that my role would be to instill sheer terror in the mindset of the D.O.C. (I was six foot six, weighed 240 pounds of muscle, sported a huge afro hairstyle), who did not know how to take a black militant—especially after the massacre at Attica Prison in New York. I was young and starving for knowledge of black history and the struggles against imperialism/colonialism by people of color around the world, so I spent most of my time in prison back then (when we weren't negotiating with the system) reading Paolo Friere, Frantz Fanon, Herbert Aptheker, Carl Jung, Mao Tse Tung, Amilcar Cabral, Kwame Nkrumah, etc., and introduced my findings into our movement. I watched how the system responded to the resistance of the prisoners, and learned through trial-by-error in my approach to social education. It was learn quickly or die for most of us, and I was trained for combat leadership by the U.S. Army prior to my conviction—Leadership Preparation Course (L.P.C.) in Fort Sill, Oklahoma in 1968. My military training at age 17 was my greatest asset, with my reading and absorption of history as my second tool. At age 20 I came to learn more about resistance movements around the world than my peers (black and white), which thrust me into the forefront with Bobby as elected leaders in the struggle for prison reform.

As Bobby and I learned together, we took episodes in history (People's struggles) and revisited them in our ongoing circumstance. The dynamic that made Bobby such a good leader was that he always devised sound strategies for a given moment that always worked. He had a knack for turning the tide in our favor, and we all trusted his judgment. You could talk to him, he'd ingest what was said or going on around him, and then eloquently relate or present the cause of our struggle to the oppressor. I learned the ability to pull specifics out of a story or situation from him, and so did many others in our close circle of associates. The system still cannot to this day figure out how he does it (on apparent short notice, or immediate observation), which makes him such a great spokesman for the cause of abolition."

Being an inmate leader had its benefits, but being recognized as such also came at a price. For his political involvement, Bobby was labeled by Superintendent Robert Moore as an "unmanageable, persistent troublemaker." He was transferred yet again, this time to the federal institution in Marion, Illinois, one of the nation's first "supermax" prisons. The Inmate Advisory Council pressured the administration to bring Bobby back to Walpole, and after several years, were ultimately successful.

However, the Walpole that Bobby had left had now become a racially tense, high violence institution. He and the other leaders were determined to restore a united prisoner front; it was the only way to face the administration with success. Bobby had his work cut out for him, and set about informing, explaining, cajoling, and influencing any inmate he came across. Ralph Hamm, as a large and physically intimidating figure, quietly but effectively represented the physical force behind the agenda. Together they laid down the new law which applied to all prisoners; there would be a moratorium on all inmate conflicts, effective immediately. Fighting was strictly prohibited. Disagreements were to be put on hold. The prison population would unite as one against the administration, and the hard-core would not tolerate any inmate pushing a minor issue which could undermine their authority. Adherence to the directive was not optional; violations of the order would be considered ceding power to the guards and administration, and all inmates were put on notice that anyone compromising their goals would be dealt with harshly. Bobby addressed the inmates in Walpole's auditorium with a fiery speech, laying out the expectations of all prisoners. They would stand up together and fight. "We will speak as one. Do not, under any circumstances, contradict or argue with each other in front of the man. We can have private conversations later, but in front of them we are together," he told them. Inmates overwhelmingly stood and cheered in support.

During his absence from Walpole, Bobby was appointed chairman of the Inmate Advisory Council when Eddie Mello was sent to segregation. He agreed to assume the post, but with certain non-negotiable conditions attached. Foremost was the sole authority to disband the council at his discretion. For the council to maintain credibility and integrity, he needed a mechanism by which he could pull the plug if he discovered any abuses. The IAC would be legitimate or not exist at all. Specifically, he did not want select groups of inmates attempting to manipulate the council and its negotiation efforts for personal gain. He had discovered that a few pockets of men who had acquired some level of power were resistant to the IAC's plans, not wanting to surrender their personal perks for the overall good. But Bobby insisted that the IAC would be representative of all inmates, and not a lobbying committee for a select powerful few. Any negotiations that occurred were to be made on behalf of all prisoners. He also insisted that no individual was to go behind the council's back and negotiate directly with the institution; only the IAC was to negotiate. As chairman, he demanded that all council business be legitimate, above-board, and transparent. The council agreed, and Bobby's demands were incorporated into the bylaws. Walpole's administration was not pleased with the new provisions, but recognized they had no power to dictate the IAC's rules.

Bobby took his role as chairman seriously. It was understood that during negotiations, no prisoner would contradict any statement Bobby made as chairman. As a rule, any inmate disagreements would be handled in private caucus. There, argument and dissent was acceptable, but under no circumstances were the council members to betray its united front in the presence of the administration.

The unity and sense of purpose fueling the inmates' council was deeply concerning to the administration. With the inmates now acting as one under the IAC, they could no longer be ignored. Administrative officials quickly offered some minor concessions as appeasement, but the IAC rejected most of them; the prisoners knew momentum was on their side and they believed the prison officials were trying to derail it.

The prison population overwhelmingly voted to make the NPRA their representative body. Bobby immediately exercised his right to dissolve the IAC and was elected the NPRA's first president. At the time, the concept of creating a representative body exclusively composed of incarcerated men was a powerful new concept. For the first time, the DOC would be forced into dealing directly with the men they controlled. Though the DOC recognized the NPRA as a legitimate organization, the State Labor Relations Board had not yet ruled on the application for official union certification. If granted union status, they agreed their goal would be the same as the IAC's: to maximize inmate self-determination within the institutions and to educate the public about the futility of large institutions. The administration recognized the Walpole chapter of the NPRA as the official representative body of the inmates, and would be forced to sit across the table from them, hear their concerns, and negotiate.

During one highly contentious negotiation session held in the visiting room, the NPRA board of directors and supporters sat opposite the institution's administrators and representatives. Amidst a tense atmosphere, Bobby rose to vehemently advocate on behalf of the prisoners, laying out a number of issues and stating their positions, blunt in his assessment of the institution's actions. When one administrator replied with a snide remark, the prisoners reacted immediately. They had zero tolerance for disrespect and condescension and were on their feet surging forward. Bobby didn't notice this, as the men were seated behind him. He saw a number of frightened looks on the faces he was speaking to, just as rushing bodies appeared in his peripheral vision. He automatically thrust his hand out in a stop position. Everyone froze in place. Without stopping his speech, Bobby slowly and calmly indicated with the same hand for everyone to sit back down. Without hesitation the men stopped in their tracks and returned to their seats. The administration was stunned, completely taken aback. While they were relieved to have avoided a violent confrontation, they had just witnessed a telling event. The inmates showed restraint and obedience at the chairman's direction, and acted with a focused, singular purpose. Bobby had demonstrated both his influence and the power of the board of directors, which terrified the administration. *What if he had ordered them to riot?* Bobby remained on his feet, and without missing a beat, continued his argument.

Bobby attacked a number of institutional regulations that inmates believed were arbitrary or unnecessary. For many of the existing regulations, they may have been logical at the time of adoption, but the passage of time had rendered them obsolete. The Department of Correction never bothered to update the regulations or to review and remove such rules although no longer applicable or useful. Prisoners were also frustrated by regulations which had no logical basis. Men might disagree with a rule, but could accept it as long as the rule was fair and related to a legitimate institutional purpose. The most hated were the "catch all" rules that could be applied to sanction an inmate in any situation where no specific rule directly applied. Anyone could receive a disciplinary violation if a guard determined he was "acting suspicious." Because the regulation was so ambiguous, the punishable behavior was defined by the staff's subjective interpretation (which could be just about anything) and subjected to rampant abuse. Compounding the problem, there was no existing process for inmates to challenge the rules. Unfair rules, lack of meaningful programs, and ongoing abuses all contributed to frustration and anger.

The NPRA demanded that all outdated and unnecessary regulations be removed. They further demanded the DOC, for all existing regulations, articulate its logical basis and put it on the record. If a regulation had no demonstrable legitimacy, it must be discarded, ensuring, rules which were clear and consistent, allowing prisoners to operate within clear boundaries, and promoting institutional safety.

When the inmates communicated with one another, worked together, and ultimately unified under a common vision, the very real possibility for change invigorated their cause. It was this mindset that positioned the inmate population to embrace change, to propose implementation of new ideas. Despite the positive tone encompassing the prison, the NPRA was not blind to a basic reality; without DOC endorsement, their vision would never become reality.

Walpole in the early 1970s was a time period which provided a window of opportunity for the entire penal system to be overhauled, and to move forward after generations of stagnation. But there was resistance, especially from the guards' union. It positioned itself as the NPRA's enemy, and fiercely protested all NPRA suggestions for progressive measures. While NPRA's vision might lead to a more humane version of the current system, it would also lead to a smaller prison system— one which required more counselors and teachers and fewer guards. If the NPRA succeeded, many would lose their jobs and benefits.

The NPRA's vision gained momentum in late 1971 when John Boone was hired to serve as the first black Commissioner of Corrections in Massachusetts. Boone's philosophy was a departure from the typical law and order approach in punishing lawbreakers. He believed that punishment alone served no greater purpose: by failing to achieve a positive result, there was no benefit to either inmates or society. Boone believed that while punishment may be justified at times, rehabilitation was critical to the success of the penal system given the fact that the large majority of inmates would return to society at some point. Under the punishment model, having learned nothing positive or helpful, inmates ultimately become embittered and destined to fail. Boone reasoned that the issue was not individualized, but rather it was a societal problem. Thus, prisoner rehabilitation would by necessity need to involve the larger community, and that the prisoners needed to have a role in any meaningful changes. He believed in treating people fairly, and finding workable solutions for solving problems. Boone's arrival in Massachusetts was fortunate for the NPRA, as its vision aligned with his ideas, and Boone soon pledged his full support. Like Jerome Miller, Boone's public stance supporting inmates was a highly controversial decision fraught with career risks. Bobby told news reporters:

> *The guys have a lot of hope in Boone. They think he's a fair man. He's not weak; he's not a pussy like the legislators think he is. You screw up and he'll lock you up, but he's for justice. The guy comes on real. Boone's concept is to treat a man like a human being and he'll react like one.*

While Boone was respected by inmates, he was instantly unpopular with the guards' union. In their view, prisoner self-determination was a nonsense concept and a dangerous one as well. They believed they could not effectively and safely provide security for inmates if they were required to share any level of power with them. As such, Boone's ideas were perceived as a direct threat not only to their livelihood, but to their safety as well. His philosophy not only called for increased prisoner participation in running the institutions, but also a decreased population through attrition. Guards saw this as writing on the wall that their role in operating the prisons would be reduced significantly, resulting in a loss of power, control, and ultimately jobs. Boone soon went from distrusted newcomer to declared enemy.

Shortly after the formal establishment of the NPRA at Walpole, Raymond Porelle was appointed to serve as Walpole's superintendent. The NPRA was gaining momentum, but the temporary alliances it was built upon were instable and not likely to endure in the long term. Porelle, who was known for his aggressive control tactics, threatened the balance the moment he arrived in Walpole. He made it clear that he was not interested in negotiating with inmates, or ceding any power into their hands. In his view, the prisoners were to be told what to do, not the other way around, so he imposed strict new regulations. Tensions immediately began to rise, while prisoners struggled to maintain their pledge of nonviolence.

The breaking point came when Porelle ordered a full facility shakedown just hours before the Kwanzaa holiday celebration. Many had planned family visits, had prepared food, and were very much looking forward to the day. Black inmates were furious. While they were previously reserved about the NPRA and its agenda, the incident solidified the black population's solidarity with the white population as, together, they rioted.

Porelle responded with a strong show of force. Once the rioting was quelled, he imposed an indefinite lockdown which began on December 29, 1972 and lasted until March 7, 1973. No inmate was permitted to leave his cell. All visitation rights were suspended, and inmates were not allowed to shower. Inmates continued to be defiant, and agreed to a work stoppage. They refused to clean, mop, cook, do laundry; any task the inmates handled for the day to day operation of the prison. The mass refusal to work effectively shut down the institution. In short time, Walpole became filthy and unsanitary, the building a disgusting place for the inmates to live and the guards to work. Food and trash piled up on the tiers. The smell of garbage, bodily functions, and unclean humans hung thick in the stale air. Frustrated guards lashed out at the inmates, delivering brutal beatings and continuous harassment. Despite the suffering they endured, the inmates refused to waver from their goal, and continued to maintain a unified front against the institution.

In an effort to ease tensions, Commissioner Boone permitted outside observers to enter Walpole to monitor the internal situation. Guards were outraged and reacted by refusing to punch in on schedule, and soon after by walking off the job. A large crowd gathered in the prison parking lot, with protesting guards shouting anti-administration slogans, including racial slurs such as "Boone the Coon." Inside the prison, the NPRA had been preparing for a guard walkout. For them, it would be a golden opportunity to demonstrate to the observers—and society—that they were capable of self-sufficiency. They agreed that they must prove that they could run the institution effectively and free of violence, but more importantly that the guards' presence was completely unnecessary to running an efficient and nonviolent institution.

For the NPRA, the ultimate goal was to send inmates leaving prison back in to society better equipped to succeed than when they came in. To that end, the NPRA set about advancing its philosophy of incarceration, sharing innovative ideas regarding re-entry, rehabilitation, vocation training, education, and halfway houses. Now was the time to show the public that this was the course of action that was in everyone's best interest, the course that made the most sense, the course that works. When a Senate panel was formed to investigate the poor conditions inside the prisons, Bobby jumped at the chance to testify:

> *Rehabilitative programs in here affect less than ten percent of the population. Maybe we could give companies a tax deduction to come in and set up programs. There's no rehabilitation in making license plates. You should put a fork in the road and give a man an opportunity to better himself.*

Meanwhile, the guards attacked Boone and the NPRA under the guise of protesting legitimate labor issues. By casting every grievance as a "security issue" the union was effectively trying to control DOC policy instead of addressing actual labor conditions or concerns. Most unpopular amongst them was the outsider observer program. Historically, the guards had benefitted from the public's lack of access to actions behind the prison walls and now the observer program made those walls transparent. They documented the guards' walkout, noted who was refusing to work on which shifts, and which workers showed up but refused to perform vital tasks of the job. The observers also documented the efficiency of the NPRA, noting a smooth running of the prison's functions with no reports of violence. Their constant presence and meticulous documentation of everything they witnessed made it very difficult for Walpole's guards to not only mistreat the prisoners, but to be able to put on an unfavorable spin on the prisoner's efforts. Soon thereafter, the guards unanimously decided to strike. The governor responded by declaring a state of emergency, and through court order, they were forced back to work. Many still refused. Those who did show up refused to work the cell blocks.

Outside observers reported that between March 15 and May 18, when the NPRA fully controlled Walpole State Prison, there were no rapes, assaults, or murders. To the surprise of many, the men were in fact running the prison, and running it well. In a press conference, Bobby reported details of the stable environment, citing there had been no problems at all. An inmate working in the kitchen said, "Prior to this, we'd be stealing food. They can't steal it now because it's *our* food." The inmates, under the NPRA's leadership, controlled themselves and ran the institution efficiently and peacefully, which further angered the guards' union. At all times the NPRA insisted the inmates follow its self-imposed code of discipline, reflecting the inmates' own value system and ideals of respect. Albert DeSalvo himself told reporters the situation was "cool." When asked about inmate disagreements he said, "We'll calm it right down. We are unity." While the balance was precarious, the inmate population respected the decree. The NPRA moved forward implementing programs and continued the operation of all day-to-day functions. NPRA Treasurer Robert Dussault said, "We don't want to run the prison. We just want a say in how it's run. This is our home."

As the guards slowly began to reappear in the prison blocks, the stage was set for an attempt to reestablish control. They wanted the public to know the problems in Walpole were created by the prisoners, and that they would no longer be running the prison. When the guards stepped up the harassment and beatings, Boone was under intense pressure to regain control of the institution. As a result, a task force was assembled, the outside observer program was discontinued, and a "takeback" plan was devised. The stage was set for a showdown.

The NPRA desperately wanted to retain control, but the Walpole administration, now led by Superintendent Walter Waitkevitch, stonewalled any negotiation attempts. Bobby sensed the rising inmate tensions and urged them to maintain a unified front against the administration, but he knew the situation was quickly spiraling out of control and violence was inevitable. He reminded them that the prisoners' moral high ground, and public support, flowed from their nonviolent behavior. Bobby urged the population to remain calm, saying, "The last thing we need is to act violently. Don't give them a reason to respond to us with force." He convinced the men to voluntarily return to their cells in preparation for the state police entry into the blocks.

The state police takeback plan called for an aggressive sweep into the blocks to regain control by use of overwhelming force, regardless of whether the prisoners were offering resistance. Though the prisoners were calm and passive, the troopers charged the blocks running behind riot shields, as if a full scale riot was underway. Prisoners were extracted from their cells, dragged onto the tiers, and beaten with batons. Inmates, at this point, could no longer remain passive and began fierce retaliation. Complete pandemonium soon enveloped the prison. Tear gas canisters exploded, burning the men's eyes. Deafening shotgun blasts reverberated throughout the halls. Although police later claimed the shots were for warning purposes only, several inmates suffered gunshot wounds. For hours, the culmination of tension, the ultimate failure of an experiment, had exploded into chaos and violence with many men—mostly inmates—suffering injury. In the end, the administration had re-established control, and the prison was no longer run by the prisoners. Many men were severely beaten and sent to segregation, with the NPRA leaders were specifically targeted. Bobby himself was clubbed repeatedly, thrown down a staircase while cuffed behind the back, and dragged across the flats over broken glass. Once the brute force ended, the entire prison population was again placed on indefinite lockdown.

The NPRA could not continue to run without its leadership. During the post-riot lockdown, the DOC revoked it's recognition of the NPRA as the inmates' representative body. To further dismantle the NPRA, new regulations controlled all prisoner movement and communication, effectively preventing the organization from meeting, planning, and existing. Feeling defeated, the prisoners' tenuous allegiance to racial unity began to quickly fade. Tensions and conflicts which had been placed on hold were now reactivated, and the code of discipline dictated by the NPRA went unenforced in the absence of its key members. Within a short time, inmate on inmate violence returned, with renewed threats, dozens of assaults, and two brutal murders occurring. Taking advantage of the situation, the administration used the incidents to publicly justify, after the fact, the aggressive tactics used during the takeback. By now, any previous DOC interest in rehabilitation and reform had been abandoned in favor of strict control and punishment. With the prison now back under control, John Boone was forced to resign.

Several months later, the NPRA learned that their union certification application had been denied. In a small victory, the decision reflected that the NPRA had convinced the SLRB that prisoners, as a class, met the definition of "worker" under the law. However, the SLRB made clear in the written decision that it lacked authority to control the DOC, and would not interfere with the Commissioner's power over all DOC inmates. For the NPRA, the news was a crushing defeat. Failure to achieve full recognition as a workers' union rendered the organization impotent, and severely undermined the entire mission of the NPRA. Soon thereafter, Bobby relinquished his role as NPRA president.

> *It was a very interesting experiment. It was a shame it didn't jump off, but at least we learned from it. Now, they're talking about re-entry, and all the things we were talking about over thirty years ago. But they're going to stop short of that step because once you start reducing recidivism, you threaten job security. That's the bottom line. The whole system relies on it, the court system relies on it.*
>
> *Once you got into the union concept you gotta say I'm going to be free or I'm going to be dead. I have an acute feeling and understanding for freedom. I know what it is. The average John Q. Citizen doesn't have a clue. He buys into the propaganda of the government claiming we are free, but doesn't have a clue what that means. But that is the whole concept of prisons, they're a farce. The concept of security is a farce. The bottom line is the average prisoner is not going to attempt to escape. To make that move, I*

put my life on the line. Any one of three towers can open up on me and kill me. Then once I hit the street the cops are out there to kill me. That's a big piece to take on. For me, I would prefer death than living on my knees inside a prison for the rest of my life. Fuck that, not going there. If you're going to shoot me off the wall, cool. Don't wound me and cripple me, so I'm in a wheelchair. Put it through my head! This is the mindset about freedom, what we had been fighting for.

Prisons run only with the specific consent of the prisoners. If prisoners withdraw their consent, the prisons can't run. We proved that point.

Bobby had given his full attention and energy to advance the NPRA agenda, and was both physically and mentally exhausted now that the fight was over. It was a noble cause, and he had given it everything he had, but he no longer had the energy to regroup and re-engage in a battle which had become futile. He still believed in the cause and was proud of their achievements, but for the time being it was dead. But despite the setback, he wasn't ready to give up. He quietly began considering a new plan, something which would benefit only himself. *"Time to plan another escape,"* he thought.

CHAPTER ELEVEN

Since boyhood, Bobby's intense curiosity drove him to figure out how things worked. As a school kid, he disliked academics in general but did enjoy basic science classes, and as he got older, he developed a strong interest in studying psychology, sociology, biology, chemistry, and anatomy. In prison, he became starved for knowledge, spending hours digesting any textbook he could get his hands on. He found particular interest in medical texts, and he focused on learning about the diagnostic information and symptomology for all kinds of health problems. He studied diligently, as if preparing for final exams. The information he learned not only stimulated his intellect, but was of practical use. If he could make a false but convincing medical complaint to the staff by describing realistic details of his alleged ailment, he knew he'd be sent to an off-site hospital. He also knew that if he could get to the hospital, he could get outside.

After playing out a number of scenarios in his head, Bobby decided that he could realistically feign a heart problem. He visited the infirmary clutching his chest one morning, his face contorted into a tight grimace. A doctor examined him while Bobby provided details of the symptoms he was supposedly suffering. His theory that his claims would be taken seriously was correct, but no ambulance was called. Instead, he was scheduled for a succession of five appointments at nearby Pondville Hospital. Armed guards would escort him to and from each trip. "I was thinking that I would have five tries at this. One of them would have to work," he said.

The first appointment did not go as planned. At the hospital he was ushered directly into a small changing room. The guards ordered him to step behind the hanging privacy sheet, remove his clothing, and put on a hospital johnnie. The changing area was sparse, nothing more than a bench and a padded chair. He needed to act fast and find a hiding spot for the shank stashed in his zip-up boot, which went undetected during the standard pat-down. Acting quickly, Bobby removed the cushion from the chair, unzipped the back, and hid the weapon in the foam padding. Then he changed clothing and waited to be examined by a doctor. He'd get the shank later.

His original plan was to undergo the exam, then make a move as he was being escorted to the hospital exit. First, he would return to the changing area and put his prison clothes back on, retrieve the knife from its hiding place, and conceal it on his body. Two guards would be present. From the front, one would have to reach around Bobby's torso to secure his waist chain. Bobby would raise his hands to give him access, and would have the knife concealed under the coat he'd be holding in his hands. As soon as the guard bent over and reached around him, he would be vulnerable. Bobby would lock his elbows, press the knife to his throat, snatch his gun from the holster, and draw down on the other armed guard. Then he'd be out the door.

But he had no idea what was going to happen during his examination. Concerned about his variety of health issues, the doctor ordered a battery of tests including a full rectal examination. Bobby hadn't expected this test do be done and was nervous. At that time, the standard equipment for the procedure was not designed with comfort in mind. While he was unexcited about being probed, he figured it would be over quickly, and was well worth enduring to carry out his plan. *"Mind over matter,"* he told himself.

The doctor directed him to climb on the table, stay on his knees, and put his behind in the air. Despite his mental preparation for the procedure, he was caught off guard by the probe as it was inserted in a less-than-gentle manner. "It felt like I was being torn apart," he said. When it was finally over, Bobby collapsed as if he'd just received the beating of a lifetime. He rolled over onto his back, breathing heavily, struggling to regain his composure. One of the guards showed some compassion, saying, "Bobby, you stay there, I'll get your clothes." He wanted to protest but wasn't able to speak. The guard was gone before he could form any words, and he thought, "*Oh shit, the knife!*" But he returned a few moments later and tossed the clothes on the bed, saying nothing. Bobby dressed very slowly, and was packed back into the DOC van to return to Walpole. He wondered if the knife was still in its hiding place.

Bobby was scheduled to have his thyroid gland examined during the second trip. While sitting on a bench in the corridor waiting to see a doctor, a medic approached and handed him a shot glass filled with clear fluid. Without thinking much about it, Bobby downed it.

"Wait, what did I just drink?" he asked.

"Radioactive iodine."

The moment the medic identified the liquid, Bobby processed its taste, a sickening acidic flavor in his mouth and throat.

"Why didn't you tell me that before I drank that shit!" The medic gave an indifferent shrug and turned to the guard and said, "Ok, that's it for now. Bring him back tomorrow." With the visit abruptly ending, combined with his severe nausea, it was clear to Bobby that he'd be going back to Walpole without making a move.

On his third trip, Bobby knew it would not be his day from the very beginning. When two guards came to bring him out, he recognized Arthur, an old school guard he knew to be a decent person. Arthur had never disrespected him, and so Bobby saw no reason to treat him poorly. Bobby didn't like many guards, but he had formed a civil and mutually respectful relationship with this particular man over the years. As much as Bobby wanted to execute his plan, it just didn't feel right to jack up Arthur. Figuring he had two more appointments left, he decided he would just have to try again later and aborted the plan. As he was getting in the van, Bobby felt defeated.

"Oh, fuck it," he said under his breath.

"What's the matter, Bobby?" Arthur asked.

"Nothing."

Bobby ditched the shank for his next visit. By this time he'd acquired a fake zip gun which would give him more flexibility in the timing of his plan. If he could successfully smuggle the phony weapon inside the hospital, he knew he'd be home free.

Two rookie guards Bobby had never seen before brought him back to Pondville. This was a good sign. They brought him into the now familiar changing area and he stripped down to his cotton boxer shorts with the zip gun secured by tape to his inner thigh. He was then transported down to the new man section where he would undergo a routine strip search. Taking advantage of the new guards' inexperience, he did not follow the standard protocol of bending over and spreading his cheeks. Instead, he did a very quick, half-hearted version and then looked at them with an annoyed facial expression as if to ask, *"Are you satisfied?"* They were aware of Bobby by reputation and were reluctant to challenge him. They looked at each other and shrugged, figuring he'd know the routine better than they would.

Neither man had noticed the zip gun. "Alright you're all set, get your clothes back on," they said.

Bobby planned to overtake them while still inside the hospital, hoping to maximize the time span he'd need to calculate any risks and weigh his options. But he hit a snag right away. The changing room curtain didn't fully close, and he was still within the guards' view as he undressed. Trying to remove and stash the zip gun without being seen would be difficult. Bobby then heard multiple voices talking outside of the dressing area, and thought, *"How many people are out there to deal with?"* He had to assess the situation quickly, so he improvised by emerging from behind the curtain clutching his stomach, pretending to suffer from gas pains.

The voices he'd heard were gone; it was just the two new guards now, one in uniform and the other wearing a suit. Bobby thought he'd come too far to not follow through with the plan. *"Fuck it, let's see how it goes,"* he thought.

"I just took the medication, it's killing my stomach. Is that a bathroom over there?" he said, pointing to a door just up the corridor.

"Yeah, that's a bathroom."

He turned to face the curtain area, pulled out the zip gun, and spun back around. The suited guard to his left was about ten feet away and Bobby was certain he was armed, so he drew down on him first. He stepped back and reached for his gun. Bobby's phony weapon would be no match against a real service revolver and he was too far away to rush him. For a split second, he considered throwing the zip gun at him, but it was far too light to cause any harm. *"If this were a real gun, I'd be forced to shoot this idiot. I can't let him pull his gun out and shoot me,"* he thought.

The uniformed guard was much closer, standing just several feet off to Bobby's right. Bobby turned and redirected his weapon straight at him. Without hesitation, he threw his hands up in surrender. His knees gave out and he stumbled backward several steps, his body slapping up against the wall. Bobby turned back to the other man laid out the situation.

"Pull it out and I'll blow his fucking brains out," he said.

Bobby then thought, *"Oh shit, bad move. Why would this guy care if I blew this other guy's brains out?"* But the threat succeeded, the suited guard put his hands up, not wanting the responsibility for another's life on him. Bobby played it cool, his face remaining hard while inside he was intensely relieved. Shooting two guards was not something he wanted to do. And had the guard drawn his weapon, he'd have blown Bobby's head off. The bluff was a desperate move, a mistake, and he was genuinely surprised it worked.

Bobby ordered the men into the tiny bathroom nearby to avoid a standoff. Once inside, he ordered both men to put their hands on the wall, high above their heads, and to not move a muscle. One had to straddle the toilet to find wall space, while the other had to reach over the sink. With his right hand, Bobby patted the suited man down. He felt the around the waistline and found what he was looking for—a .38 Colt Cobra. Extracting the gun from its holster, he slowly turned it over in his hand. Savoring the weight of the piece, the sound of the bullets shifting in the cylinder, he was in awe, physically feeling the power resonate all the way up his arm. Moments earlier he had a harmless makeshift gun and came very close to being shot. Now, he had a six-round special police load in his hand. He was in control.

Bobby wanted to break out right then, but decided to first check the uniformed guard to make sure he wouldn't be shot in the back on the way out. As soon as he touched him, he could barely believe his luck as his hand landed directly on *another* .38 Colt Cobra. Twelve rounds of firepower were more than he needed, enough for him to handle just about any situation. Feeling energized, he thought to himself, *"There's no way I'm not getting away."*

Another quick pat-down of both guards yielded no other weapons. Bobby sternly warned them not to move and began gathering up his clothes. He then wrapped the waist chain around himself, securing it only by tucking it into the front of his t-shirt, and then dropping both into the front of his pants; the chain was still visible in the back. He draped the jacket over his hands to give the appearance of being cuffed, but underneath he was actually gripping the two pistols, one aimed at each guard. The three headed for the exit, with one man next to him and the other several feet in front of him. The zip gun was still in his pocket.

Bobby walked them up the corridor, and they asked if he preferred taking the elevator or the stairs to the ground floor. Bobby opted for the cover of the stairwell. They reached the bottom and headed for the checkout desk by the back entrance. Before they got there, Bobby directed the men to tell the discharge receptionist that they had forgotten some paperwork at the institution, that they were leaving to retrieve it, and would be returning shortly. Just as he gave those orders, the receptionist called over to them not to leave yet, they had to process paperwork for the exit. The men delivered the bogus information as directed. In plain sight with a number of witnesses, Bobby was led out of the hospital by two guards. Nobody realized it was an escape in progress.

Once outside, Bobby was on high alert, his paranoia kicking into high gear. Wanting to be ready to respond in an instant, he became hyper-observant, looking rapidly in all directions, interpreting even the smallest detail as a plot for his capture. As the three men descended the long ramp exiting the rear of the hospital, Bobby clocked two maintenance men on landscaping duty. He locked eyes with one man who stared back at him, while slowly pushing a broom over and over the same spot, as if in a cinematic slow motion scene. Bobby thought, *"Oh shit, they've got me in a squeeze play."* He took a deep breath and cocked both revolvers, steeling himself for a shootout. His mind was scattered, playing out dozens of scenarios, anticipating anything that might happen. Bobby didn't know how the situation going to turn out, but in his mind one thing was for sure: no matter what happened, he was not going back to prison today.

They made it to the vehicle without incident. The suited guard got in the back, behind the grill, while the uniformed guard took the driver's seat. Bobby took the passenger seat as a transportation guard. As they began slowly rolling away from the building, Bobby watched intensely for any sign of ambush. Further down the way, they cruised past the sweeper, who did not even raise a glance from his job to notice them. Bobby let out a breath to relieve tension but remained on high alert.

The longer Bobby spent with his captives, the more chances they had to alert a cop, fight back, or for something to go wrong. He had to ditch them, and fast. He decided he would have them drive the vehicle to a nearby wooded area, a good cover location, away from the sightlines of passing motorists. But when they arrived at the spot he had in mind, he saw the landscape had changed significantly since he'd last been there. All of the trees he had remembered had been cut down by developers; the area was too exposed. Saying nothing, he allowed the vehicle to continue toward Route 1 as he scrambled to think of a backup plan. The decision was forced upon him, as a split in the road would send them either north toward Boston or south toward Rhode Island. Not wanting to cross state lines, Bobby decided on the northern route. Soon, highway signs indicated the Blue Hill Reservation was up ahead. He had a new idea.

The driver attempted to sound calm and rational, hoping to steer Bobby away from choosing a plan which would result in his death. His chatter betrayed his inner nervousness. "Please just leave the guns, you don't need those. Drop them somewhere where they can be retrieved later," he pleaded.

Bobby did not respond. In this situation, he wanted his hostages as calm as possible. If allowing the guard to talk helped work out his nerves, Bobby would let him. Relaxed captives, he reasoned, decreased the potential for problems. The guard continued his one-sided conversation and eventually became more relaxed. Neither man heard the soft click as Bobby brought the hammers of the revolvers back down.

Cruising toward the Blue Hills, they spotted a cop positioned on the side of the road monitoring the roadway for speeders. The two men heard the distinctive sound of the two hammers cocking, clicking into place.

"You two better be cool," Bobby warned.

The driver waved to the cop as they passed, he waved back. Bobby's stress was reaching peak level, but he felt much better when they arrived at the Blue Hills Reservation parking lot. He was comfortable with this location, as he was familiar with the area from his childhood. They parked in a space in the remotest area of the lot, far away from all other vehicles. Bobby could recall some of the trails he hiked years before, and he ordered them out of the vehicle to head up the path toward the observatory.

Bobby headed up the trail with the two men leading, the loaded guns still pointed at their backs. They continued deep into the forest, further and further away from the highway and parking lot. The guards were clearly nervous, assuming they'd be shot and left for dead, but Bobby had no interest in harming them unless it was completely necessary. When they reached a clearing Bobby explained to them his plan. They would be cuffed to each other by the wrists, wrapped around a small tree. They would not suffer more than some minor discomfort, and someone would likely find them within a few hours. So long as they cooperated, he told them, their lives were not in danger. One caveat: no tricks would be tolerated. Relieved that they were not about to be executed, they enthusiastically agreed to cooperate. As Bobby reached for the cuffs, he instantly realized there was a big problem. No cuffs.

Bobby grabbed one guard by the arm. He said to the other man, "You sit and wait right here. The only place you can go is up. We come back and you're gone, you'll come back down and he'll be dead here."

He quickly complied and sat down where he stood while the other guard accompanied Bobby back down the trail to the car. He was told to enter the vehicle and retrieve the cuffs. Bobby watched him very carefully as he searched around the driver's seat area. For a brief moment, Bobby saw his hand go under the seat, triggering a loud spring release sound. The guard looked scared, as if he'd just been caught doing something wrong, but quickly said, "I think the other guy has the cuffs." Bobby did not appreciate the stall tactics, and his patience was depleting quickly. When they returned, the abandoned guard was red-faced and nervous looking, cuffs in hand.

Bobby cuffed them around a slender tree and directed the pair to sit on the ground. He wasted no time in heading for the trail back to the vehicle, but suddenly stopped in his tracks and returned to the two captives. When they noticed Bobby returning, they cowered in anticipation. "You can play with this while I'm gone," he said, as he tossed the zip gun toward them.

Heading back toward the parking lot, Bobby felt confident. Other than the cuff debacle, everything had gone to plan, and he was pleased he didn't need to resort to violence. Prison had taught him that there was no need for unnecessary violence, and to a lesser extent, rudeness. Walpole had taught him that he could be very firm, yet still respectful, in getting what he needed from people. Usually, it was unnecessary to embarrass or degrade someone; acting disrespectfully toward them only triggered their resolve to resist. In fact, he was somewhat proud of the fact he had treated his captives well. *They've been cooperative and I'm going to be out of here,* he thought. Until he got back to the car.

Bobby attempted to start the car several times. The engine groaned and sputtered but would not turn over. He tried again and again, his anger multiplying with each failed attempt. Flashing back in his mind, he pictured the guard playing around under the seat, and the latch sound. He thought, *He was probably hitting a killswitch. That motherfucker!* Bobby felt betrayed. He had done what he needed to do without being disrespectful or abusive toward them. Now, he felt foolish and angry for having treated them so well.

He got out, slammed the door, and for the third time headed up the trail. He approached the captives with a businesslike gait. The men whispered excitedly, saying, "He's coming back! Why is he here?" From the look on Bobby's face, they understood their fears were justified. The first guard now

197

had his own weapon pointed directly at his face, hammer cocked. "You motherfuckers...," Bobby said. He froze in the moment which he truly believed would be his last. "He had completely checked out, he wasn't there," Bobby said later.

He looked at the other man. "What did you do to the car?"

"We've been having trouble with the ignition on that vehicle for a while now," he said.

Bobby looked at him for a time, processing the situation, and slowly lowered the hammer. He did recall other guards discussing the ignition problem on one of his earlier hospital visits. Once he was satisfied the vehicle problem was legitimate, that they weren't making excuses to buy time, he had no further reason to threaten the men. *"Ok, I have to get out of here right now,"* he thought.

He left the men cuffed to the tree, and made his way on foot back to the highway. Though risky, Bobby had no choice but to attempt to hitchhike out of the area in broad daylight. Out on the road, he stuck out his thumb and tried to appear as casual as possible. Luck was on his side; within a few minutes an obliging stranger stopped and offered a ride. They had friendly conversation on the way to Boston as the driver unwittingly assisted the escaped convict. The two guards were found hours later by a pair of telephone workers who were able to break the handcuffs and transport them to a local police station.

Department of Correction Commissioner Frank Hall was concerned enough with the episode to order the creation of a task force to investigate how Bobby was successfully able to escape, and to recommend changes. The committee issued a report after a month of interviews, and cited staff shortages and outdated procedures as major problems which contributed to making

Bobby's escape possible. While the DOC was not publicly blamed for failure to prevent the escape (the guards were not held directly responsible either), the report contained several eyebrow-raising facts. Both guards had only been on the job for only a few months and had no background or training to qualify them as correctional officers. Also, neither man had been granted special police status as required by law to accompany any inmate—especially a lifer and known escape artist like Bobby—off prison grounds. Finally, both guards were unable to produce permits for the .38 caliber guns Bobby relieved them of. Commissioner Hall immediately ordered all Massachusetts facility superintendents to review and revise security procedures for transporting inmates, and specifically to avoid using inexperienced officers in the process.

The following summer, Bobby was arrested in Cherry Hill, New Jersey, along with a three man crew for robbing an armored car. While on escape he had spent most of his time in Ft. Lauderdale, doing odd jobs and keeping a very low profile. Eventually, he made contacts through men he'd served time with, and was asked to participate in some robberies. Desperate for money, he agreed. But he didn't know the men well and the job was not executed according to plan. The group fled the robbery but was caught after the state police raised a drawbridge and trapped the gang in traffic. At the time of the arrest, the men were in possession of over $130,000 in stolen cash. After the bust, the others drew federal sentences of fifteen years apiece. Bobby got the same sentence, plus three additional years. The extra time was for cutting a hole in the prison wall while awaiting trial.

When he got back to Norfolk County in Massachusetts, he had to undergo a series of tests for classification. As part of the process, he spoke with the head psychologist. "I know you're going to plead not guilty. But you did escape," the doctor said. Bobby replied, "My lawyer doesn't want me to talk about it. But, let's say hypothetically, a prisoner from Walpole is brought over to Pondville Hospital, and the prisoner goes in—hypothetically. Without any explanation, the guards just suddenly leave with the prisoner. They bring him to Mattapan, go to a side street, throw down on him, take the handcuffs off, and tell him to go screw. Is that an escape?"

The psychologist appeared uncomfortable with the topic and quickly excused himself from the room. Bobby laughed when he left. He knew the case against him would be tough to prove. Nobody had seen him escape, and he was never caught with the guns. Turning himself in was not an option given the state police beatings he had previously suffered. If his case went to trial, it had the potential to become a media event with bad exposure for the entire Department of Corrections. The state reached out to Bobby's lawyer to work out a plea and avoid any problems.

But Bobby wasn't looking for a deal; he wanted a trial. He envisioned a highly politicized trial, attacking his attackers in a very public forum, indicting the DOC for all of its incompetence. His lawyer, however, was disinterested in publicity, and told Bobby his first priority was to negotiate a reduced sentence for him. It could be done, he assured Bobby, but made it clear he would not touch the bigger issues. Bobby continued to apply pressure and he only relented when his attorney threatened to discontinue representation.

The District Attorney's office offered Bobby six concurrent three-to-five year sentences for each of the six charges, which included kidnapping, escape, and gun charges. He felt that the offer was too good to be true—because it was. The catch was that the time had to be served on-and-after the life sentence he was already serving. On advice of counsel, he took the deal. The good part, either not realized by the prosecution or not cared about, was that he already had a three-to-five year sentence, on-and-after, for his previous escape. Any sentence for a felony committed within a prison was prohibited by state law from being served concurrently with other sentences; it had to be served on-and-after. The plea, as structured, forced the on-and-after sentences from both escapes to become concurrent, effectively cancelling out any additional time for the Pondville Hospital incident. Bobby was happy with that, and was sent back to Walpole.

Former Commissioner John Boone publicly commented on Bobby's escape, saying, "For the several months I knew him, Mr. Dellelo was always nonviolently and in a self-sacrificing way trying to pursue change in the correctional system. Apparently he gave up...The public should feel incensed about this new crime of escape, but we ought to remember this was a man who pulled together a responsible organization of 440 men."

* * *

A couple years later in Walpole, Arthur—the respectful guard—approached Bobby in his cell with an air of amusement.

"Thanks," he said.

"For what?"

"You know what. When I brought you to the hospital before the escape, I know what you meant by 'fuck it.' You could have taken me out and chose not to."

Both men shared a laugh. It didn't work this time, but Bobby resolved to keep trying or die in the process. "It's the duty of every prisoner to escape if he can. You just can't hurt anybody when you do," he said.

CHAPTER TWELVE

When a correctional institution makes heavy use of solitary confinement, it is the hallmark of a poorly run system, serving as the rug under which they sweep problems out of public view. When staff fails to effectively control members of the general population, because of inefficiency or incompetency, they simply reassign men to solitary confinement. The use of isolation is their convenient tool to dispose of problems instead of dealing with deeper issues of security and control.

The use of isolation in prisons has long been justified as an essential security measure. Prison administrations have always claimed that dangerous and violent individuals—the so-called "worst of the worst"—must be separated from the rest of the population in order to preserve the safety and well-being of guards and inmates alike. Solitary confinement has been traditionally regarded as the only effective way to control inmate behavior and reduce violence, gang organization, and escapes: other methods just don't work. Prison officials also claim isolation has value in that it allows time and space for the inmate to reflect upon his actions. Theoretically, sensory deprivation would eliminate distractions and force the wrongdoer to engage in self-reflection. Through this thought process, he would reconsider his decisions and become motivated to change his behavior and act consistently with the rules of both the institution and society. He would either be broken into conformity or suffer indefinitely in isolation. Furthermore, the discomfort of isolation would serve as a strong deterrent to future bad behavior.

Isolation as a tool for control thrives in modern American prisons. Its use, though heavily criticized as legalized torture, is steadily expanding. "Supermax" prisons (ultra-secure facilities in which all cells are solitary) have sprung up around the country, and the results are disturbing. Prison officials have expanded the justifications for its use, as the definition of a "security concern" has stretched to the degree that it can be interpreted as "any reason." For practical purposes this means sending inmates to isolation for minor infractions which do not threaten institutional security, such as not obeying a guard fast enough, alleged gang membership, possessing contraband, or acting "suspicious." Isolation was once used to control the most violent but now applies to any inmate who crosses the administration or staff, even at the most trivial level. Essentially, anyone can be sent there upon staff whim.

> *Walpole State Prison has the DDU, the Departmental Disciplinary Unit, which is the solitary unit. The DDU was originally DSU, Departmental Segregation Unit, the sign had the big squares D-S-U. When Weld came in, they took the 'S' off and put up a 'D' in its place. Block Ten was DSU, and the guys sued the Department of Corrections. The state supreme court said that segregation was not punitive, it was simply a separation from general population, and that an inmate in segregation was entitled, consistent with security, to all the same programs as men in population. So they changed it.*

As the name implies, the unit exists for no other purpose than punishment, the "end of the line" for inmates who break prison rules. Physical conditions in an isolation cell are not comfortable by any standard. In DDU, the living space is an eight-by-twelve foot cell, with a ten-foot high ceiling. Through a heavy steel door, a vertical rectangle Plexiglas window (27 inches tall, 3 inches wide) affords a view of a drab tan wall directly opposite the cell and a few feet of barren corridor. At the outer wall window, a limited view of the prison yard walls yields an equally unimpressive visual. Every cell bed in the unit is made of a four-inch slab of concrete affixed to the outside cinder block wall with a thin mattress on top. Just inside the door sits a stainless steel toilet/sink combination, with a wall-mounted metallic sheet above it serving as a shatter-proof mirror. Overhead fluorescent lights illuminate the room, often left on around the clock. The sparse room is sealed by a heavy iron door which partitions the inmate from the world beyond.

> *Now, the heating device on the roof, I don't know where it came from but it was constantly breaking down. The air conditioning was breaking down and they were constantly fixing that. To the prisoner inside, in the winter time when the heating unit breaks down, you're freezing cold in there. They had to give out two blankets and that wasn't even really helping you. The prisoners become paranoid and think that they have purposely pumped cold air in there, because it doesn't take that long to fix something. I observed them with the cranes taking the units off the roof and putting new ones in there. So you really knew that it was a breakdown, it wasn't like they were planning, they may have dragged their feet but it was more mechanical problems. It was very cold in there. But the problem is that the situational variable again. That affects, it models your behavior, and you're now paranoid.*

All meals are eaten in the cells. Guards distribute fixed menu meals on cafeteria-style lunch trays through the door slot, with empty trays collected back through the same opening. The small portions, lack of variety, and low quality food draw constant complaints, but there is no other choice. Despite the poor meals, many do look forward to the meal distribution time, as it is the only human contact they might have for days and weeks at a time.

DDU inmates are permitted one hour of release time from his cell every twenty-four hours, with a cap of five hours total per week. Otherwise, the only other time an inmate leaves his cell is during a contraband search. Often, an inmate is ordered to stand in the corridor while his cell is thoroughly tossed by a team of guards. He is then allowed to return to the cell, but then is ordered to undergo a strip search: any cell exit subjects the inmate to a possible strip search, which is conducted purely at staff discretion. Inmates have reported being strip searched despite being cuffed and shackled the entire time out of his cell, and had no direct contact with anyone other than guards. The policy has a chilling effect, as many men will discourage family and friends from visiting in order to avoid the humiliating searches. Even a simple trip to the shower requires heavy security. Three guards escort the inmate to the showers and supervise the ten minute process: remove chains, provide soap and razor, shower in view of guards, chained again, return to cell. To maximize isolation, only one inmate at a time is allowed to pass through the corridors. The only time DDU inmates ever see each other face to face is during outdoor activity, which is strictly controlled. DDU inmates have no general yard to use as recreation. Instead, thirty-foot-long cages are available for exercise if weather permits. Each narrow cage resembles the layout of a dog kennel, designed to prevent individual physical contact. Although the grim surroundings provide little to look at, most DDU inmates consider the relative freedom of pacing in the dog cage to be the highlight of their day.

Gradually, well-behaved inmates can earn perks such as a radio, a small black and white television, access to a very limited selection of books, and some no-contact visits with family and friends. Though not very stimulating to the average citizen, prisoners place a high premium on any tool or activity which may distract them from the passage of time. Of course, all privileges may be revoked at any time for any infraction.

DDU provides a lonesome existence without the benefit of peacefulness associated with solitude. Incessant noise makes rest nearly impossible; persistent sleep deprivation is one of the most common inmate complaints. Empty corridors amplify sound, making the noise of guards' hourly rounds loud enough to wake even the heaviest sleeper throughout the night. Inmates are constantly jarred awake by a prison soundtrack of loud voices, boots stomping, buzzers sounding, keys rattling, men yelling, and steel doors slamming. The cycle lasts the duration of the night, every night Guards need to move about and perform shift duties, but inmates believe the noise is unnecessary and intentional—a result of their solitary-induced paranoia and hyper-stimulation.

> *We got the sensory deprivation of sleep modifying behavior. The two guards coming down the corridor, besides just the banging and stuff, they're talking about nonsensical things, loud. They all have these combat boots on and they're walking on cement floors. So it's like they're goose-stepping down the tier having conversations. And you hear a voice say, 'Shut the fuck up ya piece of shit!' The guards yell back and then everybody starts chiming in. So there's no way you're sleeping. Believe me, you'd have to be on some serious drugs, knocked out cold, to not wake up for this. To this day, I still wake up every forty-five minutes. Even when I was on heavy painkillers for my knee injury, the noise woke me up.*

Hostility between guards and inmates is a constant in DDU, with guards always having the upper hand. But the control techniques which guards believe are effective are often counterproductive: brutal and arbitrary displays of power fail to achieve any sort of positive result, while the constant dehumanization of inmates breeds anger and hate. Heavy-handed control techniques not only fail to control, but often serve to create a more dangerous environment.

> *Guards don't understand that the way they treat prisoners compromises their own safety and undermines the most important goal of the corrections system, which is control. But you're conditioning somebody to defy authority. You're in control of what? You've lost control. Your situational variable, that you don't understand, is happening. It is conditioning and programming people to be antisocial, and that isn't what you want. This is someone that you say has aberrant behavior, now you're compounding it. You're exacerbating what you said was the problem in the first place.*

DDU prisoners quickly realize that self-determination of any kind has been completely stripped away. Over time, most acquiesce to the idea they no longer control the arc of their own lives. They reach a point of acceptance, and fully surrender to authority in a condition of learned helplessness. Instead of living a life of constant denial and defiance, he is encouraged to completely embrace his lack of control and his total dependency on others. Though not all prisoners follow this course, many do. As distasteful as it may be for prisoners to abandon their personal integrity and discard a defiant stance against authority, the benefits are several. Forsaking the fight conserves much needed energy, both physical and mental, and increases odds of prison survival. Guards tend to focus on perceived troublemakers, and conversely, usually don't bother those who passively serve their time and are not viewed as a problem. In addition to favorable treatment, passivity may lead to a better cell assignment, a desirable work duty, and having small infractions being overlooked. However, the hard-core prisoners tend to consciously reject all authority and offer resistance at every chance. While that behavior is usually counterproductive—risking longer sentencing, loss of good time, enhanced mistreatment—they do it anyway. For these men, it is a fight in principle; it's about personal dignity and the desperate attempt to maintain it. They are undeterred and refuse to fall in line, despite the futility of their efforts.

Inmates in DDU literally exist at the guards' mercy. Corrections policy affords guards enormous power to control the prison population, and with such power comes the potential for abuse. Official prison policy is often ignored, and discipline is routinely meted out for personal vendettas. Inconsistent and selective enforcement of rules are rampant, fueling a sense of injustice across the prison. Most prisoners have learned not to bother to complain about unfair treatment, as he'd likely be punished for attempting to report guard misconduct.

Guys get beat up in there a lot. You hear the conversations that they have the most dangerous job. Well, coming out of a cell, there's two wickers, two little doors, one high and one low. To get out of the cell I have to put cuffs on, so I'm cuffed with my hands behind my back. Once the cuffs are on my hands they open the bottom wicker and they put shackles on my ankles. When that's done, they give a signal and the doors open up. I got two guards on my arm, I got one on each side of me plus I got guards in the corridor. How am I going to attack you? Now going downstairs, when you got a guard on each side of you, they dictate how fast or how slow you go. So if they really want to play with you they can pick up the speed. The chain link is only sixteen inches, so if they're moving you fast, these shackles are cutting up your legs. Now, when you get on the stairs, it's a notorious situation. The stairs, there's no cameras there. Guys 'fall' down stairs. That's where a lot of beatings occur. There was no part of DDU that you can't hear. Every door has a speaker on it so you can hear a corridor area conversation no problem, you know what's going on. So it isn't like nobody knew that they were beating this guy up in the corridor.

Now the type of guard that's in there, all of them weren't bastards but the vast majority of them were. The guards that work in there are generally people who can't make it in general population. It's like a punitive action to put a guard in there. So you have that as the guy controlling you and that whole attitude is in there. Guards that overstep the line in population and beating guys up, they stash them in there. The beating up behavior doesn't stop, it's just re-directed so it's not seen out in population.

For prison guards, both corrections culture and dangerous work blurs the line between professional punishment and personal grudge. The opportunities for abuse and means to do so are plentiful. Inmates usually feel helpless in DDU, and often become overwhelmed by the feeling. They know a guard will usually get away with assaulting them; in fact, it could easily lead to a bogus charge and more time in solitary. The frustration is extreme. However, inmates manage to retaliate in various ways—stabbings, assaults, spitting, and verbal abuse. Sometimes they resort to more creative means. In the book *When the Prisoners Ran Walpole*, Bobby remarked:

We were locked in 24/7 and we were mad. We didn't have anything to fight back with so we used bullfrogs. A bullfrog was a pile of shit. We would throw it at the control room. If you caught your bullfrog on a piece of paper, it was a bullfrog on a lily pad; in a milk container, it was a steamer. We spit at everyone who came onto the blocks. We threw our food out of our cells. And then refused to clean it up. Our runners went on strike. The guards wouldn't clean it up and so it built up. The place, well, smelled like shit.

Such tactics may provide a temporary sense of empowerment, but those victories are typically short-lived. Payback from guards is a certainty, and always swift and brutal. While inmates expect retribution, there is very little that can be done to prepare for it. The guards are able to act with near impunity, and have many tools at their disposal to exact revenge—beatings, cell searches, strip searches, withheld food, destroyed personal property, denied visitation. Bobby himself recalls being a frequent target of "random" cell searches. Searches were always conducted at strange times, usually in the middle of the night to add to the inconvenience and discomfort. Often, the routine occurred on consecutive days, sometimes five or six days in a row. Guards would approach, pound on his cell door to awaken him and order him to immediately exit the cell. The searches took approximately forty-five minutes, and Bobby had to stand by as they tossed his cell. He knew better than to complain, as it would slow the process even more. When a search ended, they never found any contraband but his personal effects were always strewn about, confiscated, or destroyed. He noticed no other cells were being searched. He said, "Their message was clear: *We can do this whenever we want, as many times as we want, for any reason we want. Don't forget that.*"

By law, food cannot be withheld as punishment. But if a guard wants to antagonize a particular individual, he can render a meal inedible by spitting or sneezing on the food, dropping it on the floor, vigorously shaking the container and destroying the meal. Some men receive intentionally small portions, usually served cold. While violence is common, inmates consider messing with their food to be beyond fair play, even between enemy camps. They have no choice but to bitterly accept their treatment and continue waiting for revenge opportunities.

Guard culture, handed down through generations, perpetuates the hostile guard/prisoner relationship. New recruits, often the most likely to treat inmates as humans, are quickly discouraged from doing so by jaded veterans. They are warned that inmates are not to be viewed as individuals: *Humanization will lead to your manipulation. Do not let that happen.* New recruits are taught to assume a hostile position from the very start, and to avoid using respect and trust. They learn that in order to effectively control, it is necessary to overlook inmates' humanity, to disregard them as living people. One guards' union official said publicly:

> *Let's think about why the person's sitting in the cell 23 hours a day locked down. Because he murdered somebody. Stabbed an officer. Did something so egregious inside the prison system that he now has to be locked away even from the inmate population. So I'm never going to sympathize with the inmate. That's not my job.*

This mindset defines the guard culture, and by extension their behavior. Unnecessarily yelling orders, using derogatory terms, assuming a condescending attitude, and utilizing excessive force are all part of the prison environment, a climate of emotional detachment and indifference toward inmate suffering. For them, inmates' physical or emotional needs are irrelevant; the priority is security. Guards spend long hours within the institution, and, much like the inmates they watch over, they are trying to survive the difficulties of prison as well. They are taught to shut down natural feelings of empathy, and to use alienation and emotional distance as defense mechanisms; otherwise the institution will break them in the same way it does many inmates. Thus, rationality, caring, and sympathy are not perceived as dignified behavior, but rather as a professional weakness. Those who try to break the cultural norm become quickly ostracized.

While an inmate's sentence length cannot be extended by prison officials, they have unlimited discretion to assign and extend an inmate's DDU time, which cannot be appealed in court. When an inmate fails to behave in isolation, he loses credit for that month toward his DDU stay. This system produces a revolving door effect: isolation causes men to act out, they get more time, they act out, get more time. The usual procedures and constitutional protections for an accused man—hearings, evidence, appeal—do not apply. Ultimately, the inmate has no recourse whatsoever. He is powerless.

Guys complained a lot, but most were not looking to be coddled. They just wanted to be treated fairly, like human beings whose dignity was acknowledged with a basic level of respect.

* * *

In 1994, the Court TV network contacted the Massachusetts DOC with a proposal for a story about solitary confinement. Though the prison system was typically secretive when it came to media curiosity, a camera crew was granted rare permission to shoot footage inside Walpole's DDU to observe conditions and profile several employees and inmates. While the guards welcomed the cameras in, the inmates were skeptical. The inmates believed the camera presence would serve to advance guards' agenda, producing propaganda to curry public favor as leverage in future contract negotiations. It was rumored the crew would come in, seek out a few designated "dangerous" or "crazy" individuals to interview, to demonstrate that guards have a very dangerous job. The guards' union would then be better positioned to demand higher pay, less oversight, and more discretion in doing their jobs.

Inside DDU, Bobby and others had no idea cameras were coming in. He could hear a number of voices in the corridor, unusual for DDU. He then heard a lieutenant saying, "You gotta talk to this guy, you need to hear from him." At that moment, his door wicker opened and the officer's face appeared.

"Bobby, you want to talk to these people?" he asked.

"Who?"

"It's a camera crew, from Court TV."

"Yeah, I'll talk to them," he said.

So now the guy comes over first, without the camera, and he was talking to me because he wants to get a feel for what I'm going to be talking about. So when I spoke articulately and started to run down the conditions of the prison and DDU he kept turning and looking toward the guards, like, 'Is what he's saying true?' And he kept looking at this one lieutenant, and he would nod his head, like he was co-signing what I was saying. Now he gets excited, and the other guy with the camera he's like, 'Whoa, we want to get this guy.' He says, 'Would you be willing to say this on camera?' And again I said, 'Absolutely.'

Bobby was thrilled to have an opportunity to make his voice heard. Crouching down to speak through the rectangular opening, with his face partially obscured, Bobby spoke in a subdued and thoughtful tone. He knew his camera time would be limited, and didn't want to squander it by ranting about his own mistreatment. Walpole's issues were not about him as an individual; he wanted to address the larger issues and speak out on behalf of all prisoners. He decided it would be best to discuss those who were least able to advocate for themselves and articulate their suffering; the scores of mentally ill men surrounding him. Bobby was always bothered at how mentally ill individuals were warehoused away in solitary and, while the effects were devastating to them, the institution was wholly unconcerned. Bobby wanted the world to know that while such a policy was routine and common, it was inherently wrong, both morally and legally. Bobby told the camera crew:

> *You accept if you violate rules and regulations that you're going to be punished. But then there's a fine line between what's punishment and what torture is. A guy that's behaving in an odd manner because of being psychologically unbalanced is a lot different than what I knowingly did—I escaped. I knew what I was doing. But an inmate that's having a psychotic episode, and as a consequence of that behavior is put into DDU, something is very wrong with that. That, I have a problem dealing with.*

Charlie Chase, a notorious discipline problem at Walpole, was also interviewed. Despite his antics for the camera and extensive disciplinary record, he appeared to be a lucid individual who understood his situation and surroundings. Chase was serving a life sentence for a second-degree murder conviction in 1991, and shortly after his arrival at Walpole he gained a reputation for his violent outbursts. There were hardly any rules he didn't violate, everything from fighting inmates and guards to trashing his cell to possessing contraband. It wasn't long before he was sent to DDU. Once there, his behavior did not fare any better; in fact, it deteriorated. His impulse control, already poor, became even worse in the heavily restricted environment. Chase threw feces and urine at guards. He would steal razor blades and mutilate himself, and, with his own blood he painted swastikas on the cell walls. He yelled and screamed constantly, threatening everyone around him, and made numerous futile escape attempts. He was out of control.

During some of Charlie's more violent episodes, he was extracted from his cell. After refusing to comply with orders, guards in full riot gear stormed his cell and physically overpowered him. Each time, he put up full resistance, despite being outnumbered, and often ended up injured. Every incident was handled internally, each earning him additional time in the DDU. Chase told the camera crew he believed all of the action taken against him was a conspiracy to keep him in DDU forever. But his irrational behavior was dismissed by the guards. When asked if he thought Charlie was crazy, one DDU guard said, "No, I don't think so. He likes to come across like that, but no, I don't think he's crazy." Another guard was blunt in his assessment: "He's a clown. Maybe that's not the right opinion, but it's true. It's not so bad in there. If we gave them a washer and dryer they'd still complain."

* * *

In recent decades solitary confinement units have become a convenient dumping ground for mentally ill. With deep budget cuts resulting in mental hospital closures, many patients have ended up in prisons—which are in the business of punishment and security, not mental health services. They are a lost population in an environment which does not know, or want to know, how to treat them. Accordingly, they are warehoused out of the way, in solitary where they can be easily controlled, and where nobody sees them descend into further illness.

Prison guards handle mentally ill inmates no different than any other inmate. Their job description and training does not include social work or counseling skills, compassion, or behavioral analysis. If an inmate has a psychotic outburst on an upper tier, guards typically follow a "no harm, no foul" policy—let the inmate yell and scream until he runs out of energy. That the episode severely annoys and disrupts other inmates trying to sleep, study, meditate, or simply do his time in peace is of no concern. As long as the inmate behavior does not directly require guard involvement, he is basically ignored.

Charlie Chase was hardly the only DDU inmate who behaved poorly. Many others, out of frustration and delusion, physically harmed themselves. They punched walls or repeatedly slammed their heads. In some cases, men smeared human waste on the cell windows and walls or even their bodies. Some refused to eat, take medication, or leave the cell for a shower, all of which would trigger a violent cell extraction. Others cut themselves, swallowed inedible objects, or found a way to attempt suicide. They often succeeded.

> *The institution needs segregation because they don't know how to run the goddamn prison. The mentally ill that come into the prison, you can't control them out in the population. Problems that they don't know how to deal with, they stash in there. I had a guy on the tier with me, big black guy, he was three cells down from me. Every morning from around six in the morning until around eleven at night. This guy was arguing with an imaginary person in his cell. I mean a full-blown conversation, you could walk by the cell and he'd be yelling at somebody on the bed, 'Motherfucker! I'll kill you!' Screaming and ranting and raving. There's no question—this guy is nuts. He's in a psychotic episode and he belongs in a mental institution. As longs as he kept it up there on the tier, they leave him alone. If he comes downstairs and gets near the guards with that insanity, the goon squad will jump this guy, beat the shit out of him, charge him with assaulting the guards and put him in the DDU. They won't give him a court case, but*

he'll get sentenced to DDU. Now if you assaulted the guard, that's a felony. By law, the superintendent is required to notify the district attorney's office. The act of beating him up is a criminal act, and the cover up is a criminal act too. And this poor bastard's in there. So what they do is, mentally ill people that they can't control and can't send to Bridgewater, they hit them with bogus charges and put them into DDU. That's what I was telling them on the TV show, I said look, there's a minimum of two dozen people in this block that are mentally ill. All this block is doing is exacerbating their mental illness. They're going to drop these people directly from this block into the street. That's criminal behavior. To do that to society is outrageous.

For the most part, the public, is unconcerned with the detrimental effects of solitary on any inmate, regardless of mental stability. Even those who have studied the issues acknowledge initial skepticism. Dr. Stuart Grassian of Harvard Medical School has extensively studied the harmful effects of isolation on prisoners for decades and is a recognized authority on the effects of solitary confinement. But prior to conducting any studies, Dr. Grassian himself admits that he did not believe isolation was seriously harmful. At the time, he subscribed to the popular opinion that inmates were manipulative by nature, and assumed inmates' claims of suffering were likely self-serving fabrications. But Dr. Grassian was surprised by the results of his own studies. Evidence he gathered and analyzed showed that isolated men did in fact suffer greatly, on many levels, and in very real ways. Further, he found evidence that inmates did not typically exaggerate their condition for dubious purposes. In fact, the men he studied were often reluctant to discuss their mental states; and if they did discuss any suffering, it was often in a dismissive or understated manner. Grassian said:

In my opinion, solitary confinement—that is confinement of a prisoner alone in a cell for all or nearly all of the day, with minimal environmental stimulation and minimal opportunity for social interaction—can cause severe psychiatric harm. This harm includes a specific syndrome which has been reported by many clinicians in a variety of settings, all of which have in common features of inadequate, noxious and/or restricted environmental and social stimulation. In more severe cases, this syndrome is associated with agitation, self-destructive behavior, and overt psychotic disorganization.

In addition, solitary confinement often results in severe exacerbation of a previously existing mental condition or in the appearance of a mental illness where none had been observed before. Even among inmates who did not develop overt psychiatric illness as a result of confinement in solitary, such confinement almost inevitably imposes significant psychological pain during the period of isolated confinement and often significantly impairs the inmate's capacity to adapt successfully to the broader prison environment.

Grassian described symptoms he observed in solitary inmates as "a major, clinically distinguishable psychiatric syndrome." One of the more pronounced symptoms he noticed was the extreme reaction to minor stimuli. Common prison sounds such as a tapping sound from the ventilation system, footsteps in the corridor, or the sound of a faucet dripping could trigger massive anxiety or furious outbursts of anger. Some men began to process background noise as human voices which relayed messages to the inmate, often of a highly disturbing or violent nature. Isolation in a tightly confined space caused men to suffer panic attacks of varying intensity. Men reported feeling overwhelmed by the idea that they have been forgotten about and will never be released. Due to the cramped confines of the cells, subjects reported a crushing sensation of claustrophobia, an inescapable sensation of the walls shrinking closer and closer, much like being buried alive. Visual hallucinations were not uncommon, with men losing the ability to discern dreams from reality. Others struggled with diminished memory capabilities and loss of ability to concentrate. Dr. Grassian also found that men in isolation frequently suffered extreme paranoia. Many men reported imaginary bodily pain, believing a deadly disease was permeating his body. They soon became hopeless and lost the ability to control impulses, often hurting themselves or engaging in other destructive behavior, and were haunted by obsessional thoughts of death.

Free citizens live day to day on highly regulated schedules, which provide a sense of time passage and progress. With no clocks, calendars, or windows to view the outside, men in DDU cells have just the opposite experience. Days and weeks without a schedule strip men of their grounding, leaving them disconnected from the outside world, and feeling both disoriented and restless. Without the ability to properly calculate time, solitary inmates can become severely anxious, often over matters that would seem trivial to the average citizen. Isolated men dwell on the uncertainty of having basic needs met: *When am I going to eat? How long until I get out? When is my next visit? When do I get a shower? Have they forgotten about me in here?* Men without the ability to keep this anxiety in check frequently spiral downward into hallucinations, hyperventilation, panic attacks, or even full nervous breakdowns. While some DDU inmates manage to find effective coping mechanism to deal with their environment, nobody is entirely immune from the negative effects of isolation. Dr. Grassian observed that extreme anxiety, hallucinations, and varying degrees of loss of reality occurred in just about all isolated inmates. Prisoners are forced into a "sink or swim" situation; either come to terms with the restricted world or lose sanity.

Dr. Grassian interviewed Charlie Chase and reviewed his psychiatric history as he prepared to give expert testimony in a prisoner class action lawsuit. He told the New York Times:

> *The paradigm in corrections is if the inmates are acting badly you punish them, and if you punish them hard enough they won't do it again. But to think that a person like Charlie Chase is going to learn from that is nonsense. A lot of disruptive behavior in prisons is not so much a carefully calculated response, with a calculation of means and ends, as it is just someone being wildly out of control. The coolest, cruelest and most calculating of criminals are damn smart enough never to get themselves thrown into solitary confinement.*

CHAPTER THIRTEEN

In early '93 at Walpole, they were gonna put photograph IDs on everybody. It's supposed to start the first of the year. Guys don't want to do it, wearing these tags, and there's a lot of resistance. But everybody knows that come the first, you're gonna have to wear these things or you get a ticket and other punishments. So now, the guards being the idiots that they tend to be, one night at suppertime meal, when your blocks getting ready to go to the dining room, they announce that you have to wear your ID to go to chow. We refused to go. We didn't know this was going to happen; this was a spontaneous reaction. In the entire prison, only twelve people went to the chow hall.

The institution caused a hunger strike. They wouldn't allow you into the chow hall unless you wore the tag. They were supposed to do this on the first of December, not in the middle of the month. Nobody's going to chow, basically, you now have a hunger strike. But a lot of us had a lot of food. We refused to go to the chow hall, we shared our food. They closed the canteen down so you couldn't get more food, but we had already stocked up—that was one of the benefits of having money from drugs. So we had the money to buy all kinds of food. We didn't hoard it; somebody would cook the meal and everybody would get a taste of the meal. You weren't going to starve.

Now they're panicking. Murphy was the deputy, he was the Superintendent in Old Colony. They called me and couple other guys out, 'What's the problem?' I said, 'The problem is you said you weren't going to do that until the first of January. In the middle of the month without any warning, you can't do that.

This hunger strike wasn't planned, this was a spontaneous reaction. You're in big trouble.'

So now the hunger strike held for so long, they panicked. They started shipping people out to all the other institutions. Guys who couldn't normally get transferred got transferred so that there was no leadership to take control. Because now the prisoners organized spontaneously and someone like me could take absolute control! And they don't want to go through that again.

So three of us go to Old Colony: Me, Mikey DuPont, and Jeff Sinnott. Mikey DuPont's a jailhouse lawyer. We're going out and we've got two cars, and at that time there was a seatbelt law. Prisoners in the car don't have a seatbelt on. When we stop at Rt. 1A, the car behind us plows into us, and when we get to Old Colony, we've got serious whiplash. Describing what happened, Mikey says, 'We gotta get a lawsuit going.' The law is you have to wear a seatbelt. We didn't have seatbelts on, so we have grounds for a lawsuit. Mikey wanted to take the lead on filing the case, so we just went along with it, figuring why not.

We go down to Old Colony, I never seen this place before. We come in through the back trap. I say, 'Look at this fucking place. I can see great potential here...it's just fences, no electricity. I circled the yard one time and found at least three holes. The next day walking around the yard I said, 'I'm out of here!'

O nce at Bridgewater, Bobby and the others were assigned to the orientation block like all new arrivals. The next morning he hit the yard to take care of preliminary business. It was time for reconnaissance: check out the prison yard layout, learn who the players on the yard were, gain information about the guards, and most importantly, establish his position within the prison hierarchy.

At Old Colony, Bobby quickly saw that everyone possessed at least one weapon, mostly crude variations of knives or picks. At the time he arrived, there was construction underway in several sections of the facility, and while scrutinizing the building from the yard, Bobby noticed that the civilian construction crew often neglected to pick up scrap wood, metal rods, and other debris. Because of the relatively lax security, he easily accessed the construction sites to find something he could fashion into a knife or pick. "I wasn't going to be the only man without a weapon," Bobby said.

After a week in Bridgewater, Mikey approached Bobby in the yard. He was excited to announce he had prepared a civil complaint alleging negligence against the DOC relating to the van accident. Bobby listened as he detailed his legal strategy for a big money personal injury lawsuit. After a minute he held up a hand, cutting Mikey off.

"Take my name out of the lawsuit."

"But this is a winner; we got them dead in the water on this one." Mikey was confused.

"Michael, listen to me. I hear another drummer. I'm going home."

Mikey laughed, but wasn't so sure it was a joke.

Bobby continued to search for—and found—many cracks in the security all over the facility. Having inspected the yard only a few times in his short stay, he discovered he had a number of options to explore. Within a few more days, he saw even more opportunities. He started making plans.

There are long corridors, and units come off of the corridors, and there are two wings to the unit, and there's a round-shaped yard between the two blocks with a twelve-foot wall with concertina wire around it. So each unit has a yard, plus there's a big yard outside. One-third of the institution is a big yard.

The control rooms in each of the blocks were made with tempered glass windows, which is like really hard material. The door leading to the yard beside it has no bars, just big windows. You can get through them, but it'd take you twenty minutes with a sledge hammer to bash through it. Unless you took that black rubber out, and you put alcohol in there, you lit it, let the window get cherry red hot, take a bucket of cold water and hit it and then just kick the whole thing out.

The door has a little box up in the corner of it, with a little stick piece coming up, it's a celluloid switch. Sixteenth of an inch left or right will set the alarm off. What it does is when the door opens, there's a light up on the roof. It's on a pole with a small red light on top. Every door that leads outside has this pole above it. There are four towers and they're all above the level of the roof, so any tower can clearly see the tops of the roofs. When a red light goes on, you instantly know a door right there had opened up.

The insanity of it is they don't know what they're building. You look at the door, and two feet above the door is a metal plate right there, an electrical plate. You open that up, guess what's there? The wire to the door into the roof! So if you cut it low, cut it high, the light does not go on when you open the door.

They got these little poles, everybody thinks they're lightning rods, every ten feet along the edge of the roof. When you look at it you say electricity goes to the highest point. You have a ventilator that's at least three feet higher than this thing. Why would the electricity go to this thing and not to this metal

224

ventilator? Well, I got the book from the American Correctional Association, of all the institutions around the country. And guess what it's also got in it? Advertisements for correctional material. And guess what they got in there? This gizmo. It's a capacitance fence. If you get between two of these things, you set an alarm off. They know exactly where someone's coming off the roof. Sophisticated electronics.

Two cells share a ventilator. Up on the roof is a ventilator and on the side of the ventilator is a funny looking tube with a clip on the top and the bottom. Well if you open this ventilator and you disconnect this clip, you set an alarm off. That's all cute, but there is no part of the building inside the prison that touches the fence or gets near it or goes beyond it. So what you're suggesting is I'd work my way to the roof, have to circumvent this one on the vent, have to circumvent the thing somehow to go over there. Why would I climb up on the roof to climb down to go over the fence when the door downstairs can be circumvented, the window can be circumvented? You got all this electronics stuff up on the roof! For what purpose? It serves absolutely no purpose and you just spent lots of money on it. It's the tinsel effect.

In No Man's Land, the outer fence is fifteen feet high and it curves in. There are eleven strands of wire. On the pole where the wire connects to, between each strand is a razor blade a few inches long. When you walk around the yard, the fence going around the yard, it's stainless steel. The sun hits it, it flashes. You look and see they've got razor blades up there. But no, they got double strand of concertina wire. Why would I climb up and over this fence when there are holes all around it? They have a cyclone fence under the ground, an upper cyclone fence goes over it under the ground, so that if you dig underneath you

225

run into the fence. That makes sense, except there's a couple of spots where it's at least this much above ground, the length of this, and then this one overlaps this one above grounds. There's brads holding them together and at the pole there's a thicker wire twisted together on the inside. Now, if you take a lock, turn it around, stick it into the brad and pull it guess what this thing does? Opens up. So all you gotta do is pull these brads, pull the piece that's twisted, if I put a lock behind it, the thing, it's case-hardened steel, it's not going to break. If I put it on there, put my foot on the fence and pull, the fence unwraps. Pull the fence, go underneath it. Why would I climb over this?

In the yard there's a fence runs this way then another fence connects, and there's a pole at the end. This fence connects to the pole, the other fence connects to the pole. How does it connect to the pole? One, two, three brads are holding it to the pole. Cut, cut, pulls away from the fence. I just walk out the fence. Why would I climb over and cut my ass going over concertina wire when I could make two cuts and walk through the fence?

The inefficiency and incompetency of the overall security was laughable.

* * *

Joe Correira was a career bank robber out of Boston's Charlestown neighborhood, a small enclave in the shadow of the Tobin Bridge known as a longtime breeding ground for criminals of all types, particularly bank robbers. Like Bobby, Joe was a transfer out of Walpole, a lifer with nothing to lose. Despite the fifteen-year age difference, Bobby recognized him as someone who could hold his own. When Joe began having cellmate problems, Bobby stepped in and arranged to have him transferred in as his own cellmate. The men got along well, but more importantly, Bobby found Joe to be trustworthy. Soon enough, it was time to discuss future plans together.

Bobby knew to be both patient and extremely cautious in these kinds of situations. Plotting an escape with a partner required explicit communication, and it was not as if he could sit down with Joe in the cafeteria and openly discuss plans. The entire block was wired with two-way speakers; he had to assume anybody could be listening at any time. If a guard spotted Bobby and Joe up in their cell talking, all he'd need to do is flip a switch and could pick up the voices as clearly as if he were sitting in the room with them. Even soft voices could be detected, so any verbal exchanges about the plan were forbidden. In a note to Joe, Bobby scrawled, "Do not speak. This place is wired. Do not trust anyone." Bobby thought about communicating with Joe in code, but dismissed the idea as both tedious and easily intercepted. Besides, this sort of plan required such meticulous preparation that using code would create too many opportunities for misunderstandings, which could get them both killed. They also had to worry about rats: if an informant knew anything of the plot, it could be offered up to the administration for preferential treatment or a reduced sentence.

One of the rules that we had, I had written it to Joe, because over ninety-five percent of the cellblock are stool pigeons. If you're not going to kill them, leave them alone. We treated everybody equally; nobody in the block was scared of us. So no bad vibes are coming from their stool pigeons about me and Joe into the administration. So I said leave the stool pigeons alone. Because you're running with me, if he gets scared and tells the man some bogus story, I get shook down and lose everything in my cell. Then I won't blame him, I'll blame you.

Bobby began tracking his observations of Bridgewater's surveillance equipment and techniques, and had to do it knowing he was being watched. He had already ascertained that any conversation in the yard could be heard in the control room. In the cellblocks, the control room was surrounded by tempered glass, totally soundproofed, requiring an inmate to shout to even be vaguely heard. However in the adjacent corridors, the small slot to pass papers, as well as the air space at the bottom of the door, conveyed sounds and voices very clearly. During a typical daily routine, Bobby would need to pass by five cellblocks to reach the yard. He could clearly hear, "Dellelo's passing post one, Dellelo's passing post two," as he progressed toward the outer yard. The first time he heard it, he ignored it and chalked it up to hyper-awareness. But as it continued to happen with consistency, he thought, *"Oh shit, I'm being tracked."*

Guards routinely conducted random searches of inmates across the yard. Every time Bobby went to the yard, without exception, he was one of the "random" men searched. Searches were not simple street-style pat downs used by the police. The selected inmate or inmates had to be escorted from the yard to a basement area, stripped down and searched thoroughly. Bobby, and other inmates, noticed that when he reached the yard, two K-9 vehicles were already positioned at opposite ends. Guys in the yard would see the trucks pull up and say, "Hey, Bobby's coming out." And sure enough, minutes later he appeared in the yard and was escorted to the basement. Playing cards one time, an inmate came over with a pass slip. Someone had taken notes on the reverse side and accidentally passed it on to the inmate. In handwritten pen, the slip had Bobby's name at the top and a list of all people he was interacting with, talking to, and generally associating with. His suspicions of being tracked were confirmed.

As further preparation, Bobby and Joe strolled the yard having conversations with the full intention of being overheard. They passed notes, which were destroyed immediately upon reading, in which they would lay out plans to discuss prison life while walking the yard or in other wired hotspots. Bobby would casually mention how he had come to terms with life behind bars, and hoped to grow old peacefully, free from the intense longing to be back on the outside. Joe would ruefully agree, adding his own comments that prison life wasn't so bad. Furthermore, he'd say, he had nothing on the outside to look forward to even if he were released one day. Both men would agree that they were actually scared of ever being outside again, afraid of failing to adapt to a society that has changed so much during their years locked away. To anyone listening, it was the idle talk of two lifers, mellowed by the passage of time and the grim acceptance of death before freedom.

We talked like that often. It lulled them to sleep, thinking we were passive lifers. We were never seen as potential escapees.

A couple times a year they have a cookout in the block, that little yard. They got the barrels cut in half with the grills on them. Me and Joe would do the cooking. You could buy hotdogs, hamburgers, chicken, and other food. We'd spend maybe sixty bucks, and they had refrigerators. You had a bag with your name on it, all our shit was in there. My brother Louie, he'd come up to Walpole at Christmas time, with over $400 dollars on just meat. When that came in, other guys are getting cereal, cookies, and other stupid shit you could buy in the canteen. They had it brought in on Christmas day. The IPS does the processing of the food. As soon as mine came in they gave it to me right away. They do not want to play with this. They know the kind of money that is sitting here. There are steaks, steak tips, pork chops,

*I mean Louie bought some great meats. They said
they'd get it to me real quick because we are not
taking any responsibility for it going bad. Does this
look like a guy that's escaping? And we know the
game of the listening devices, so in different spots, we
choreographed the conversation. It's all about living
happily ever after in the prison. Lulled them right to
sleep.*

Because the plan required consideration of so many
uncontrollable variables, Bobby and Joe were constantly in a
state of high alert. Though Bridgewater was officially designated
a medium security facility, it was a medium security in name
only—it was in fact a maximum security institution. Bobby and
Joe, as previously labelled "escape risks," were not supposed to be
in Bridgewater in the first place, the DOC was becoming
increasingly comfortable in sending more high-risk men to the
facility. This concerned Bobby, as those types of inmates would
bring heat, subjecting everyone to an overall higher level of
scrutiny. Even worse, someone might try an escape attempt
before they did.

One afternoon, Bobby and Joe were walking the yard,
tracing the perimeter over and over, and continuing their usual
discussion about life in prison. Very quickly and without looking,
Bobby pointed to a section of fence abutting the lookout tower
which housed the main entrance to the institution.

"Right there," he said softly. Joe instantly knew what he
meant.

That Friday afternoon Joe picked the lock to a restricted
area and stole the operating manual for the prison yard's
microwave alarm system. On the street, Joe had worked
sporadically as an electrician to supplement his criminal income.
He had demonstrated his skills in the prison shop, and was

trusted to work electrical maintenance and other jobs which gave him access to restricted areas throughout the institution. By exploiting the opportunity, he and Bobby poured over the stolen manual in their cell for the entire weekend, backward and forward, until they had practically memorized the entire contents. Early Monday morning, Joe slipped it safely back into place completely unnoticed. By that time, both men felt confident that they knew as much, if not more, as the prison maintenance staff about the operation of the alarm system.

The manual revealed valuable information which gave them a clear picture of what they were up against. They learned that the prison's high-end microwave system utilized a microwave dish approximately two feet in diameter, which beamed twelve feet on either side of the disc, totaling twenty-six feet. Bobby knew that "No Man's Land"—the area between the inner and outer fences—was only twenty-one feet in length. He deduced that top-level security could not possibly be employed in that zone because not only would the presence of either fence set it off, but the slightest variance could trigger a false alarm. Wind blowing against the fence, plants growing into the beam zone, rain or weather effects on the immediate terrain could all be enough to create a false trigger. The second level of microwave security spanned about eight feet, a two-foot diameter dish with only three-foot beams on either side. Two of the dishes, facing opposite directions, were less than two feet away from the fence. This level of security could be eliminated as a possibility. According to the manual, bottom-level security required a person to actually pass directly in front of the dish to set off the alarm. Two opposite-facing dishes, a signal sender and receiver, had lights perched atop which flashed when the beam was broken. Tower guards armed with shotguns would then know to shoot between the lights, because the prospective escapee would be there. If this was the extent of the security system, Bobby liked his chances.

To confirm that he was dealing with the lowest possible microwave security measures, he struck up a conversation with an IPS lieutenant.

"That microwave system is the stupidest thing in the world."

"Why do you say that, Bobby?"

"I could easily crawl under that thing without setting it off."

"You think so?"

"Yeah, definitely."

A week later, the IPS team was seen making adjustments to the system. To test its effectiveness, one officer crawled under the beam and did not trigger the alarm. Accordingly, they adjusted all microwave dishes to beam in a lower position to pick up anyone passing so close to the ground. Bobby and Joe watched in amazement. If the beam was low enough to detect crawlers, it would also be extremely easy to jump over. They laughed to themselves; it was as if they were being given a demonstration on how to dodge detection. Now, they had definitive confirmation that Old Colony's security was minimal at best. It was time to make specific plans.

Bobby and Joe carefully worked out the escape details, but did have one disagreement: the question of *when*. Joe wanted to go at night, using the cover of darkness to slip away. Bobby, who loved to indulge counterintuitive reasoning, pushed for a daytime operation. To make his case, he had Joe look out the cell window late at night to note the harsh glare of spotlights illuminating No

Man's Land. He pointed out how the lights appeared even brighter when contrasted with the surrounding pitch blackness. Conversely, Bobby showed him the colors in the daytime—blue skies, green grass, white clouds. The daylight, he argued, would provide a better camouflage from the tower guards' view forty feet above. In addition, they'd catch everyone off guard. Nobody would anticipate something as brazen as a daytime escape.

On October 31st, 1993, a Sunday morning, the plan went into motion just after 8:00 a.m. From the towers, guards spotted a fight which had erupted at the far end of the prison yard. Guards in all four towers immediately trained binoculars on the spot to assess the situation, identify any participants, and, especially, to look for weapons. Every guard on duty heard the prison-wide security alarm wailing and rushed toward the action. On the yard, inmates surrounded the fighters, cheering them on and making it difficult for guards to break it up. At the time, very few people were aware that the fight had been staged to occur at that exact moment.

With the temporary diversion, Bobby and Joe moved. The head guard in their unit took off toward the fight, but locked the block behind him, leaving them stranded in the block's individual walled-in yard. The two grabbed one of the several wooden picnic tables, quickly dragged it over to the wall, and flipped it lengthwise to create a ladder up toward the twelve-foot summit. At the top of the fence, they carefully and quickly stepped in between the concertina wire, and, once cleared, jumped to the grass below. Back inside the block some friends hurried the table back to its usual location. Staying close to the fence, Bobby and Joe tried to appear inconspicuous as they approached the No Man's Land fence just below the main tower. They were fully visible from the main parking lot, so if a car came by, they turned and casually pointed up toward the windows to give the impression that they were on work detail. Bobby had selected a specific point of the fence, which he had pointed out to Joe earlier, due to disc positioning. The area abutted the main entrance tower, with a large plate glass window overlooking the yard to the right and the perpendicular No Man's Land. They scaled the fence in the corner, directly under the tower window as a guard watched the disturbance in the opposite direction. To get to the top, they had fashioned a climbing hook out of the thick metal handles from the inmate lockers, which were typically confiscated by IPS because they were often converted into shanks. Bobby and Joe took theirs and bent the handles into a "z" formation. They took one and bent it in, lodging it in the fence at head level, then got up on it to use it as a foot support in order to reach the wire. Bypassing the concertina wire and the intertwined barbed wire, they passed over the fence top within feet of the guards standing in the window, distracted by the fight. Bobby said, "If they had simply turned to the left, we would have been caught red-handed. They could have easily shot and killed us."

Having studied the alarm system, Bobby and Joe knew how No Man's Land was wired. The disc facing them along the fencing was deactivated during daytime hours. They knew this because the beam would pick up visitor traffic at the main entrance and would be falsely triggered dozens of times per day. The infrared alarm could occasionally be heard at night, but never during the day. The second disc in No Man's Land faced outward, with the back side approximately six feet from the bordering fence. Bobby and Joe scaled the fence in the area where they simply walked behind the disc, easily breaching the high-tech security system. Reaching the outer fence, they repeated the same climbing process as the first fence. Less than three minutes after the fight broke out, Bobby and Joe were standing outside of the prison walls, the first official escapees from Old Colony.

In the morning daylight they walked across the front lawn along the fence, crossed over the access road leading to the main parking lot, and disappeared into the woods leading to the main road a short distance away. Just as they entered the wooded area, Bobby took one last glance back to read if there had been any detection. In the distance he saw several inmates watching, who clearly just witnessed their escape. Bobby recognized a couple as stool pigeons, and froze for a moment, thinking, *"Oh shit, here comes the sirens."* Then one of the guys broke into a wide grin, pumped his fist, and gave the thumbs up signal.

They may have been stool pigeons, but because we never disrespected anybody, they held their mud. They did that because they identified with us. We were like friends, convicts, their guys. So when we went, they went with us. It was like yes! We got those bastards!

They had chosen to move on a Sunday morning mainly because it was a slow traffic day. No prisoners were transported to or from the facility, and no DOC vehicles would be on the road. The only exposure would be to civilian vehicles or possibly local police. When they emerged from the woods, they walked quickly, listening for the prison emergency sirens during the short walk to reach Route 44 running east/west. About a half-mile down the road, they reached a traffic rotary where they entered at a convenience store, got some snacks and drinks, and called a local taxi service to bring them to Taunton, some ten miles away. From there, the plan was to board a bus, blend in with the passengers, and head directly to Boston. However, the infrequent travel which made a Sunday escape so appealing suddenly became a liability. At the bus station, they checked the transportation schedule and learned there was no service to Boston that day.

Despite the probability that they had not yet been discovered as missing, they were still racing against the clock to get as far from the immediate area as possible. They brainstormed and settled on the least risky plan, calling a taxi company. Minutes later a cabbie pulled in to the lot and agreed to drive them straight to Boston for a flat rate. He barely noticed his passengers. By 11:00 a.m., Bobby and Joe were dropped off in front of the Boston Herald building, standing on a street corner as free men for the first time in years. They could hardly believe it.

It would be another few hours until the sirens went off back in Bridgewater.

* * *

Though free, Bobby and Joe were far from safe. They were wanted men, and could be killed if not careful. If they were to survive outside of the prison walls, they had no time to waste enjoying their newfound freedom. It was time to take care of business. Crossing over the bridge into Chinatown, they walked straight into downtown, and made it to a coffee shop opposite Park Street Station, the same location where Bobby had been arrested thirty years earlier. They got coffee and used the payphone bank just outside, with Joe making calls to arrange for weapons, and Bobby working the phones for money and a place to stay. Within an hour they had about $600 to get started. They set about blending in with the population by shedding the clothes on their backs, buying nondescript civilian clothing. The pair entered a downtown department store, buying flannel shirts, blue jeans, t-shirts, and boots. After changing clothes and eating a hot meal in a diner, they felt good, finally coming down from the excitement of the day, feeling simultaneously exhilarated and exhausted. It took a few more phone calls, but by nightfall they were laying low in a safe house across the Charles River in Cambridge.

When news of the escape broke, DOC Commissioner Maloney was livid. Not only was the lax security at Old Colony exposed, but backroom political dealings had become public knowledge. When Bridgewater opened, the facilities budget had been approved in part due to Maloney's promises of a medium-security facility. He publicly declared that no dangerous inmates would be housed at Old Colony, thus alleviating the small town's reluctance due to safety concerns. But after the escape, the public was demanding to know why convicted murderers, serving life sentences and considered high escape risks, were serving time at a medium security facility. Even worse, the town's fears were realized when such men were not only present, but had escaped into their community. Because the escape occurred on October 31st, all Halloween activities were cancelled in Bridgewater and the surrounding towns. State troopers with shotguns were searching the area, aided by helicopters and dogs, with orders of "shoot to kill." Headlines warning of escaped killers on the loose went out across the print and televised media.

Bridgewater Prison Superintendent Paul Murphy, already despised by both administrators and prisoners, was called in by the Commissioner who wasted no time lambasting him for the public embarrassment. He ordered Murphy to stand in the yard, at the point in the fence where Bobby and Joe had gone over, to personally guard the area until it was fixed. Bobby heard later from inmates how pathetic he looked standing in the rain, hat pulled low, and seething with anger. The entire time he was in full view of numerous inmates, all of whom reveled in his humiliation. Bobby couldn't have chosen a better person to embarrass by escaping if he tried.

The Superintendent of the entire Bridgewater complex was called in by the Commissioner for the same treatment, but also had to answer to the town. At a board meeting, he sat opposite an angry panel of selectmen in a rickety folding chair with his papers on his lap, while they grilled him about the incident and the lies which had enabled it. He had very few answers, none of which were acceptable to the board. In a desperate attempt to deflect the heat, he meekly offered a solution that was too little, too late. All lifers—who should not have been there in the first place—would be immediately transferred out of Bridgewater.

The escape not only hurt the reputations of individuals, but the entire DOC agency as well. A spokeswoman for the department made a sheepish admission to the media the next day.

> "While the motion-detected system that surrounds the medium-security prison was activated at the time of the escape, the alarm had been turned off because it was triggered too often by the hundreds of visitors and employees who enter the prison's main gate," Correction Department spokeswoman Robin Bavaro said.

Furthering the embarrassment, the DOC admitted that construction of the windows in the guard tower created a partial blind spot in the area where the men went over the wall, mere feet away from the guards in daylight hours. Also, nine days prior to the escape, a guard noticed Joe Correira as he examined the outer fencing. The suspicious behavior triggered a shakedown of his cell, but no plans or tools which indicated an escape plot were discovered.

In the following days, the media detailed out the two men's criminal credentials as various local and state law enforcement desperately searched for the pair:

> Some guards called him "Houdini" and others called him "Superman." The names came quickly for Robert Dellelo after a perfectly timed escape from prison in Norfolk on a foggy night in 1968.
>
> Yesterday, the convicted cop killer was gone again.
>
> His accomplice Joseph Correira, in the Halloween break from a medium-security prison in Bridgewater has also tasted freedom on the lam, but only once.
>
> Prison officials consider both men extremely dangerous.
>
> Dellelo staged his first escape in September 1968, when he left a plaster dummy in his Norfolk prison bed, used a key to unlock a jail door and scaled a 20-foot, electrified fence.
>
> In 1973, he drew a fake gun on his guards and took their guns. He drove them to Milton, where he chained them to a tree and walked away. He was captured nine months later in New Jersey.

Police received numerous tips from the public, but none panned out. They interviewed family members of both men, who expressed concern for their well-being and hope for a peaceful end to the situation. Neither family offered any tips on how to catch the men. Just when it was looking like the pair got away clean and would never be heard from again, someone called the Cambridge police. They had been spotted.

Bobby and Joe lasted twenty-four days on the street. They hid out in Cambridge the entire time, at an apartment across the street from the courthouse, with two women companions. On the night of the capture, the women offered to cook Bobby and Joe a large Thanksgiving dinner. Bobby drove them over to Somerville, where they bought all the holiday supplies at the Twin City Plaza supermarket. As the women cooked and the night began to fall, Bobby considered going for a bike ride, both to kill time and to enjoy the unusually warm November weather. Normally, he didn't venture out in public unless absolutely necessary. But at this point he'd been free a few weeks and was beginning to feel cooped up. Also, it seemed as if the heat had begun to subside. The escape story had blown over and the media had moved on. Even so, Bobby knew he was taking a chance if he went outside because his face had been all over the news. He decided to go out anyway.

As he was readying to leave the house, the telephone rang and one of the women answered. Bobby watched her as she listened intently, a look of surprise on her face. She hung up and said, "The police have the place surrounded. They have shotguns." Bobby lifted the shade and peeked out the second floor window, seeing flashing blue lights and cops everywhere. Bobby yelled to Joe and they ran to the back side of the house. He yanked open a window hoping he could jump and run for it.

"Don't even try it! Do not try to come out that window!" a voice shouted over a loudspeaker.

Bobby directed both women downstairs to the front door. As innocent bystanders, he wanted to make sure they were safe in the event the situation turned violent. Also, he'd been caught off guard and needed to stall for time. By surrendering the women he might buy himself a few more minutes to figure something out. But the women were freaked out and didn't want to go outside. Bobby reassured them, "Just walk out the door. Just hold your hands up high in the air and go out." Finally, one grabbed the door, swung it open and proceeded out with her

240

hands up as instructed. Bobby remained just inside the doorway with the other woman, encouraging her, "Go ahead, do what she just did." She hesitated, but then exited the door. As she passed through the doorway, her right hand reached out and switched on the overhead light. Bobby was spotted immediately.

"Dellelo don't move!"

His mind raced. For one second he thought to turn and run up the stairs, but he'd be killed before reaching the second step. He instinctively felt his waistband, but realized he had forgotten to bring his gun downstairs with him. There was no way out at this point. He knew he was trapped. His mind raced, and he thought, *If they had just gone out the door, we could have tried some other way of out of here.* Unarmed and surrounded, Bobby called up the stairs.

"Hey Joe, it's over. I got shotguns on me, I cannot move."

"You can't make it back up the stairs?"

"There's no way. They got my ass."

"Oh shit...ok. I'm just gonna clean up what I can up here."

"Alright."

Taking a deep breath, Bobby pushed through the screen door with his hands above his head, and slowly walked out to the waiting police. He exaggerated his submission; he didn't want there to be any mistake about his surrender. If he even remotely appeared to be going for a weapon he'd be dead.

"Where's Joe?" someone asked.

"He's upstairs and he's gonna come down. Be cool, now, nobody's looking to cause any problems."

At the station before they move us to jail they make us wear these hospital johnnies, with the little plastic slippers. Joe's pissed about it. Now they got us in drag and you're gonna have all these reporters and cameras, and make us walk out there with dresses on? He's mad, I'm not mad; I'm prepared for this one. They take Joe out first, then after a while they come get me. Now as you come to the door, it's a double door. Once you come out of the cell area, there's a double door, and the light all along the door is pure white. All the cameras are on there. So we get in front of the door, and I got them all around me. A state police captain, Wood, he said, 'Get over here, you were involved in this, get in this.' I got them on each side of me, and holding my arms and they're all around me. They open the door and we start walking out, and he's holding my arm tight. He's got my arm like this, and he's acting like he doesn't see the cameras. The theatrics would make you want to vomit. As we're walking and everybody's looking stern and proud, performing for the cameras, I'm pulling the johnnie up. Now, I'm walking swinging my dick, it's bouncing back and forth. Everybody is roaring, all the reporters are laughing their asses off. These idiots can't understand why they laughing. Wood looks down says, 'Oh no!' and pulls the thing down. Once he gets the johnnie down, he jumps back into position, I swear, he grabs my arm again and acts like nothing happened. You think that's the end of it? We start walking, up comes the johnnie, and the dick is bouncing back and forth off my legs. Everybody's roaring laughing.

They put me in the DOC vehicle. They got a screw sitting beside me, two in the front. It's funny, these four girls come by. They stop at the window, giving a thumbs up, and said, 'Yeah!' And on the news it said Dellelo showed us more than we were expecting to see. What they did is they blacked off the bottom,

242

and I'm smiling and laughing with this big dumb grin. Guys would say, 'What were you laughing about? What the hell were you so happy for?' And when I explained they said, 'Oh go ahead!' And the four girls, no letters from them. I guess I didn't impress them that much!

The day following the capture, Captain Curt Wood of the DOC's Fugitive Apprehension Unit offered the media details of the escape:

-During their 22 days of freedom, they seldom ventured far from Somerville and Cambridge. They were planning a major robbery for yesterday or today, then had intended to flee the state.

-Other occupants of the apartment appear to have been friends of friends of the fugitives, and were not accessories in the escape or planned robbery.

Captain Wood had met Bobby several times over the years when visiting prisons around the state. While he described Bobby as "the ultimate con man," he also pointed out that he was a model prisoner. Furthermore, knew Bobby well enough to know he was a likeable personality and also very intelligent. "He was smart enough to know Wednesday night that he didn't have a chance," Wood told reporters.

* * *

A couple weeks after his return to Walpole, a local news reporter came to the prison to interview Bobby. He was brought in from DSU, and sat in a folding chair surrounded by guards while wearing leg irons, handcuffs, and a waist chain. An interview with a local reporter was broadcast on the evening news. He recalled:

I had no ID or social security to work under. If people didn't give me money to survive, I would have been compelled to commit a robbery in order to get money to survive with. It was a very scary situation being on the street. If they caught me in a certain situation, I'm going to get killed.

Some of the things I did out there, I stood on the Mass. Ave. bridge looking at the stars, looking at the moon, looking at the Boston skyline. I spent a half hour just doing that. I was in the Aquarium for over 3 ½ hours just going around looking at things. I was like a tourist in my own city. It gave back humanity to me; it gave back senses of feeling that got lost for thirty-one years.

Bobby remembered discussing how his experience on the street triggered long-dormant emotion, feelings he lost in Walpole:

In Harvard Square where the Coop is there's a whole family, mother, father, daughter, son and a dog, sleeping in the doorway. You see a woman sitting with a sign saying, 'I'm a homeless mother willing to work for food.' This isn't some junkie or some bum. That was really disturbing; I could never keep the change in my pocket...these were people that were hurting. To see in Harvard Square, the elite walking by! I always gave my change away, I could never keep it. When I first saw it, I kinda got a tear in my eye, it really hurt me. After, in retrospect, it felt good that I could feel like that again because inside prison you lose that feeling, you lose that humanity.

The segment closed by reporting that Bobby was now serving time in MCI-Cedar Junction, where he was housed in the solitary unit called Ten Block, "one of the toughest units in one the toughest prisons in the country." If convicted for escape he would receive additional time on-and-after his life sentence—despite the physiological impossibility of actually serving it.

Several months later, Bobby received a message in solitary confinement from the IPS lieutenant he'd discussed the alarm system with prior to the escape. A guard approached, looking cautiously up and down the hall and said in a loud whisper, "This is coming from him, not from me. He said, 'You motherfucker! You will never be forgiven for this one!'" Envisioning his angry face, Bobby laughed hysterically. The entire escape incident, with all of its risks, was validated in that moment. "We took them so smooth, it was really beautiful. It was a good escape," he said.

* * *

Bobby and Joe were already serving life sentences, so they were not very concerned about receiving additional time on top of their sentences. Both men were given an administrative punishment of five years in Walpole's DDU for the escape.

The pair was arrested pursuant to a court order, requiring them to be brought into court "forthwith and without delay." Twenty-six months after their arrest, both men languished in solitary without ever having been brought to court to face the escape charge. Bobby and Joe each wanted to file a motion for a new trial in their original cases, but could not because they had not yet resolved the escape charges. As legally savvy inmates, they knew if they sought new trials prior to settling the escape matter, they would be hit with the maximum sentence of ten years apiece.

Public defenders were appointed to Bobby and Joe free of charge through the Committee for Public Counsel Services. Bobby was experienced with public defenders, and he knew how the game would be played. Many times he watched as defense

245

lawyers pursued the case in a manner which suited their best financial interest, by needlessly continuing cases *ad nauseum* to log hours and maximize their legal fees. He figured they'd be brought into court, shackled and held in the waiting cell, and three or four hours later be informed that the case was continued for a couple of months. They'd have to come back again and again, with no advancement in the case. While they sat in a cell, the lawyers were billing the hours.

Bobby and Joe both sent certified letters to their respective attorneys, demanding an immediate trial without undue delay. Neither man cared about the actual outcome, they explained, as they were serving natural life sentences. Because of this, they were beyond the punishment of the court—additional time on top of a life sentence was pure semantics. The outcome of the trial was a secondary issue for Bobby; it was more important to him that a trial would expose the DOC for the twenty-six month delay, a clear violation of due process. When Bobby and Joe raised the subject with their respective lawyers, neither wanted anything to do with it. Now, the lawyers were trying to prolong their cases while simultaneously sidestepping the constitutional issues involved. Bobby and Joe sent certified letters to establish the record of attorney inaction. Later, they'd have grounds to appeal for ineffective assistance of counsel if needed.

Finally, a *habeas* was issued, ordering both men to appear in court for early November. The previous day the defense attorneys received yet another certified letter, signed by both Bobby and Joe, detailing their plan of action. The lawyers went into a panic, as both men would be entitled to be present in court for the motion to dismiss; due process allows a defendant to be present for any critical stage in the criminal process. A hastily scheduled meeting between the defense counsel, the prosecution, and a judge was held soon thereafter.

Three months later, Bobby's cousin Jack came to visit. He had gone to the courthouse, as he did on occasion, to check the docket on Bobby's behalf. Showing Bobby a photocopy of the docket entry, he pointed to the bottom entry which reflected the escape charges. Just to the right of the charge, highlighted in yellow marker, was the word "dismissed." Bobby shook his head and laughed. He was disappointed he wouldn't have the chance to raise the larger issues, as he'd been preparing for a righteous battle. In the end, he still felt pretty good about not receiving any additional time for escaping from prison. "They fucked up, all to my benefit," he said.

DDU director Phil Harrington passed by Bobby's cell a few days later. Bobby always called him "Harry" to his face, an intentionally disrespectful gesture, one that set Harrington off into a wild rage if any other prisoner used the name.

"What's up?" he asked tentatively.

"Check this out," Bobby said as he slid the paper through the crack. "Look at the highlighted part." He took a moment to process the words he was looking at, and then his eyes got wide, face turning red.

"How the fuck did you do that?"

"See Harry, you think what happened in Old Colony was an escape. That wasn't an escape. That was a furlough." Pointing to the paper in his hand, he said, "That's the fucking escape!"

Harrington was livid, and stormed off without another word. In DDU, where genuine happiness almost never occurred, Bobby was thrilled. He had gotten over on the system and beat them at their own game, and in that moment, nothing felt better.

CHAPTER FOURTEEN

O ver the years, Bobby had become accustomed to life in solitary confinement. He'd been sent there many times, with stints ranging in length from a weekend to two years, depending on his offense. Despite the challenging conditions, Bobby felt he was psychologically healthy and he had developed the necessary mental toughness to endure isolation. He didn't enjoy the experience by any means, but he was not afraid to go there if necessary. Still, even with his prior isolation experience, he wasn't prepared for the punishment he was handed after his Bridgewater escape. Labeled an "active escape risk" by the prison administration, he was given five consecutive years in the DDU. Bobby hadn't spent nearly that much time in isolation at any one stint, and when he arrived in DDU, he steeled himself for what was ahead.

The grim effects of isolation did not immediately reveal themselves. For the first few weeks, Bobby almost enjoyed the time alone. There were some benefits: he had a bed, meals, personal space. All of the politics and posturing of the general population were suddenly of no concern. Isolation also brought a measure of safety, as he was physically shielded from attacks by other inmates, and he no longer needed to work to maintain alliances for safety. Best of all, he had a little privacy. With the elimination of all the daily general population distractions he was allowed to think and write more clearly, his mind more sharply focused. Bobby's initial assessment of his situation was positive, and he felt confident. "It didn't seem so bad...*at first*," he said.

For Bobby, the greatest source of his mental endurance was fueled by defiance. He found energy and strength through active resistance of his confinement and steadfastly refusing to acknowledge the authority of his cell, the guards, the administration, and the prison walls. If in his mind he was free, he knew, he could find the ability to survive inside the box. His life, he decided, would not be defined by the conditions of his incarceration. In his refusal to be a victim, he found the wherewithal to avoid the hopeless abyss so many men fell into. If he could adapt to the worst possible situation, he reasoned, any punishment they gave him was impotent.

Although Bobby had a coping strategy, the ability to control his emotions and mental well-being did not come easily. He was intelligent, confident, and in good physical shape, but he was not impervious to the hard realities of life in DDU. Over time, he could feel himself slipping, becoming slowly overwhelmed by madness. He began frequently waking up due to horrible, violent dreams. Sometimes the obsessional fantasies commandeered his thoughts in the middle of the day as he did his routine activities of reading and exercising. When meals were delivered through the meal slot, he envisioned attacking the guard opening his door. "I pictured killing him with my bare hands. I had thoughts of cutting off the guards' heads and rolling them down the corridor like a bowling ball," he said. The loneliness, hallucinations, and sensory deprivation, over time, stole his ability to recognize differences between reality and creations of the mind. Bobby thought his television was talking to him directly, advising him to kill people along with other bizarre directives.

I was in there maybe a few months and I had to see my lawyer because I had the escape charges. I had a list of things I had to discuss with the lawyer. So I had to prepare the whole scenario, what's got to be done. When I get out there, seeing the lawyer, you're in a big room. It's gotta be fifteen by twenty feet at least. One side is glass squared windows, and a guard sitting out there observing you. There's a big desk in the middle of the room with a big camera pointing right down. They could actually read what you're doing. But now, the guard moves, I look at him, I come back, I lost the conversation. It's like a memory blank. The lawyer moves her hand to pick up a paper. I follow the hand. Once it comes back, I lost the conversation. You think you're losing your mind. I never experienced that kind of chaos. I had no rational explanation for it. The more I tried to understand it, the more confusing it became. Because every time she moved, it disrupted my mind process, I couldn't get out of there fast enough. When I got back to the cell, I still had the list, and I realized I didn't get anything done on it. It was like, 'What the hell just happened to me?' Because now I'm in control because there's nothing moving on me. My mind is coming back together and I'm reflecting on what just happened. I couldn't understand it.

To keep sharp, Bobby did everything he could within the confines of his cell: paced, slept, meditated, daydreamed, wrote, stretched, did push-ups and sit-ups. When he could get the materials from the book cart, he immersed himself in literature, textbooks, manuals, and encyclopedias. Due to the limited reading selection, he read whatever was available regardless of interest, anything which helped to keep his mind active and engaged. More importantly, his intense reading regimen distracted him from dwelling upon negative thoughts, and the painfully slow passage of time.

Bobby's studies in psychology proved to be a key to his DDU survival. If he could understand his condition, he reasoned, he could find the resolve to cope, to become better equipped to survive. He spent hours scouring sociology, psychology, and philosophy textbooks looking for answers, not as an intellectual pursuit but as part of his struggle to survive. "Fortunately, I was able to realize what was going on. I understood solitary was slowly dragging me down," he said. When he hallucinated and thought that the television was speaking to him directly, he learned to recognize the violent fantasies as a non-reality, a symptom of his isolation. He consciously ignored those voices and reminded himself of his situation, and not to fall into the trap. In turn, he could modify his behavior and comprehend this bizarre universe he was experiencing was not abnormal under the circumstances.

Because he had developed an understanding of the ways in which his mind worked, he was able to identify and avoid some of the common pitfalls many others became ensnared in. He studied the concept of the situational variable, in which an individual's actions are controlled and guided by the particular situation and circumstances surrounding that individual. He understood he must adapt, and by doing so he may engage in certain behaviors to survive that he would never consider engaging in otherwise. In prison, men turn to violence, manipulation, homosexuality, lying, and drug use—all of which may be abnormal activities to him on the street. But prison is an artificial environment where the rules of normal behavior do not apply. Behavior which may appear to be insane or irrational to a free man is routine and completely normal for prisoners. Bobby allowed this concept to guide him and to make sense of his surroundings.

> *It's the situation that alters the behavior. The condition of confinement alters behavior. The Stanford Prison experiment, they took some college students, randomly broke them into two groups. One group was prison guards, one group was the prisoners. They had to cancel the experiment; the guards immediately acted abusive and the prisoners revolted. Exactly what happened in that experiment is what happens in jails today and since the beginning of time. The condition of confinement, the*

251

situational variable, you put a human being in a certain kind of condition, he reacts to that condition. And that condition can mold behavior and its profound differences.

In solitary confinement you are adjusting to an abnormal normal. You are adjusting to insanity.

* * *

Not all time served in DDU was a total loss for Bobby. Even while serving in the most isolated environment known to society, he was able to achieve a significant and remarkable feat, something very few in his situation would be able to do. He made a close friend—and one who would challenge him in new ways.

Writer Susannah Sheffer first travelled to Walpole to meet Bobby in the fall of 1997. By then she had been working for over a year with former prisoner Dwight Harrison to write his life story. They spent hours each week talking about his crimes, addiction, victims, and time behind bars, which Sheffer organized and developed into a cohesive narrative built upon themes of loss and redemption. Sheffer noticed early on in the process that Harrison often referred to Bobby Dellelo, with whom he had served many years in prison, as an influential figure in his life. Dwight spoke highly of him as a person, inmate, friend, and teacher, detailing the ways in which Bobby led him to gain insight into his own life. Eventually, in his memoir *In a Dark Time*, Dwight would reflect Bobby's influence upon him:

'You ought to sign up for the GED,' Bobby had said. At 40, Bobby had been in prison for 18 years and in juvenile reform schools before that. Nicknamed 'Big Head,' Bobby was clearly one of the guys who ran the place. I hadn't exchanged more than a few words with him, but I always noticed how he carried himself, like he was claiming the ground he walked on. A whitened stripe cut through the center of his black hair.

'Why should I sign up for their programs?' I assumed Bobby would understand contempt for anything that belonged to the prison. 'This isn't about them, it's about you,' he said. 'Why are you doubting yourself?'

How did he know? How could he tell that underneath my disdain for official programs was the fear that I wouldn't pass the test anyway? To get away from the discomfort of being seen so clearly, I jumped to another excuse.

'I got natural life,' Bobby answered. 'You think I'm going to let that stop me?' That was Bobby. He took truth and held you right up to it, squirming and trying to look away, and he kept holding you there, steady, until something settled inside you and you realized you could stand to look. And then the looking showed you something you've never seen before. Excuses didn't work. Everything you tried to hide from yourself you couldn't hide from Bobby.

Harrison wrote to Bobby and explained how he and Sheffer were working out his life story, and asked if he'd be willing to sit with her for a visit and share some of his perspectives. This was no small favor; for Bobby to place Sheffer on his visitor list he'd have to bump someone else, possibly a family member, off the list. But Harrison trusted Bobby would do it if asked, and shortly thereafter, he did add her name as a visitor. "Somewhere along the way, a year into my work with Dwight, I sort of said 'Where is Bobby?' Sheffer said. "These figures [in Harrison's life] I was hearing about, so many were so historical. I wasn't really focused on 'where are they now?' because so many were no longer living. But I realized that Bobby was still alive, and the present-day reality of it sort of hit me. Dwight said he was in DDU, which I

253

had been hearing about a lot anyway, of course. I began to put that in my mind, that reality of Bobby as not just a character in a story but alive and somewhere. I understood that Dwight was prohibited from visiting him because ex-prisoners can't visit, so he wasn't in touch with him. But somewhere in those conversations, the notion that Bobby was there came up, and I had never visited a maximum security prison and was writing this thing, and it would really be a good idea for me to visit and see for myself. It sort of came together that it would be a way to cover several bases at once, to both meet Bobby and get a sense of him in a reality kind of way, and to hear his memories of Dwight. It somehow emerged that getting Bobby's memories of the same time would be very interesting. And why not? It was almost like an excuse to go in and see. I thought I would go once, which became a hilarious joke later because that's not what happened."

Sheffer and Harrison traveled to Walpole together. Ironically, Harrison was barred from entering the place he had been forbidden to leave for so many years, but he wanted to be part of the experience of introducing the two friends, to the extent that that was possible. Sheffer, for her part, was intensely curious to meet the man she'd heard so much about.

All DDU visits are limited to one hour, and Sheffer wanted to make it count. She entered DDU and saw Bobby being escorted toward the glass through which they would meet. He was cuffed, wore a waist chain, and was shuffling toward her while shackled around the ankles. He smiled in a friendly but reserved manner. She could sense he was curious about her.

And he was curious. He later remembered thinking, *"Why was she here? What did she want from this? What was she like?"* DDU prevented him from interacting with hardly anyone, much less meeting a new person, and it was even less likely that that person would be a woman. However, he figured if Harrison had asked, the reason behind the request was trustworthy.

At first, Harrison was the subject of the conversation, but they soon felt comfortable moving on to a deeper level of discussion. The conversation flowed naturally, despite the awkwardness of two strangers meeting in a highly restricted environment. Sheffer soon felt comfortable enough to allow her writer's curiosity to trump caution and pushed beyond the safety of neutral ground. Harrison was put aside as a topic, and she began directly inquiring about Bobby's life and perspectives. He was surprised, but took the questions seriously, and responded thoughtfully.

By the conclusion of the whirlwind meeting, Sheffer found herself fascinated by the conversation and the whole experience of meeting Bobby. She was physically prevented by the glass partition to shake hands or hug before she departed, but felt that a simple farewell was inadequate. Bobby offered a "glass handshake," his open hand directly on the glass, signaling for her to do the same. As they exchanged goodbyes, and Bobby asked her, "Give Dwight a hug for me." When she reached the parking lot, she honored his request.

Later, reflecting back on the meeting, Sheffer felt there was so much left to be discussed, so many questions which had been raised but remained unanswered. Bobby was intriguing to her; his insight to Dwight, his perspective as a lifer, his personal philosophies, and his inquisitive personality. She wanted to comprehend how he had lived without freedom in solitary conditions, how he survived, and how he preserved his sanity. She said, "Very early on, he said to me, 'I have had to work to maintain my sanity, humanity, compassion, and individuality in this environment.' I thought, 'Unbelievable.' To choose those four words! Each one is a world of complexity to think about. That

255

those would be the four words he would say, and identify as important. That he's alluding to how he's had to work to maintain them. I recall being completely captivated by it, as if it were a teaser for something it might be possible to learn a lot more about...how in the world has he done that? How has he managed to maintain those qualities? Sanity, humanity, compassion and individuality. I can't say it enough. So in a sense, eventually I found myself on a mission to understand that, how did he do that?"

In the following months, she followed up by writing to thank him for granting the visit, and cautiously offered to return for another if he was open to the idea. He quickly responded, "Absolutely."

Bobby never took Sheffer off his visitor's list. She returned regularly to Walpole, where she continued to talk with him about Harrison and to share drafts of the manuscript she and Harrison were working on. Over time, they became closer and talked about Bobby's experiences as well. It was as if, seeing what Sheffer was doing with Harrison and the kind of insights they were developing, Bobby grew curious about having some of the same kinds of conversations.

"Bobby was not exempt from the paranoia prisoners often feel," Sheffer recalled. "You're in a complicated situation, you're not being irrationally paranoid, because it's true, and you actually are being watched. So we developed sort of a code language. One of the reasons that Bobby sort of enjoyed me at the outset, I think, is that because I'm a writer, I got a kick out of that, having to come up with a code to talk about whatever he didn't want the guards to follow, which included details of how he was actually feeling. Initially I couldn't get my head around the fact that you couldn't step outside and privately confer; there was no way to have a momentary pause outside of the surveillance.

You could never get that moment. So how do you develop the code while being watched? But in a way that's kind of a bizarre intellectual exercise. We'd have these super convoluted exchanges where you'd have a code name for yourself. You'd say, 'I had coffee with ...' and give your code name, as though you had had coffee with someone else. It was crazy. I was reading over some of my old letters to him and some of the contortions we went through were hilarious. But he loved it and his intellect loved it, I think, that we could spar with it and figure it out. We'd have to have code names for other people, but how do you establish that while you're sitting there talking? You'd have to say, 'The friend of...' and with the eye contact you kind of established that you were actually referring to that same individual. Occasionally you could see a hand gesture out of view of the camera that would try to explain further.

Bobby is so used to being the teacher. He was always in the teaching role for other people; he's smarter than most people. He'd been in an explanatory mode for years, I think, and sometimes I would challenge him and we'd spar because I'd perceive him as being patronizing, because his favorite thing is wanting to explain. Of course, there were so many things I knew I didn't know, so I'd take that posture: 'Yes Bobby, teach me. I'm open to it.' But then we'd have this other thing going on where he'd be vesting me with the teacher role. And I think he really drank that up like a thirsty person, having someone who could be his teacher in some ways. It's hard to describe this without sounding self-aggrandizing, but he hadn't had that situation a lot in prison, where there was someone who could challenge him in these specific ways. Hearing about all this, Dwight would say to me that Bobby had met his match in me because I would challenge him and bring him to areas where he wasn't comfortable. He kept telling me, 'Do that, do that, make me squirm,' and he meant, 'Make me think about things that are hard to confront.'

The whole structure of the visit, it's so short, you're so aware of the time pressure. But it also means you drink the experience straight up, you get right to it. Once we had established together that there were particular things he wanted to explore during our conversations, I had a certain amount of authority to bring him back to those areas, using the authority of the clock and the authority of our agreed-upon agenda. I'd rest on the confidence on that he's asked me to do this. When he digressed into other things, I'd say, 'Bobby look at the time,' and he'd say, 'Yeah, help me out.' He meant, help me focus, help me deal with these difficult topics. He'd outright ask for the help. It's a tough thing to do with someone in any situation, let alone in that situation of a prison visiting room. You're making them uncomfortable because you're pushing them into personal territory, but if you're doing it, you have to believe they want you to.

If there's anything that is true about Bobby, it is his fascination with learning and his ability to see everything as a learning opportunity, almost to the point of hilarity. I mean he could be transferred to Ten Block and say, 'It's fascinating, it's good,' and find twelve reasons to convince you why that was actually a good thing. But that did not mean he was out of touch with reality. When things were bad, he knew they were bad. He was not off on some other planet, saying, 'No, it's fine', when the situation was terrible. Still, his habit of putting a positive spin on everything, which was maybe a coping strategy, was incredible."

Sheffer probed Bobby about his life, carefully encouraging him to discuss his emotional history and current emotional life, realms that she understood were largely inaccessible to him at first. As part of his DDU survival, Bobby had put his emotions aside, operating on an almost purely intellectual level; he understood this about himself and very deliberately wanted to address it. He told her outright that he both wanted to explore with her some of the kinds of issues she was exploring with Harrison and that he was ambivalent about doing so. Keeping this tension in mind, Sheffer developed a balance between asking probing questions and respecting the coping mechanisms he designed and relied upon to survive DDU.

"He was struggling with how open to be. Very early on he actually managed to tell me this, to write me this very moving long letter about wanting to be open and revealing in terms of his emotional life. I knew that if you ask a person to be open and emotional, it's very likely that at some point you're going to get to all this raw stuff. But could he do that when the whole point of survival in DDU is to not to open yourself in that way? It was so complicated, but he shared the dilemma with me explicitly, which was all the more interesting and moving.

Prison survival forces you to shut down your emotions, and Bobby knew that but also had a real agenda about endeavoring not to let himself be taken over by prison. He wanted to see what they were doing to him and to work to compensate for it. So he kind of identified this subtle thing as a something that was happening: I'm shutting down my emotions. It's incredible, yes, but Bobby had an ability to be an anthropologist about his own life, to see what was happening and how he was being affected. It's like how he responded when he realized that in isolation you lose the ability to read other people's nonverbal cues. When Bobby discovered that, he set himself on a corrective course, essentially doing things such as provoking the guards into some kind of nonverbal response so that he could keep up his ability to read body language. Who in the world would know that that's what this prisoner is doing? He's training himself to not lose that ability to read people. He did that in DDU all the time: I see this happening to me, let me take steps to deal with it. So that was part of his survival. When he was up to his edge, up to the threshold of capacity emotionally, you could tell. You'd see him get this look on his face and I could tell it was really hard for him, he was at his edge.

What I came to understand only gradually was that all of this was also part of his preparation for getting out of prison. He had really identified that he was going to need to be better at this—understanding his emotions—when he got out. 'Here is the harm that prison has done to me, and part of my self-defined pre-release program from within DDU will be to work on it.' Self-defined, or self-created, because nobody was formally working with him on this. This was all in the spirit of 'things I can take care of before release,' which I didn't understand at the outset, because my understanding was that he was serving a natural life sentence and would never be getting out. When Bobby would say things like, 'I'm not going to die in prison,' I didn't know how to think about it, and I think I didn't really understand it. It seemed like something he needed to believe to survive, and so I thought, no way am I puncturing that bubble. But I didn't think he was talking about a real possibility. The litigation that he was working on when I first met him, I do remember early on thinking, 'Let it drag out, let him have hope, let him have a reason to keep going.' But again, I didn't expect that litigation to work.

Bobby was telling me that dying in prison was not an option for him, not happening. I perceived myself as visiting Bobby partly to understand the experience of a lifer. My understanding was, he wasn't getting out, he was serving natural life. But that turned out not to be what happened and so what I was learning was something else entirely. A lot of what I thought I was getting asked to learn about this experience of visiting him was about the impossibility, about the fact that he'd never get out and how to handle that. I came to the determination that I would stand up for him getting out, that it was safe to do that and that I felt right about it, but I also I thought it's not going to come to anything because he's not getting out.

Meanwhile, during the years I visited him in prison, there was a lot to learn. Right alongside the 'I'm not going to die in prison' thing was his repeated assertion: 'I'm not in prison.' The endless hours that went into understanding the ways in which he meant that! The brief way to summarize it is that he meant, 'I don't live as if I am a prisoner.' It goes back to his point about maintaining his sanity, humanity, compassion, and individuality. Now, none of this meant he was superhuman, or immune to the effects of DDU. But I think Bobby is an extraordinary study in resilience.

So did I see the effects of DDU on him? Yes, though it took time. Initially, in the early days of DDU, we did what I shorthanded as the glass handshake; each putting a hand up to the glass at the end of the visit. I couldn't help being acutely aware of the glass. I was aware that he hadn't touched anybody, and the deprivation of that. He had said to me very early on, 'The hardest thing for me would be to think that someone on the outside was sad for me.' Which was a conundrum because I would in fact feel sad, I would feel what he was missing. It's hard not to, when you visit someone in DDU. When you get out of a visit, you appreciate everything around you. That feeling would come up at other times, too. Whenever I would see vistas or oceans, any great expanse, I would think of Bobby not seeing it. It gave poignancy but also vividness to everything, like I'm seeing it for him; it gave richness to my experience. So sometimes that's how I felt about the glass, that he doesn't want me to focus on what he is not allowed to experience. He wrote to me one time, he said, 'In spite of the glass, we touched spiritually and emotionally.' He was saying that kind of touch is real, so in that sense we do shake hands at the end of a visit. I got to a place where I saw it as he did, that the glass handshake was like a triumph over the circumstances. In DDU everything is stacked against forming a human connection, and yet we had one. It was like a victory because we beat them. They don't want you to be human, and you were human for an hour. I thought that was so triumphant. Then at one point I was talking to Dwight about it, saying that in a way this means the glass handshake is as good as a regular handshake, and his response surprised me. He said, 'Bobby's been in prison too long.' He agreed that the glass handshake is about transcending the environment, but it's also about loss. This took me aback, but in a useful way that made me really grasp the paradox of it. It's a coping strategy of extraordinary proportions to experience a handshake through glass not as a deprivation but as a triumph. That is true, but then here is Dwight saying, 'But also, it's a loss not to have the other kind of handshake. Don't forget it.' Later, Bobby could see that. I actually told him about what Dwight had said—that he'd been in prison too long—and Bobby looked really wistfully out in the distance and said, 'He's probably right.'

So both were true. But I continued to find Bobby's ability to construct comfort mechanisms for himself extraordinary. One time I asked him, 'What do you do when you feel like you want to break down the walls?' I just felt that he had to have some of that intolerable feeling, he couldn't be coping all the time. To his credit, he didn't say he never felt that; he answered the question. He told me this whole thing about how dogs were important to him as a child, and how he was basically able to recreate the memory of cuddling his dog and falling asleep holding his dog, and how that would chill him out when he felt that prison was intolerable. He doesn't really see how strong that was, but it is. To be able to recreate that feeling, in the depths of prison when you have not held that dog or anybody for decades, and to let that work for you? Some people just can't do it. Bobby had to ability to do it with his mind. It's easy to imagine a prisoner thinking of the memory of holding his dog and feeling unbearable yearning, feeling the lack and almost be not being able to bear it, the fact that you're not actually holding the dog. Bobby went there and used it as comfort.

I'm giving these glimpses of this very private resilience. No matter what you say or do throughout the day, at the end of it you're alone in your cell in the middle of the night. You either can or you can't deal with that. The dealing is at that level. It's not only dealing with prison and the people, it's also dealing with the reality of that it's three in the morning and I'm alone."

Others around him were dealing with similar issues, and Bobby felt genuine concern about them as well. He hoped he could use his findings to guide other DDU men and to provide insight to the outside world as to exactly how the Department of Correction treated its population. Bobby eventually wrote an article about his isolation experience which was reprinted in several periodicals, some of which made their way back into the prison. Reactions from his fellow inmates were strong. Soon after the articles began circulating around, an inmate with a fearsome reputation approached Bobby in the yard. The man relayed his frustration, how DDU had stolen his ability to enjoy anything, especially the joy of visiting with his wife and children. He had very much looked forward to each visit with his family, but his easy loss of focus, inability to articulate thoughts, and emotional distance all diminished the quality of the visits. After his family left, he felt emptier and more alone than before, an agonizing pain bordering on intolerable. Bobby validated his experience, as he'd been there too. He spent hours showing him that the problem wasn't caused by his personal weakness, it was the environment that forced his reactions, and that his experiences were hardly unique. Though horrible, the conditions and suffering he complained of were quite common amongst isolated individuals. Once he understood his suffering was shared, and that he was not going insane, he found solace and strength in that knowledge. "I read that article," he said, holding back tears. "Man, that's exactly what happened to me. I thought I was losing my fucking mind."

In time, a slow trickle of inmates emerged from the population to share their stories with Bobby, repeating the same themes again and again. While he attempted to remain detached as he listened, he was surprised to find himself reacting emotionally to their tales. He was offering himself as an expert on the subject, a rock to which others could turn to make sense of the madness. But while he was validating their experiences, they were also validating his. He spent so much energy helping others through the ordeal of DDU that he had hadn't given much attention to his own issues. He began to realize the same thing he helped others come to terms with; that his personal experience was shared by many others, and they too had suffered equally as much. The revelation hit him like a brick.

Bobby spent over five years in DDU before he was released back into general population. While happy to have regained a social life, he struggled with the mental and emotional problems he had developed in isolation. Crowds made him anxious, and he was paranoid about old conflicts with inmates. He was overstimulated by the people, the sounds, and the hustle of a busy prison. Often, it was overwhelming. But as time passed, he began to feel slight improvements and committed himself to keeping a positive attitude. As part of that effort, he made a point of helping others through the same process. Bobby noticed that when former DDU men spoke to others, they exhibited very little body language, with hands at their sides or arms folded, all the direct result of lengthy periods of time without social interaction. Bobby encouraged them to become animated when speaking, consciously using their hands and body as a speech enhancement. "Move like a guinea, talk like a greaser!" he'd joke with the others, pantomiming stereotypical gestures made popular by cinema mafioso. Bobby observed that many men, with effort, were able to restore the kinesthetic skills which had gone unused for so long. For some, DDU effectively obliterated the skills, and they needed to be relearned from scratch. Bobby understood this and was happy to help, reminding men to use body language as much as possible. He'd tell them, "Don't let the DDU steal anything from you permanently. Now, use your hands."

> *After five years and one month in DDU I went to what they called the Mods, which was a special sixty-man unit. I was in there for a while before they moved me into population, which wasn't a bad idea. Because if you go directly into population, your paranoia is very high and people are in your space. It was tough getting used to people near me. A lot of these young kids they talk tough but they don't mean anything. But when you say certain things to me they have a different meaning. That's what I operate on, and you can't operate that way. They would run their mouths, and for a while I was jacking these young kids up left and right. And you learn that these kids don't really mean anything, this is a game that they play, a lot of talk. But after DDU I was quick to take action. I had to re-learn how to deal with those situations.*

* * *

Solitary confinement does not work. What they do is they give flat sentences. Ten years in DDU. Well, your whole program just went out the window, and you actually lost control of the individual. They keep talking about control, but they have no understanding of what control is. They think locking you in a cell, keeping the door locked 24/7 is control. That's not control—that's losing control. Control is when you can take a guy, get him into a group, and then move him through a system, controlling the movement. So that when he hits population the attitude and behavior that got him in is pretty much extinguished. So you had the ability to properly control, they had the goose that could lay the golden egg. You could humanely modify behavior without torturing somebody. You could take a man and move him back and forth, depending on the behavior.

In Massachusetts, you have two sets of laws. One's thirty-nine the other one is forty. One's on isolation, one's on segregation. But isolation is punitive; you can no longer be in isolation forevermore. In '55 they changed the law. You can only be in isolation for fifteen days max, at one time. If there was a group of charges, no more than thirty days for a group of charges, with one day off at the fifteen day mark. So if I had fifty charges on me, the most you can have me do in isolation is thirty days with one day off. Usually it was like three days. I would lose, for every day in isolation, three days of good time. It made sense, the max I could lose was forty-five days. It was in my control. Then, they changed that. DOC could take all my good time. So when you take a year of good time, that's like a year in the House of Correction. But you're in state prison, so technically DOC is giving me a year in Walpole State Prison on bogus disciplinary nonsense. The 'get tough on crime' idea made absolutely no sense inside the prison. But

266

you had the isolation statute, then you had segregation.

DDU is a violation of law. Guys argued in court that DDU was isolation and it couldn't last more than fifteen days. The SJC said no, it's not isolation, and they lost the suit. I kept telling the lawyers you're arguing the wrong argument. It's segregation, a disciplinary segregation, but under Massachusetts law it cannot be punitive. It has to be a DSU not a DDU, and you're entitled to programs. As a DDU you get no programs. It's a violation of law. The Department of Correction, by statute, is required to rehabilitate prisoners. It's statutorily mandated for all prisoners, including the ones in DDU. The only exception would be the guy that's in isolation. And that's understandable because it's only a fifteen day period. You wouldn't radically upset rehabilitative programs if you had to get punished for acting out.

We had 777 come in around '71, which was the furlough programs. It was a Republican, Governor Sargent, he got that put in place. Then later we get Weld in, he destroys it. So it's a roller coaster ride, a pendulum, it swings in both directions depending upon the politics of the time.

You can't rehabilitate prisons, and that's why I push for the abolition of prisons. You have to abolish prisons, and it's the method that you do it that makes sense. The law requires the Department of Correction to rehabilitate prisoners. We should be fighting to force DOC to rehabilitate all prisoners, to provide the proper programs for them to do it. If you are successful there, you're going to reduce the amount of prisoners in the system, the recidivism rate is going to go way down, you're saving money, you're closing prisons. DOC and guards' union do not have a vested interest in rehabilitating prisoners. The classic example is these privatized prisons. You have shareholders. You rehabilitate the product, you're fired. Are you insane? You're going to put us out of business? This is a money making operation. And that's the insanity.

If you want to reduce the recidivism rate, you have to be smart on crime. Isolation is an example of being stupid on crime. These men will return to the community one day. You have to ask yourself, 'Do I want them to come out better than when they went in, or come out worse?'

CHAPTER FIFTEEN

During his five years in DDU, with few opportunities for productivity, Bobby wanted to focus on something positive. He began thinking about his case, and how he was so young and legally ignorant at the time of his trial and appeal. He always felt that his defense lawyer did a poor job representing him, and his reading of the law over the years caused him to believe he had genuine issues to appeal which were never raised. Bobby gathered his papers, and nearly thirty years after his original appeal, he threw himself into a full re-examination of his case.

> *So now I can do a motion for a new trial, I can put all my energy and time into that sucker. Ironically, had you put me in DDU for one or two years, I wouldn't have done that. I wouldn't have bothered. I would have been planning my next escape.*

In 1965, Bobby appealed his first-degree murder conviction. Represented by his original trial attorney, the only issue raised for appellate consideration was that he was improperly denied a motion for a directed verdict of not guilty. She argued that the prosecution failed to show evidence for each of the basic elements of the crimes charged, and thus a not guilty verdict should have been ordered without the case going to the jury. The motion had been filed during trial at the conclusion of the prosecution's case-in-chief, but was denied at the time.

Bobby also claimed the joint enterprise theory leading to his conviction was in error because Holmes was killed only after the joint behavior—the attempted robbery—had come to a conclusion. He argued that since they had mutually withdrawn from the criminal enterprise, any subsequent actions were not in furtherance of the crime. Once they pulled out of the robbery,

Nicky's behavior was not part of a joint venture. Furthermore, he had physically distanced himself from the crime to the extent that he was not in proximity to the murder. Thus, the joint venture theory was misapplied to his case, and his murder conviction should not stand.

The Massachusetts Supreme Judicial Court heard the appeal on May 3, 1965. Addressing the withdrawal from joint venture argument, the court stated:

> The jury, viewing the events objectively, could reasonably conclude that the two men broke off the undertaking upon the sounding of the alarm, not because they did not wish to proceed with it, but because they knew that if they persisted in it they faced imminent capture; that both had a common purpose to resist capture...and that resorting to shooting was likely as a means to accomplish that common purpose. There must be an appreciable interval between the alleged termination and the fatal shooting. Even though the attempted or accomplished crime of robbery may technically be said to be complete, if the homicide is committed while the killer is engaged in one of the elements incident to the crime such as an escape or flight, the killing is referable to the robbery; and whether the act of escape or flight is a continuous part of the attempted or accomplished crime is for the jury to determine. Here the jury could find that from the moment the criminals entered the jewelry shop for the purpose of robbery to the moment of the defendant's capture, that the defendant was continuously engaged in violence or threats of violence involving the use of a loaded pistol, that both his and Yasaian's acts were referable to the attempted robbery, and that their acts provided mutual support throughout. The assault upon Officer McGrail facilitated the escape of Yasaian as

well as of the defendant. The fatal shooting of Detective Holmes by Yasaian followed immediately. The fact that the defendant and Yasaian ran in different directions upon leaving the Dexter Building could be found to be concerted action, designed to cause dispersion of the police in pursuit. These acts, all in rapid sequence, could be found to be parts of a single brief transaction.

The court ruled that the issue of withdrawal from the joint venture was a matter of fact for the jury to find, and their decision that the robbery was not over at the time of the murder was reasonable, and therefore, the original decision to deny the directed verdict motion would stand. Bobby's defense counsel explained to him that, barring an extreme long shot, he was going to spend the rest of his life in prison.

By 1997, his third consecutive year in DDU for the Bridgewater escape, Bobby set to work on his appeal. He sought to challenge some issues his lawyer failed to raise with the goal of having his conviction vacated, and to win the right to a new trial, and even possibly gaining his freedom. After reading all of the law he could get his hands on, which was limited, he poured over the trial transcripts. Bobby had devoted innumerable hours to this end, but had not sought the help of any legal professionals. Lawyers hadn't been very helpful to him in the past, and he believed they actually hurt his chances at acquittal and successful appeal. In fact, a CPCS screening attorney sent him a dismissive letter, essentially advising him to give up the fight because there were no valid issues to appeal. At this point, he figured going forward *pro se* was more beneficial than leaving his case up to yet another underpaid and disinterested defense attorney. Though Bobby had no formal legal training, he had studied law intensively; he'd read cases and statutes for years and had a strong understanding of how courts interpreted applicable law. In his own case, he found issue after issue to challenge, and he wanted the court to consider each and every one. With nothing to lose and everything to gain, he began writing.

In August of 1997, Bobby completed and filed his Motion for New Trial. In his memorandum supporting the motion, Bobby first argued that the trial judge used prejudicial language in his presentation of the defense attorney during his closing jury instructions. He also pointed out that the trial judge's jury charge was unfair because his characterization created an impermissible presumption of guilt and caused the burden of proof to shift to himself as the defendant. Further, he asserted that trial judge defined "reasonable doubt" in terms which were confusing and contradictory to the jury, and effectively created a lower standard of proof for the Commonwealth. Therefore, he claimed, his due process rights under the Fourteenth Amendment were violated, his trial was irreparably unfair, and his conviction was constitutionally improper. As such, the only proper remedy would be the granting of a new trial.

Bobby eagerly awaited a hearing date to be scheduled, but it never happened. Years passed by and the court took no action on the case—no hearings, no rulings made, nothing. As a *pro se* defendant filing an appeal from a DDU cell, he had extremely limited communication abilities, and no leverage to push the matter forward. The Commonwealth understood this, never bothering to file a motion in opposition. When the court ignored his pleading, he had no outside assistance to bring his case forward. So he sat in DDU and waited for something to happen.

By March of 1999, Bobby was released to general population after serving over five years in DDU. His first priority was to follow up on his stalled appeal, bringing him straight to Walpole's main law library. Once he accessed the resources there, he realized the original motion was heavily flawed due to the inadequate resources available to him in DDU. He set to work revising and refining the motion, and submitted a new revised version exactly three years to the day from the original filing. Therein he argued that the court must allow his original motion to be amended because that motion was written "under extreme duress, with inadequate access to the institution's law library, and, under extreme conditions of punitive and deprivatory confinement, while serving a five (5) year sentence in the Department of Corrections Departmental Disciplinary Unit (D.D.U.) for escaping." As support for this claim, Bobby detailed the small sampling of random and outdated law books provided to him on a pushcart occasionally brought through DDU. He also attached as an exhibit letters he sent to Walpole's Director of Treatment, chronicling his repeated requests to access law books from the institution's main library. One reply to his requests read:

> Please be advised that I reviewed your correspondence and have spoken with the Librarian. The best course of action available requires you to define specifically what your legal issue is so that the Librarian can assign an inmate law clerk to research what areas of law you will need and make the appropriate copies for you. Unfortunately, the law books you are requesting are in constant use by the inmates housed in population and therefore cannot be removed from the Main Law Library.

Thus, despite his most diligent research efforts, he was provided with materials which were grossly inadequate to provide any meaningful legal research toward his motion for a new trial. Because no action had ever been taken on the original motion, and no oppositional motion had ever been filed by the Commonwealth, Bobby argued to the court that granting the

273

motion would in no way prejudice the state, and would allow justice to govern the issues. The court agreed.

Though Bobby's access to proper materials was now better than in isolation, he was still in prison and resources remained very limited. Despite this, he extensively researched supporting cases for claims made in the original motion, and was able to find stronger, more relevant precedent to bolster his position. The new materials he uncovered allowed him to recast his claims in more succinct and cohesive language and to omit outdated and irrelevant cases he previously cited. Additionally, he discovered further grounds beyond his original claims on which to base his motion, such as Ineffective Assistance of Counsel, Prior Bad Acts, and Improper Prosecutor's Closing.

One key difference between the original pleading and the amended version was that this time around Bobby had assistance of counsel. Since his release from DDU, he had the ability to communicate with CPCS, who assigned veteran attorney Nancy Dolberg, an associate of a prestigious Boston law firm, to his case. This proved incredibly fortunate. Dolberg possessed a very credible legal reputation, knew the law, and firmly understood the issues involved. Unlike so many of Bobby's past lawyers, she listened to him, soliciting his opinions and viewpoints without judgment or dismissiveness. She trusted Bobby enough to the degree that she assumed an advisory position, allowing him to determine his own legal strategy and argue the issues he wanted the court to hear. Dolberg contributed her writing skills to increase the persuasiveness of his arguments, assisted him in finding the best case law as support, and helped focus his legal arguments. By the time Bobby completed the final draft of his memorandum, he was excited. He was certain they had a winner. Dolberg agreed.

The new motion reiterated his earlier argument made with regard to the judge's jury instructions causing an impermissible shift of the burden of proof to the defendant. In 1979, the Supreme Court held in *Sandstrom v. Montana* that the burden of proof in a criminal case lies solely with the prosecution, and the state must prove each and every element of a criminal charge beyond a reasonable doubt, and that the defendant is under no obligation to prove anything. Bobby acknowledged that he did not make this objection at trial, which would preclude him from raising the issue on appeal, but his original appeal was heard and denied in 1965, long before the *Sandstrom* decision. As such, there was no way he or his attorney could have recognized a constitutional error which had not yet been clarified by the nation's highest court. Now that this due process principle had been clearly established, Bobby argued he was entitled to now raise them for consideration.

He also challenged the jury charge regarding presumption of innocence as both misleading and confusing. Quoting the transcript, the trial judge's statement read:

> A defendant need not present evidence of his innocence. He has the right to remain inactive and secure **until** the Government goes forward with evidence to prove him guilty..." [Emphasis added].

Bobby vehemently argued that this judicial instruction contradicted the principle that a defendant is presumed innocent until proven guilty, and that the presumption endures throughout the entirety of the criminal process. The charge, as read, suggested to the jury that Bobby's right to be presumed innocent lasted only "until" the state began producing evidence against him. Then, from that moment forward, he would no longer enjoy a presumption of innocence and the burden would shift to him to offer evidence of his innocence. In doing so, the judge effectively instructed the jury to ignore a critical aspect of due process.

Under the Sixth Amendment, any criminal defendant has the right to be represented by adequate counsel at trial. Bobby argued that because his attorney failed to provide him with competent legal representation, he was deprived of this right. Since he had the same lawyer for both the trial and immediate appeal, he cited numerous examples of incompetence from both proceedings to support the claim for a new trial. Specifically it was her repetitive failures to object to highly prejudicial evidence offered by the prosecution. Not only did the jury hear the statements, but the failure to object prevented genuine issues from being raised on appeal.

Finally, the motion directly addressed the multiple improper statements made by the prosecution during closing arguments. In a criminal trial, the state is required to review the evidence presented to prove the charges, and highlight reasonable inferences made therefrom; it cannot improperly appeal to emotion through inflammatory statements, misstate the evidence, or address facts not in evidence. All of these happened during the trial without defense counsel objecting. The transcript read:

> Now, whose idea was this robbery? Would you say the defendant, from your observation of him, would have the capacity, would have the brains, would have the know-how, would have the experience in juggling guns to plan this robbery? Or would you say, as he would want you to believe, that it was little baby-faced Yasaian?

> Do you think for a moment this man would have hesitated in shooting Officer McGrail in that doorway if Officer McGrail wasn't reaching for his

gun? Men of his type don't run risks. If McGrail had raised his hands the way poor Officer Holmes did, you may rest assured he would have shot Officer McGrail then and there. And when they were in that cab, if he felt that the odds were one hundred in his favor and zero in favor of Sgt. Chennette, he would have shot Sgt. Chennette then and there. That is why he had the guns. That is why he had this load of ammunition.

The prosecution speculated to the jury that Bobby had the intent to harm police officers. No evidence existed to support the suggestion as to what Bobby may or may not have done; he simply defended himself by saying he had nothing to do with the murder. In fact, the testimony from Officer McGrail supported Bobby.

Q. Now, Officer, the defendant could have killed you, couldn't he?

A. Very definitely.

Q. He didn't use his gun, did he?

A. No, he didn't, ma'am.

Q. He didn't take his gun and pistol whip you, did he?

A. No, he did not.

McGrail later testified:

Q: And did he have a gun at that time?

A. Yes, he did.

Q. It was still in his hand?

A. Yes, it was.

Q. Did you open the door of the cab?

A. On the right hand side.

Q. Could he have killed you then?

A. Yes, he could have.

Bobby also cited improper statements made during closing arguments. Not only did the prosecutor ignore his presumption of innocence, but misstated the evidence to the jury as well:

Those of you who have previous jury experience know that very seldom do these seasoned criminals come forward and say, 'Yes, I did it. I want to take what is coming to me.' Oh, no; oh, no—because of their experience in criminality, they concoct devious defense and devious schemes to beat the law. And it is very interesting to note, as the case progresses, they abandon one theory of defense and go on to another.

Now, as the case started, it was obvious to all of you that this man was going to defend his case on the theory that he never was in Kopelman's; that everybody was mistaken; that Bernard Kopelman didn't see him; that Irving Kopelman didn't recognize him; or that Officer Buckley of the M.D.C. was mistaken. That was his theory of defense. However, when the time came that Mr. Whalley took the stand, and that was the gentleman who was the janitor in another jeweler's building and identified him as being with Yasaian in his building on November 1, he got kind of panicky. You remember, he ran off that dock, came down here and insisting on putting on the silk stocking. Thinking that the silk stocking would hide his face. Well, it was apparent that once he put on that silk stocking, there was nothing in that stocking to hide his face or his features. From that point on the defendant's theory of defense changed. He no longer was going to rely on the fact that he wasn't there. He was going to admit that he was there and such he did when he took the stand if you remember.

However, now it becomes necessary for his experienced criminal mind to devise another defense, to devise an avenue of sympathy with the jury. And what is his scheme of defense now? Now that the first has failed? It is one that when he went to the police station, he was abused by the police.

Bobby's main defense claim had always been withdrawal from the joint enterprise. The prosecutor claimed that Bobby originally denied being at the scene, but then switched defense theories only after hearing witness testimony. Nothing in the record supports that Bobby's defense was, at any point, denial of presence at the scene. Claiming that was his original defense was simply a fabrication of fact; it would follow that Bobby couldn't have switched defense theories if the first asserted theory never existed to begin with. The prosecution's characterization of Bobby becoming "panicky" and suddenly changing defense strategies was an improper insinuation of guilt.

Now, Mr. Foreman and gentlemen of the jury, the time has come for you to do your duty. Remember, when you came to jury service, you were told that it was your responsibility to find the truth and to render a verdict in accordance with the truth, and I ask you to do your duty and render a verdict in accordance with the truth to find this man guilty of murder in the first degree and guilty on all other indictments.

Now, he asks for mercy. He asks for leniency. He asks for compassion. Was any compassion shown to Detective Holmes? Was any consideration given to that poor man who was shot dead while his arms were raised? However, do your duty.

Now, on the state of the evidence, the believable evidence, Mr. Foreman and gentlemen of the jury, this defendant was the captain of the team. This defendant was the one that was making the plans. This defendant was the leader. He went into Kopelman's. He was the one that went for the diamond room. He was the one that went to the place where the loot was, which, as he says, he hoped to divide with Yasaian. And now that poor baby-faced Yasaian is dead he is trying to foist the responsibility for this situation on Yasaian.

Bobby's appeal argued that the cumulative effect of the numerous impermissible statements easily met the legal standard for a new trial. The statements, taken as a whole, created a substantial likelihood that he was deprived of his due process rights and a miscarriage of justice resulted; a new trial must be granted.

Now properly backed by a competent defense attorney, Bobby's motion was unable to be ignored. The Commonwealth submitted a dismissive response in October of 2002, first pointing to the thirty-three years which had elapsed since the original trial and appeal. Thereafter, the document essentially mirrored the defendant's brief, merely responding point-by-point in the negative. Among the defensive claims the Commonwealth made was that Bobby waived any challenges to allegedly valid jury instructions by failing to object to them at trial or raise them on appeal. Even if the claims were not found to be waived, the challenges were without any merit whatsoever. Finally, even if instructional errors were made, they were irrelevant or simply harmless error which had no impact on the jury's guilty verdict.

The Commonwealth also addressed the awkward position of rebutting the claim of ineffective assistance of defense counsel by arguing that she adequately defended the case, used effective legal techniques and strategy, and how her excellent work ultimately spared Bobby the death penalty. Further, she further acted properly in failing to raise certain issues on appeal, because those issues were not likely to be successfully heard. Similarly, her failure to seek limiting instructions regarding several issues was also proper, given the Commonwealth's assessment of the case.

Superior Court Judge Carol Ball considered the motion. Bobby won a quick victory on a preliminary matter when she agreed from the outset that Bobby could not have waived his objections by failing to raise them at trial or on direct appeal, because in 1964 (the time of his trial and appeal) the claims of constitutional error were not yet fully developed according to the *Sandstrom* decision.

Moving on to the substantive claims, Judge Ball dismissed the claims of impermissible burden shifting, citing cases to support the idea that the jury instructions, taken as a whole, sufficiently explained the concept of guilt beyond a reasonable doubt. Next, the judge addressed the jury instructions which Bobby claimed the word "until" improperly reduced his presumption of innocence. She stated:

> While not in explicit terms, the instruction here essentially states that the presumption of innocence disappears once the government introduces evidence of the defendant's guilt. It fails to emphasize that the presumption merely *begins* to disappear or that "it takes evidence to overcome the presumption of innocence." Therefore, viewing the charge in its entirety, I am not satisfied that the instruction on the defendant's presumption of innocence

sufficiently conveyed to the jury that the presumption remained with the defendant throughout the entirety of the case. Moreover, I "cannot conclude that the erroneous instruction, taken in context of the entire charge, was not prejudicial to the rights of the defendant inasmuch as it may have influenced the jury in their evaluation of the evidence." **Accordingly, Dellelo is entitled to a new trial.** [Emphasis added].

Because I have concluded that a new trial is required based on the presumption of innocence instruction, I need not reach the defendant's remaining arguments. These include challenges to the instruction regarding intent/malice aforethought, allegations of ineffective assistance of counsel and errors in the Commonwealth's closing argument.

While he would have liked the judge to rule upon all of his claims, Bobby was thrilled at the end result. With his original conviction decades old, most of the witnesses from his trial were now dead or whereabouts unknown. Furthermore, so much time had passed that any eyewitness accounts would hardly be credible or accurate testimony. In a new trial, the state would lack the tools to prove the case beyond a reasonable doubt, and therefore another trial would be highly unlikely. Suddenly, after decades behind bars, Bobby's legitimate freedom was a very real possibility.

CHAPTER SIXTEEN

The prosecutors were aware of the numerous problems in retrying a decades old case, but still wouldn't offer a plea deal. Instead, they threatened to use the original trial transcripts as evidence in the event of a new trial. Bobby objected, but Dolberg advised him that the rules of evidence would probably allow it. He argued that the transcript was inherently unreliable; the basis for the new trial, in part, was due to the allegations of ineffective assistance of counsel and prosecutorial misconduct. She thought about it for a moment, and said, "You're right." When this information was brought to the attention of the District Attorney's office, they chose to back off. If they had an unwinnable trial before them, it was a better option to negotiate a plea of some sort. For his part, Bobby was not interested in going to trial either. Over the years, he had witnessed many inmates invest an enormous effort into overturning their convictions, only to be retried and convicted again. Now that he had won a new trial, he was determined not to make that same mistake.

I said I would plead guilty to the manslaughter. They first come back with an offer of 35 to 45 years. We didn't know if they knew about the federal time. And when they came back with that, then I knew, they said I was gonna have to do some time, well that was federal time. I had like three years and seven months to do. I have 3-5 years on-and-after for the escape, so it's really not 35-45; it's actually 40 to 50.

So I said take that off, which then brings it back into the range I wanted it in to eat up the 18-year federal sentence. I'm trying to kill my on-and-afters. So that brings it back into the range and takes them out. I told her to tell him I'm 62 years old and I'm not dying in prison. So we brought it down to that. And the 5-7 years being added in there doesn't change the deal. It's still within the range but it makes it look good, the cop's family is there, it makes it look like I got this big sentence.

With Bobby's release becoming increasingly likely, Susannah Sheffer assumed the role of an unofficial pre-release counselor to help prepare him. She understood the importance of counseling to assist a released prisoner with such a jarring transition, and she knew that no official pre-release assistance was going to be offered to someone in his situation. Sheffer undertook the task to the extent that she could:

"When it seemed he was possibly getting closer to release, probably when the judge ruled on the motion, we began ratcheting up the preparation. There was a lot of concern. Everyone kept saying Massachusetts is not going to release a lifer. We no longer have the death penalty here, and one of the reasons we don't have it is because we say we have life without parole, and if someone who is serving life without parole gets released, that puts that whole idea at risk. And that seemed really valid to me, the idea that that would possibly work against him getting out. If it was going to happen, we felt that the messaging of his release was really important—how it would get talked about. Bobby's feeling initially was to do everything under the radar; that is, to have as little publicity as possible. I worked with him in a role play, just in case he was wrong and there was media coverage of the whole thing. At one point, playing a reporter, I asked, 'How do you feel about the prospect of getting out after forty years?' Immediately, Bobby says, 'I'm looking forward to it.' It was funny, so understated.

A key part of this process was that I began to introduce the idea of the Holmes family as real people, not just this abstraction from the past. Bobby had been misinformed, thinking that there

284

was no family left, that George Holmes was a single man. That was what he told me early on, and I had not bothered to look into it. It was my own fault, negligence on my part, really, not to have followed up on that. But now I went back and read the old Boston Globe articles and I saw that there were there four kids. I said to myself, damn, it was wrong not to have learned about this sooner. When I began visiting Bobby, I was not yet working with murder victims' family members, but by the time his release was approaching, I had been doing that work for years, and I knew something about the long-term impact of murder on surviving family members. I knew that these family members had to be deeply impacted by this; there's no possible way this is not still an issue. So I began to talk with Bobby about that reality. A lot of this—pursuing this line of inquiry—was for Bobby, but it was also for me. I had to have some integrity in how I was approaching this; I knew that if I'm working with him on it, it's got to work in a way that I can live with. I never wavered in my belief that it was safe to let Bobby out and that he should get out after so many years. But I had to at least hold the victims' experience in my mind as well, and, to whatever extent I could, urge Bobby to hold it. I knew we were likely never going to get to where they were going to be in favor of Bobby's release, but at least maybe we could try to minimize the harm to them in the process.

Meanwhile, we were also dealing with the question of whether the plea would work in a way that would give Bobby a sentence not more than the prison time he had already served. It's a numbers game. Are the combined numbers going to add up to less to forty years, the time he has already served, and is the victim's family going to be o.k. with that? Not that the victim's views will determine the outcome but you know it's going to influence whether the prosecutor's going to accept the plea. I think the subtext we understood from prosecutor was that he wanted to accept the plea, wanted the years to add up, because he knew he couldn't take this to trial with witnesses from 1963. Bobby was very happy to plead to manslaughter, not only for the legal reasons but to say he's not trying to say he's not guilty. We talked about this, and he told me that he wanted to let them have the conviction, both politically and because it was sort of a moral accounting. When some people call him wrongfully convicted, it irritates me because it's inaccurate and Bobby knows it. He himself says it's incorrect. Bobby consistently said to me, 'I'm guilty of the robbery, but I didn't kill anyone and I think forty years is enough prison time for a robbery.' He wanted to get out, and he thought his life sentence wasn't right, but he never said he was innocent.

So we were regularly taking about these things and also about the victim's family. I spent a ton of time with Bobby on these sorts of things: how they might feel, what to say, what not to say, just lots and lots of work on the owning of that reality, and what language does or doesn't suggest that you're owning it.

Then the day that he had his court date to plea, there was the victim's family. That was a whole other emotional thing. Those of us who were there for Bobby were trying not to be jubilant, trying to be dignified, have some decorum because these people who have suffered such a loss are here and no doubt view this differently. There's no pretending that we weren't hoping Bobby would get out of prison, but I was trying to be at least respectful here. After the plea had been accepted, the judge gave the victims the chance to speak. The youngest son, who was nine at the time of the murder, he got up and told a story that exemplified everything I had told Bobby about the family being impacted by this event for years. It was one thing after another, a tale of horror, a domino effect, all the ways in which that one tragedy in 1963 had affected this family. I watched Bobby watching that. During our most recent visit, Bobby had told me what he was going to say when he got to speak in court. It was going to be something about accounting and owning. After George Holmes's son spoke, Judge Ball turned to Bobby and asked, 'Do you have anything you want to say?' and Bobby shook his head no.

I wondered what was going on, but Bobby called me the next day and explained why he didn't speak. He said, 'I had to let him have the last word. I didn't want to mess with that at all.' He told me he was blown away by the tale the son had told, that the whole thing was so much bigger than he had thought. I said, 'It always is, Bobby, that's exactly right.' I was glad he heard that and glad it had affected him in that way. It was something he had to hear, even as the person who had only been involved in the robbery. He was so intent on calling me that next day because he wanted to explain his reasoning and didn't want me to think less of him for keeping silent. I fully accept his intent. In the moment he felt it was the most respectful thing to do. Right alongside that I recognize that not everyone will have appreciated what he was doing and it may have also been helpful to have spoken, but I respect his choice."

The judge's approval of the deal did not yet set Bobby free. The federal issue was still unresolved, so he remained in Walpole until the paperwork could be sorted out. Several days later, he was abruptly told to pack up his things, and that he was headed for court. He wasn't certain which court he was going to, but on the way, realized he was headed for the federal courthouse in Boston. Upon arrival he was secured in a holding cell to wait for confirmation that his federal sentence had been satisfied under the terms of the agreement.

It was a phone call or a fax at the very last moment where the agreement finally got solidified. Because they have certain paperwork that showed the sentence was over, that it ended at a certain time, because the federal sentence would go to date of imposition, so I had to show where that line was. So the 19 ½ -20, my release date is 1983. This was 2003, so I got like twenty years to play with here. So that wipes out the Massachusetts sentence, and the federal sentence comes up to the date of imposition. So now the time is gone. I owe no parole, no probation, you go your way and I go mine. I'm done.

After about ninety minutes, he was brought out for fingerprinting. He saw the two Walpole guards waiting, but he remained confused about what was actually happening; he didn't bother asking. Returning to his cell, he became extremely nervous, thinking, *"What skeletons are they digging out of my closet now?"* Hours passed by and Bobby's anxiety continued to escalate. When a U.S. marshal passed by the holding cell, Bobby confronted him. "What is my status?" he shouted. "What the hell is going on? Why am I still here?" The officer said nothing, but pulled a key and slowly opened the door. Bobby leaped out and got in his face, again demanding to know his status. He looked at Bobby like he was totally insane, then handed him a small bag. He said, "You're going home. Here are your clothes." Bobby stood still in disbelief. Finally, he laughed and said, "You bastard!" The marshal grinned and began taking off the chains. Moments later, Bobby was ripping the bag open, and dressing faster than he ever had in his life. It was really happening.

Bobby could see his friends and family in the waiting room as he was led back into the booking area. Like him, they had been nervously biding their time, not knowing for certain if he'd be released or if they'd be sent home because more paperwork needed to be processed or, even worse, that he needed to serve more time. Then, they saw him in civilian clothes heading down the hall. He was excited to see them through the window, and began waving and smiling, mouthing "hello" to them. Bobby then heard his sister-in-law, Lois, her voice coming from behind him. "Bobby, what are you doing?" He hadn't realized he was actually seeing them in a mirror, not through a window. He turned around and saw everyone standing behind him, giving him a strange look. "Oh shit! I thought you were over there," he said. Everyone laughed.

On November 19, 2003, his sixty-second birthday, Bobby emerged from the courthouse as a legitimately free man for the first time in over forty years. Brother Louie and his wife Lois, his cousin Jack, and Susannah Sheffer were there to greet him. They celebrated, standing in a small tight circle, exchanging hugs and congratulations, practically overwhelmed trying to process the long-awaited moment.

"So, what do you want to do now, Bobby?" Louie finally asked.

Without hesitation Bobby said, "Let's get the fuck out of here before somebody changes their mind!"

* * *

If I didn't have family there, I would have hit the streets of Boston with the blue scrubs with 'Walpole' on my back. No money, they didn't give me my money. I didn't have discharge papers. Where do I go if I got no family or nobody to go to? I'm going to have to go find people that I don't want to become obligated to.

That was the funny thing, the adjustment to the street. I had escaped three times. It wasn't the same thing on the street, because on escape, I'm armed. The mindset is different. I don't have to work for a living, I just go to a bank, and housing is not a problem. So that reality wasn't there. Come into a

*train station, a door opens, all these people come out.
When you're going straight, it's like a panic attack,
you're not used to all these people around you. On
escape, I'm carrying a pistol. That door opens, you
come out, and I'm not concerned. You act crazy, I'm
taking out my weapon. So that reality isn't there.*

*I've looked at this stuff before, how things changed.
Washington Street, Boylston Street, Essex Street, the
Combat Zone...I knew where I was but didn't
recognize anything. All four corners are gone, all
new buildings there. You look up Washington Street
and there are all these high rise buildings, where did
those come from? Where did you put them? How did
they get over there? That was very disquieting. When
me and Joe got out on escape, we went on the MBTA
end to end on all the lines to familiarize ourselves
with the city because so much had changed. When I
got out legitimately, even that changed. The whole
city, it was all changed. Everything was completely
different from how I remembered it. The world I
knew was gone.*

PART III

CHAPTER SEVENTEEN

Though the United States makes up only five percent of the planet's population, it is responsible for locking up approximately one quarter of all inmates worldwide, making the U.S. the undisputed world leader in incarceration. It hasn't always been the case. Thirty years ago, only about a half-million individuals were serving time nationwide. That figure doubled within a decade, and by the year 2000, the population had doubled yet again to over two million. By 2010, it had increased another half million. Today's inmate population of nearly 2.5 million men and women far exceeds that of any other nation (China is a distant second with 1.5 million incarcerated).

For decades, the U.S. prison population had remained stable at approximately 110 inmates per 100,000 people. It wasn't until the mid-1970s that the prison population rate increased sharply, with levels peaking in the 1980s and 1990s. At this time it was widely assumed that the rise corresponded with an increase in crime, an idea which was strongly reinforced through media. But the actual reasons for the sudden expansion were not the result of a spike in crime rates or a response to a particular crisis; rather, it was compelled by forces both more subtle and intentional. As business interests permeated the prison system in pursuit of profit opportunities, its supporting industries also experienced rapid growth and development. Prisons themselves became the new factories, a massive apparatus which required thousands of workers to operate. Prisoners would enable that growth and development.

Throughout history, a wartime economy has typically proven highly lucrative for private industries, especially those able to secure government contracts to manufacture and produce goods aiding the war effort. As Dwight Eisenhower left the Oval

Office in 1961, he warned the nation of the dangers associated with big business and government interests merging. His experience allowed him to understand the politics of a wartime economy, and he knew that traditional business interests could conflict with the moral, economic, and legal interests of the country. He cautioned that the merging of those interests (the so-called "Military Industrial Complex"), though necessary, could turn into a self-perpetuating monster, and that such unchecked power and influence threatened the very heart of democracy:

> This conjunction of an immense military establishment and a large arms industry is new in the American experience. The total influence— economic, political, and spiritual—is felt in every city, every State house, and every office of the Federal government. We recognize the imperative need for this development. Yet we must not fail to comprehend its grave implications...In the councils of government, we must guard against the acquisition of unwarranted influence, whether sought or unsought, by the military industrial complex. The potential for the disastrous rise of misplaced power exists and will persist...We must never let the weight of this combination endanger our liberties or democratic processes....
>
> Crises there will continue to be. In meeting them, whether foreign or domestic, great or small, there is a recurring temptation to feel that some spectacular and costly action could become the miraculous solution to all current difficulties.

Decades later, the Cold War began to wind down, and the Military Industrial Complex faded along with it. Industries which had boomed during wartime no longer reaped exorbitant profits as government spending slowed significantly. Business opportunists redirected their energies to other potential money makers, and soon identified the state and federal prison systems as ripe for reinvention. As the interests of government-run correctional agencies merged with the interests and goals of private industry, the relationship developed and grew into an entity which eventually became known as the Prison Industrial Complex (PIC). The PIC promotes the expansion of the prison system not as a means of public safety and protection but as a profitable venture which benefits a small number of special interest groups. Its beneficiaries heavily support policies which generate increases in prison construction and high recidivism rates to ensure prisons remain filled to capacity. The inherent conflict of interest underlying the PIC has produced devastating results: financial motives of corporations trump the moral decisions a government agency must consider, business interests yield great profits for the few while carrying an enormous price tag for many, while reason and compassion are discarded in pursuit of monetary gain. Bottom-line business strategies of the PIC may produce enormous benefit in profit to an elite few, but injustice, poverty, and racism for everyone else.

The PIC power base—the taxpayers who fund it—has been built upon a foundation of fraud. Its continued success depends heavily upon half-truths and lies, manipulated statistical data, and scare tactics, all of which have been perpetuated by media sources. While citizens are presented with dubious claims of lower crime rates and economic boosts to local economies, they are shielded from information regarding the massive expenses, the rampant corruption, and the societal havoc flowing from PIC policies and practices. The PIC fights hard to preserve the status quo, as evidenced by the millions of dollars spent every year in an effort to spin public perception. Attempting to control the flow of both positive and negative information to the public, prison profiteers employ public relations tactics which are disingenuous at best. They typically pander to some of the best hopes of society—community preservation, protection of families, safety from drugs and violence, and incapacitation of society's most dangerous individuals, while invoking the worst—fear, scapegoating, racism, and elitism. Those who profit from the Prison Industrial Complex have taken great measures to convince the public that prison expansion is inextricably linked to the best interests of the entire country, while simultaneously obscuring the enormous damage it causes.

* * *

The PIC was born amidst a series of tough anti-crime measures which both boosted the prison population and demanded more prisons to house them. The sweeping and harsh laws gained popularity following a violent uprising in 1971 that erupted at Attica State Prison in upstate New York. For the first time, long-simmering tensions hidden behind prison walls for decades were broadcast to the living rooms of the American public via television. Leading up to the outbreak of violence, inmates had vigorously protested against a variety of Attica's living conditions, but were continually ignored. Budget problems prevented much needed facility upgrades, forcing inmates to live in severely outdated and unsanitary quarters. Programs providing education and vocational training had been abolished, thereby removing key rehabilitative measures and other constructive uses of inmate time. Food and basic personal hygiene products were strictly rationed or sometimes even withheld from inmates altogether. Overcrowded conditions— 2,250 men in a prison only secure for 1,600—created incessant noise, lack of personal space, and decreased safety. Months of rising violence within the institution stirred paranoia and aggression, with nearly everyone carrying some type of concealed weapon as a survival necessity. Finally, the rise of radical political activism on both sides of the prison walls escalated racial tensions to a dangerous level. Throughout that unusually hot summer of 1971, a sense of urgency grew steadily, headed toward inevitable violence as the nonresponsive administration continued to dismiss the prisoners' concerns.

On September 8th, a series of small disturbances quickly spread throughout Attica and soon turned into a massive riot. By the time the news reached media outlets, prisoners had assumed full control of the facility and had taken hostages. Using the captives as leverage, inmate leaders issued a set of demands ranging from improved physical conditions to human rights concerns. The administration, however, steadfastly refused to negotiate and within several days the situation reached a tense stalemate. New York Governor Nelson Rockefeller was conscious of the media attention directed toward Attica and he understood the political implications of his response. Sensing he was losing control of the situation, he elected a hardline response and authorized the state police to take back the prison by use of any force necessary.

The takeback began on September 13th. All electricity flowing to the facility was cut off, and soon after, police helicopters hovered over the main yard. In a move which shocked both inmates and guards, the helicopters began dropping tear gas bombs, inciting panic as everyone scrambed to avoid the burning clouds. During the commotion the sound of gunfire erupted, with shooters from the perimeter towers assaulting the yard with a continuous barrage of bullets and buck shot. Inmates scattered throughout the main yard and onto the surrounding stairs and catwalks as they were indiscriminately sprayed with bullets through the tear gas clouds. When the shooting finally ended, dead and wounded bodies littered the yard. Early media reports incorrectly stated that many of the deaths resulted from inmates stabbing hostages, but later autopsies showed all deaths resulted from police shooting.

Twenty-nine inmates and ten hostages died that day, with several more dying later from wounds. In all, forty-three lives were lost as a direct result of the Attica uprising.

Following Attica, the issue of prison conditions was thrust into the public discussion. Intense national media attention devoted to the incident fueled public outrage over its conclusion, as many believed the incident could have resolved without a death toll. Governor Rockefeller, not wanting the blood of Attica on his hands, utilized his access to media outlets to turn public sympathy his way. Squarely blaming the prisoners for the catastrophe, he cast the incident as an example of mindless violence from aggressive and entitled inmates. Rockefeller demanded an end to the supposed leniency which had emboldened criminals, and to reclaim the streets by subsequently launching a new platform touting "tough on crime" policies. He assured the public that imposing longer sentences and mandatory penalties would increase safety and send a strong message to criminals that the days of getting off easily were over.

Rockefeller delivered on his promise by successfully enacting legislation guaranteeing longer sentences, minimum lengths of time to serve, decreasing parole eligibility, and mandatory punishments. This stricter approach to crime marked a drastic departure from previous sentencing practices in which the court system had emphasized rehabilitative efforts over punitive measures. But with Attica, Rockefeller was able to advocate for a punishment model of corrections as both necessary and long overdue. The public supported the idea, having grown weary of a system perceived as soft on crime at the expense of law-abiding citizens. Mandatory sentencing seemed to be the perfect solution for communities frustrated with anecdotes of soft judges allowing offenders to be released after serving a mere fraction of the imposed sentence. By guaranteeing a minimum amount of time to be served, the laws thwarted lenient judges while also restricting early release programs and parole possibilities. Rockefeller assured the public that no convict would be released from prison until his debt to society was paid in full.

The governor's new strategy was meant to directly target drug dealers, whom he believed to be the greatest scourge on society. Under his new legislation, sentences for drug dealing became as harsh as those for murder, as convicted dealers became eligible to receive automatic life sentences without the possibility of parole. In May 1972, Rockefeller signed his laws into effect and the era of Tough on Crime began with enthusiastic public support. The state of New York received national attention for this new agenda, and though hotly debated, many states soon enacted their own versions of the strategy, using a variety of measures:

Mandatory Miniumum Sentencing. A fixed minimum amount of time to be served for select offenses. The sentence is non-negotiable and cannot be reduced through accrual of good time sentence reductions, parole, and early release programs. Judges cannot impose alternate or lower sentences based on extenuating circumstances.

Truth in Sentencing. Sentencing terms are literal. A five-year sentence results in the convicted serving no less than five years; parole or early release cannot be granted before the minimum is served.

Increased Penalties. Longer terms of incarceration for numerous offenses, and the increased use of maximum sentences such as life sentences, life without parole, and capital offenses.

Strict Enforcement. Increased attention toward enforcing existing laws, such as minor drug possession laws or loitering, which had previously been ignored or mildly enforced. The approach authorizes a more aggressive application of the law, including increased arrests and harsher penalities for first-time offenders.

Three Strikes. Legislation requiring lengthy prison terms, including life sentences, for repeat offenders. Individuals accruing three lifetime convictions for selected offenses are qualified for the enhanced sentencing.

President Reagan promoted tough crime measures at the national level, and while riding a wave of public support declared a "War on Drugs" in the 1980s. With mandatory sentencing now implemented at the federal level, the number of arrests sharply increased and America's prisons began filling to capacity and beyond. Critics voiced concerns that severe punishments would create racial disparities, overcrowded prisons, unnecessary taxpayer burden, and would not effectively reduce crime. In fact, the rate of violent crime in the U.S. was dropping at the time. Yet the majority of the public continued to support the new laws with little concern as to their broader implications and long-term effects.

* * *

While the business dealings of the PIC mostly occur in private, its public face is represented by the elected officials who court voters with anti-crime platforms. Stump speeches often scapegoated a generic class of "criminals" who were blamed for high crime rates, increased taxes, the breakdown of moral society, or just about any problem facing society. After identifying who is responsible for the problems, politicians then cast themselves as crusaders against criminals on behalf of society's good people, promising that everyone will be safer as a result.

The tactic is as simple as it is effective. Convicts—an already unpopular and politically disadvantaged group—have no effective way to fight back. Richard Nixon successfully employed a tough-talking "us versus them" tactic when dealing with national unrest surrounding the Vietnam era anti-war movement. He declared civil disobedience to be a "corrosive doctrine" which not only undermined law and order but was also morally wrong. He singled out young protesters as the enemy, warning citizens that their disrespect of the law threatened the very foundations of democracy. While protestors fought for advances in racial equality, Nixon was dismissive of their efforts, publicly labelling them as criminals.

In the aftermath of Attica, elected officials across the political spectrum followed Rockefeller's lead and began to call for harsh crackdowns on criminal offenders. With the overwhelming public support for new anti-crime measures, both Democrats and Republicans sensed the low political risk and jumped on the scare tactic bandwagon. They sold the idea to the public that prisons were teeming with violent animals waiting to be released back to the street to victimize the innocent. The tactic worked; many citizens were frightened, and it was against this backdrop of fear that both parties began casting themselves as strict law and order types who would protect the public from these largely fictional dangerous criminals.

While devisive rhetoric serves a political purpose, the politicians who use it conveniently failed to acknowledge underlying causes of crime such as racial inequality, economic conditions, and mental health/substance abuse issues. Instead of confronting the difficult work associated with the real issues, politicians simply frame criminal behavior as the moral failures of depraved and predatory individuals who actively ignore the law and victimize others. The politician, as a false hero, then takes advantage of fear and anxiety, making farfetched promises of justice, winning cheap political victories while fundamental problems remain unaddressed.

* * *

In the 1980s, spending on prison construction for both state and federal facilities escalated to record highs to keep pace with the rapid expansion of the prison population. But conviction rates soared so quickly that government operated prisons couldn't be built fast enough to keep up with the demand. Operators of privately-run prisons seized the opportunity to compete for lucrative government contracts for goods and services with promises of higher quality service, improved cost efficiency, smoother operation, and modern security facilities. Prison-related industries of all sorts lined up to provide price gouging services and equipment for just about any institutional need, seeking to share in the billions of taxpayer dollars flowing into the system.

Today, a number of annual conventions supporting the prison industry boom are held across the country. At any such event the rabid profiteering which has engulfed the modern corrections system is on open display. While prison officials from all over the world attend to shop for the latest products, sales representatives offer professional demonstrations, savvy marketing pitches, and detailed informational brochures to convince them to spend big. Convention display booths provide products and services for everyone, catering to every facet and every position within a prison system. For the inmates, phone service rates, personal hygiene products, clothing, and shoes are all available for mass purchasing. Corrections officers are offered a variety of defensive products including lethal and non-lethal weaponry, electrically charged riot shields, body armor, boots, helmets, gloves, vests, batons, and pepper spray. For the prison administrators, modular cell displays showcase the latest in inmate bed and toilet designs, as well as razor-wire perimeter fencing, impenetrable steel doors, high tech alarm systems, high-grade video surveillance systems, and countless other products to build a safer and more secure facility. Industry conventions provide a direct forum to promote mutually beneficial relationships between government and industry, with millions of citizen-funded dollars generating enormous profits.

The business profiteers behind the PIC agressively lobby federal and state officials to promote incarceration, thereby preserving the expansion and construction of prisons across the country. Every year, millions of dollars are spent hiring professional lobbyists and lobbying firms to influence powerful lawmakers. Since 1999, Corrections Corporation of America (CCA) alone has spent over $20 million in its efforts to lobby the federal government. To assess the exact amount spent on lobbying is difficult because disclosure regulations at the state level vary according to each jurisdiction, and many do not require reporting amounts spent on lobbying. (While direct campaign donations are limited by law, there are no restrictions on the amount corporations can spend on lobbying.) However, it is known that CCA & GEO Group, Inc., the two largest private prison corporations, have combined to directly lobby over thirty-five states nationwide.

Private prison corporations pursue the twin goals of earmarking budget money for prison construction and to pass laws which increase the prison population. To this end, CEOs and high level executives intermingle with other professional organizations and associations in order to advance a pro-prison agenda. Currently, the American Legislative Exchange Council (ALEC) fosters relationships between elected officials and private businessmen in an effort to coordinate multistate efforts to this end. ALEC specializes in creating model legislation which typically advocates both free market competition and the privatization of government services. Samples of proposed legislation are passed off to legislators to demonstrate an ideal model, and through the close relationships promoted by ALEC, lawmakers do not need much convincing of the legislation's merit. Often times, bills provided to lawmakers are pushed forward and passed without any revision at all. ALEC also assists politicians with pubic relations in order to justify pro-business action and gain public support. CCA and other private prison companies pay huge membership fees to ALEC for access to government officials, and has proven to be well worth the investment. In this way, the PIC has essentially been allowed to write its own laws.

Major private prison companies have strategically donated large sums of money to candidates in states with high inmate populations to promote favorable legislation for the prison industry, and funding is typically directed at incumbent politicians regardless of party affiliation. The strategy is to gain direct access to those currently holding power rather than seeking to install handpicked candidates with business sympathies. In states such as Florida and California, the top private prison companies have contributed over $2.5 million to state level campaigns in the last decade, and not surprisingly, private prisons thrive in those states.

CCA has sought prison privatization contracts with almost all fifty states. In exchange, each state would be expected to maintain a high inmate occupancy rate, sometimes as high as ninety percent (several states have stipulated to a quota of 100% occupancy). But if numbers fell below the agreed upon occupancy rate, the state would be financially responsible to pay CCA for any unfilled beds. Essentially, each state considering such a contract would need to have laws in place to keep inmate beds filled or risk financial loss. CCA would then enjoy a risk-free business relationship with that particular state, as it now had guaranteed income—from taxpayer dollars—regardless of fluctuations in inmate population.

The PIC is a shadowy entity, and it can be difficult to discern who is working for whom. Many former high-ranking public corrections administrators go on to serve as lobbyists, consultants, or fulltime employees for private prison companies and vice versa. These highly paid individuals cash in on their contacts, relationships, and influence cultivated during the course of a career to secure prize contracts. While viewed by some as standard practice of a capitalist system, the easy reciprocity between private industry and publicly run prison systems produce negative byproducts: improper granting of favors, nepotism, insufficient oversight, inmate abuse, lack of adequate training, and facility mismanagement.

Though the Prison Industrial Complex is a web of industry dealing in goods and services, the product underlying the profits is incarcerated human beings. PIC business growth strategies focus on the preservation and expansion of its product—the inmate population—and the policies which support it. As such, private prison corporations not only lobby for longer sentences, but also to encourage legislators to block any efforts aimed at reducing the inmate population. Ideas which make moral and economic sense such as early release programs, parole, and plea bargaining are continually opposed. In short, the PIC promotes crime; it is good for business.

CCA's 2010 Annual Report is a clear example of the PIC mission:

> Our growth is generally dependent on our ability to obtain new contracts to develop and manage new correctional and detention facilities...The demand for your facilities and services could be adversely

affected by the relaxation of enforcement efforts, leniency in conviction or parole standards and sentencing practices or through the decriminalization of certain activities that are currently proscribed by our criminal laws. For instance, any changes with respect to drugs and controlled substances or illegal immigration could affect the number of persons arrested, convicted, and sentenced, thereby potentially reducing demand for correctional facilities to house them...Similarly, reductions in crime rates or resources dedicated to prevent and enforce crime could lead to reductions in arrests, convictions and sentences requiring incarceration at correctional facilities.

With the U.S. inmate population approaching 2.5 million men and women behind bars, business has been good for the prison industrialists. Large numbers of the PIC product is culled from various pools of disenfranchised and politically invisible members of society. Indeed, minorities, mentally ill, illegal immigrants, uneducated, unemployed, and drug addicted individuals—the vast majority of prisoners—are essentially powerless to fight against the machinery of the PIC. These groups have virtually no representation in government and the least means of legal defense, and are commonly regarded as the most disposable members of society. Convinced by politicians and media that these pockets of society are the enemy, mainstream society holds them wholly responsible for high crime rates. The PIC gains financially when public compassion for the prison systems' repeat customers remains nonexistent.

* * *

In 2006 the Bureau of Justice reported that fifty-six percent of all state prison inmates suffered from some type of mental illness, ranging from depression to schizophrenia. Over the last several decades, thousands of adult mental hospitals

305

shut down following government assurances that community-based support programs would be forthcoming. Those promises went unfulfilled, and the old facilities never re-opened. Hordes of mentally ill individuals, incapable of living independently, ran afoul of the law once thrown back into society without supervision. With no appropriate alternatives available, prisons evolved into the *de facto* mental hospitals of today. A prison facility is not designed with effective mental health treatment programs in mind, and often lacks the financial ability to implement proper training and staffing. But without necessary services, counseling, and medication, mentally ill individuals are often overwhelmed by the rigid, rule-driven prison environment. The result is mental breakdowns, disruptive behavior, violent outbursts against officers and inmates, and disturbingly high suicide rates.

As such, mentally ill individuals end up as collateral damage within the prison system. They are arrested more frequently and often serve longer sentences than others once incarcerated. Such individuals become stuck in a vicious circle: lack of services and housing leads to arrests, inadequate treatment in prison leads to disciplinary action, which triggers longer sentences, and results in a high likelihood of failure once released from prison. The PIC encourages this cycle and actively blocks efforts to transition the mentally ill out of prison to sustainable living situations on the street. Business forces display no moral qualms about punishing large numbers of individuals who desperately need treatment. When mentally ill men and women fill the prisons, the PIC realizes greater profit.

Minorities, particularly young minorities, have also been a steady product source for the PIC. While statistics show that there is little difference between races when it comes to buying, selling, and using drugs, African-Americans are incarcerated at an exponentially higher rate than whites. For the Caucasian population, approximately 700 individuals per 100,000 are incarcerated, while for African-Americans the figure is over 4,700.

Sentence lengths demonstrate racial disparities as well. The way in which anti-crime laws have been applied, whether intentional or not, produces a discriminating effect. In many states so-called "school zone" drug laws purport to protect children from drug dealers in and around school property. The laws create an arbitrarily set boundary (*e.g.,* within 1,000 feet of school property) and provide a mandatory minimum sentence (often two years on-and-after time) for selling drugs therein. While any law claiming to protect children typically enjoys widespread public support, school zone laws as applied protect very few children. A violation does not require an attempted or actual sale of drugs to school children; the zone merely provides a geographical dragnet for law enforcement. Prosecutors seize the opportunity to apply the enhanced penalties when drug sales between adults happen to fall within the proscribed zone. Children are rarely involved. Urban districts have so many school-zone qualified institutions (preschools, head start programs, public and private schools of all levels—colleges and universities are glaring omissions) that virtually an entire city can qualify as a school zone. A drug deal anywhere in a city, regardless of whether a child was involved, triggers the harsh penalty without increasing child safety in any way. In more sprawling suburban areas, gaps between school zones are significantly larger, and the law is invoked less far less often due to simple geography. Conversely, inner cities with much higher concentrations of minority populations are significantly impacted by this mandatory sentencing practice.

Anti-gang laws are also a popular law enforcement tool used almost exclusively against young male minorities in urban areas. Gang membership qualifies an individual for arrest in some states, as does the highly dubious "suspicion of gang activity." Whether an individual is gang-involved is determined by police using highly questionable criteria. Something as simple as wearing a certain color can be cited as evidence of gang membership, while the term "suspicion" can mean just about anything in an officer's subjective view. Police also use constitutionally suspect methods to disrupt alleged gang activity by selectively enforcing beefed-up loitering ordinances, making frequent illegal stop-and-frisks, and use of racial profiling. Rarely, if ever, are such tactics used in suburban areas against non-minorities.

Sentencing disparities between races may be the most obvious evidence of institutional racism. Under the Anti-Drug Abuse Act of 1986, penalties for crack cocaine possession and distribution were increased, while penalties for white powder cocaine remained untouched. Though essentially the same substance, the disparate treatment of crack and cocaine had racial implications. The public viewed crack as a cheap inner-city drug sold by gang members to poor, drug addicted individuals. Meanwhile, the more expensive white powder cocaine favored by wealthier suburbanites held a different perception as an occasional recreational activity amongst productive members of society. The negative image and stigma of crack use severely affected urban minorities but hardly touched college students and suburban professionals, despite the nearly identical criminal behaviors. By adding mandatory minimums and harsher first offense penalties (even allowing the death penalty for certain drug offenses), city-dwelling minorities were locked up in droves while their suburban counterparts continued selling and using relatively unscathed. To make matters worse, the law added civil penalties which exclusively impacted inner city inhabitants by allowing the government to revoke benefits upon conviction such as voting rights, food stamps, educational loans, and public housing—matters of little concern to wealthy suburban residents.

Regardless of race or social class, it is the endless pool of drug offenders in the U.S. who help keep the PIC in business. Bureau of Justice statistics show that substance abuse is a problem for forty-five percent of the federal inmate population, and as high as fifty-three percent for state-level inmates. These figures represent those who committed crimes while under the influence of drugs, committed crime to obtain drugs (or the money for them), and used drugs in close proximity to the criminal behavior.

While strict penalties for drug offenders continue to be popular, there has been no corresponding reduction in crime or improvement in public safety. In fact, prison drug abuse programs and prison alternative programs have proven to not only successfully reduce recidivism, but are also far more cost effective than incarceration. But despite the benefits to society, the forces behind the PIC have fought hard against common sense approaches to drug addicts and offenders. They push lawmakers to classify drug-related offenses and the condition of addiction as criminal behaviors rather than treating the issues as matters of public health, thereby preserving the highest possible population of inmates. Most of the drug offenders are nonviolent individuals, and pose no threat to the overall public safety; the PIC has framed the issue in a way to create the opposite perception to justify unnecessary laws and massive spending on the prison industry.

More recently, the PIC has capitalized on the growing trend of mass detention of illegal immigrants. After 9/11, scrutiny of immigrant status became one of law enforcement's highest priorities, and pushed the number of immigrant detainees to today's current figure of between 30,000 and 35,000 immigrant detainees on any particular day. Under the federal Illegal Immigrant Reform Act, federal authorities were authorized to use mandatory detention for any noncitizens convicted of a crime, while border states passed laws making it easier to detain individuals illegally entering the country. Arizona, for example, enacted legislation requiring detention of suspected illegals without documented proof of citizenship, thus requiring anyone who appeared "non-American" to carry papers at all times or risk arrest. Funding to combat illegal immigration has increased sharply, with Immigration Customs and Enforcement's (ICE) annual budget doubling since 2005. Immigrant detainees have increased in numbers far beyond the amount of beds available, adding further to overcrowding issues and promotion of prison construction. The private prison industry reaps extraordinary benefits from mass detention of immigrants, as they house over half of those detainees being held pending deportation hearings. Each body occupying a cell generates a direct profit, and provides the prison with every incentive to keep the detainee in custody for the longest time possible.

* * *

The Prison Industrial Complex would not exist without the statistical manipulations, media falsehoods, and political scare tactics its benficiaries routinely use to gain support. Through deception, the public has largely accepted the PIC's simple justification for its own existence, which is the notion that imprisoning more criminals reduces crime and makes the public safer. The PIC has successfully used media sources to spread their message. Bureau of Justice data has shown that eighty-two percent of the public base opinions about crime on information provided by mainstream media sources. Media outlets often sensationalize criminal acts to create eye-catching headlines and tantalizing news stories to draw both readers and advertising revenue, but also mislead the public by over-hyping isolated incidents to suggest that crime is out of control. Further, media outlets publicize information which serves to promote job security for those who work and benefit from a bloated system, with police and correctional officers' unions appealing to the public to leverage inflated claims of job dangerousness for higher pay and benefits. PIC corporations issue public statements and annual reports reflecting dramatic rises in prison populations, disingenuously suggesting that crime rates are on the rise, and that increased measures are necessary to fight crime.

The private prison industry is highly conscious of its public image, spending millions each year hiring marketing professionals and communications specialists to influence public perception. The strategy is to spin information to the public through various mediums including polished websites and blogs, print advertisements, press releases, and event/charity sponsorships while simultaneously using the same sources to suppress negative information. Unlike government run correctional facilities, private prison records are not readily accessible to the public and press under the Freedom of Information Act. Therefore, information regarding inmate abuse, poor living conditions, exorbitant expenditures, or any other source possibly leading to public criticism can be easily kept away from public view, allowing the PIC to maintain a positive image, public support, and profit.

Deception is vital to the PIC's success. Without it, the necessary support would not exist; public buy-in derives from the false belief that the expansion of prisons is beneficial to all. As such, the PIC has created a core of myths which are essential to maintain its support:

Violent crime is on the rise. In fact, the exact opposite has been true. Prison expansion and inmate populations dramatically expanded during a two-decade period as violent crime steadily declined. Further, studies have proven there was no link between increases in higher incaceration rates and a decline in crime rates.

Crime rates are high because criminals are punished too lightly. The public has readily accepted the notion that criminals are punished too leniently and do not fear the consequences of the law, and as a result, they continue to commit crime at will. PIC beneficiaries continue to advance the idea that tougher punishments will make criminals think twice before committing crime, and longer sentences keep bad guys locked away where they cannot victimize innocent people. But increases in severity of punishment have shown no appreciable deterrent effect in reducing crime, especially in the majority of criminal cases where drugs, alcohol, mental illness, and poverty are involved.

Prison overcrowding requires more prisons. The Tough on Crime era spawned a seven-hundred percent increase in prison population without a corresponding increase in crime. With harsher sentencing, individuals have been sent to prison more frequently and for longer terms causing state corrections departments to face unmanageable numbers of inmates. State prisons and local jails are designed to accomodate a fixed population, and are unable to accomodate the massive influx of new prisoners. Since many facilities had been operating at or near capacity for years, sudden overcrowding produces a dangerous new norm.

Outdated facilities and lack of housing space, in addition to financial limitations, place undue strain upon local corrections systems. Overcrowding issues force prison officials to be creative and produce ideas to do more with less. However, the novel solutions often trade off an institutional problem for an inmate problem. For situations where no solution is apparent, prison officials typically err on the side of administration. For budget shortfalls, officials may eliminate all non-necessary components of the prison, *i.e.,* inmate services, supplies, classes, recreation, and training. If a lack of cells is the issue, recreation space and classrooms are taken away from inmate use and outfitted with beds to serve as makeshift cells. When every possible space is occupied, segregation units fill up with inmates who broke no institutional rules to be placed there. When institutions reach the absolute capacity breaking point, they simply refuses to accept new inmates. The problem is then passed on to the court system, creating a systemwide logjam effect.

Both inmates and prison officials agree that overcrowding is a dangerous problem; too many bodies without adequate space leads to hostility and violence. Prison reform activists and abolitionists point to overcrowding as proof that far too many people are being imprisoned, and that safe, effective, and cost-efficient alternatives to prison exist to alleviate this dangerous condition. While overcrowding is both unnecessary and dangerous, those who have found profit and job security within the prison industry continue to call for a very simple, yet extremely expensive, solution: build more prisons.

Private prison facilities are superior to state-operated institutions. Assuming the premise that more prisons are necessary, the PIC industries insist the most cost efficient way to keep pace is by contracting with private prison companies. It is claimed that unlike state facilities, private prisons are of excellent quality, provide better security and services, and operate cost effectively. State run facilities, it is argued, are impossibly outdated and expensive to operate consistently with modern correctional needs. While private prisons may in fact solve some of the infrastructure problems of old and outdated facilities, they are fraught with problems themselves such as insufficient training, low pay, high staff turnover, higher volume of violence, abusive conditions, and lack of accountability.

Private prisons are not necessarily cheaper than

313

government run facilities. Studies commissioned by private prisons have manipulated statistics to show cost-effectiveness, but neutral studies have shown private prisons to be even with government services at best, and in many cases, worse. Costly lawsuits, increased safety risks, zoning disputes, and the inability to retain enough inmates to profit can all lead to massive cost overruns. Financial incentives to keep costs as low as possible causes administrators to create a system which dangerously cuts corners on matters of safety and security. So while a private prison may boast a cheaper operating cost, its services are also often of a lower quality as well.

Private prisons operate in the public interest. The PIC appears to promote public safety, while in fact it is actually the biggest supporter of criminal activity. For PIC profiteers, business is good when incarceration rates are high. It relies upon the "repeat customers" who serve time, are released, commit subsequent crimes, and return to prison. The prevention and dismantling of services to improve re-entry for inmates suggests that the prison system wants ex-cons to fail. By blocking paths to success, the PIC is promoting further crime—to the detriment of society. When those individuals inevitably return to prison, it is this failure which translates directly into profit for the prison industry.

Traditionally, the corrections system embraced a commitment to public safety and prisoner rehabilitation. Since the emergence of the PIC, the pendulum has swung in the other direction; concerns of public safety are nothing more than lip service, while rehabilitative efforts are stifled for the simple reason they in fact help keep individuals out of prison. The self-justifying nature of the PIC fosters expansion and perpetuation of a system that has little to do with crime and punishment or the protection of society. As a for-profit industry, the system promises shareholders continued growth, thus its primary goal is to grow and increase profits for those with vested business interests in the industry. In theory, if prisons were committed to protecting the public, rehabilitation and reducing recidivism would play a major role to that end. Indeed, prisons would be growing—*smaller and smaller*. A genuine system would not strive to be self-perpetuating, but rather self-destructive.

* * *

The Prison Industrial Complex owes much of its success to the policies set by a relatively unknown yet highly influential federal agency, the National Institute of Corrections (NIC). Congress authorized the creation of the NIC in 1974 as an agency to operate within the Bureau of Prisons, granting it broad powers in an attempt to rectify some of the core problems with state corrections systems across the country at the time.

Originally, NIC's primary mission was to coordinate correctional institution policies by promoting uniformity across the fifty states. To do so, NIC was to serve as an agency to centralize control, align training programs, and create a master information center. Prior to the NIC's existence, state prisons throughout the U.S. lacked a clear set of consistent operating standards, and operated mostly independently of one another; wardens were essentially free to run their own facilities as desired with almost no oversight. As a result, each individual institution had vastly differing operating procedures, training, funding, philosophy, and resources. This disorganization, over time, promoted wide-scale corruption, abuse, miscommunication, and inefficiency throughout the American corrections system. When inmates protesting the rampant poor conditions across the country turned to riots in the early 1970s, the government responded by creating the NIC.

Unfortunately, since having centralized how prisons are controlled, administered, and operated, the NIC of today has developed into a dictatorial agency, one which operates at the expense of the states. While the NIC is limited by statute to only "formulate and disseminate" policy, the NIC's role is far from advisory. Though the NIC cannot by law directly set state policy, it can—and does—dictate to states what policies should be followed, often providing model legislation to states suggesting changes in the law. In order to preserve funding, state legislatures must pass or modify laws in accordance with NIC preferences. If the state complies, funding requests are honored and possibly increased, while noncompliance leads to funding reduction or outright denial. While none of the states have any legal obligation to the NIC, they can hardly afford to not play along.

Today, the NIC has taken advantage of its lack of transparency and public accountability to serve the Prison Industrial Complex by acting in collusion with the American Corrections Association (ACA) to promote the political and business interests behind a profitable corrections system.

ACA works with NIC to audit prisons, making sure facilities are functioning smoothly, spending properly, etc. They get $7,500 per audit. Audit teams are primarily comprised of retired correctional officials. But on the important questions, the auditors exclude feedback from the most important group, the inmates. No discussion is held with prisoners, so institutions become ACA certified without any assessment of inadequate food, poor conditions, lack of medical care, excessive force and abuses. When the ACA came to Massachusetts to perform the audits, they didn't talk to prisoners, only staff. They never heard about any of the abuses, mistreatments, etc. In Walpole, two-thirds of the population is in lockdown. If the prisoners are out of control, they are not doing their job. ACA is all ex-

correctional officials but no ex-offenders included. They collect their fees, give excellent reports, and validate professional status. Institutions become certified, based on criteria which overlooks actual issues. The organization is empowered to certify the state, not the other way around as in every other field but corrections. Such a system is putting the cart before horse and wastes enormous amounts of money.

For instance, Massachusetts has no gang problems but when the NIC says, 'Here's gang money,' Massachusetts grabs the federal funding and suddenly creates gang blocks. We got four maximum end blocks, forty-five men to a block, you've got 180 cells that you're now going to have for gangs. They filled all of the 180 cells. Ninety percent of them were Spanish people. You came in prison being Spanish? Well because they have La Famiglia, they have the Latin Kings, in other states they're really big. What's in Massachusetts, it's not significant. It's not a problem in the prison. The Spanish population in the prison, population wise it's like maybe eight percent of the population, and twelve or more percent are in the prison. Why then is ninety percent of the gang block Spanish? Because they're easy targets.

The prisons stretch for reasons to seek funding. They got a kid that put a little swastika tattoo on his hand as a kid. Aryan Brotherhood, white supremacist, that's what that symbolizes. And who comes to that conclusion? Some guard who doesn't know his ass from his elbow. Studied and was trained to identify gang member tattoos. And he's told go find gang members, check out their tattoos. He's not going to come back and say there are none. Because if he says there are none, then you're not entitled to the federal grant money for this block. And this is the problem with NIC, it doesn't follow the money. It just gives

317

the money, but they should go in there and look to see if it's justified.

NIC is necessary and performs important functions, but is in need of serious modification. NIC must operate outside the influence of big business and independent from the ACA. We have to get out of the business of prisons. But we have the prison industrial complex, and there's a vested interest in perpetuating this thing. Prisoners are losing the ability to fight back because under the NIC we have a national prison system. Reading the NIC statute, they're talking about electronic devices and stuff. That's what they are doing in the prisons now, and it's scary. They're talking about training judges and judiciary—this is the executive branch. What happened to separation of powers?

What needs to happen is a shift in NIC's attitude. For example, in order to end supermax prisons, the best plan of attack would be to convince NIC that supermaxes are wrong in concept, that they are inhumane, and they produce more dangerous individuals. In essence, the idea is not smart on crime. NIC has the power to set a national policy to abolish supermaxes. If the argument succeeds, the effect would be the closure of such institutions nationwide.

The NIC is responsible for the failures of the prison system. It is NIC policy that supports a bloated and unnecessary bureaucracy which continues to grow bigger and bigger, more and more expensive. It's out of control. It is time to realize the prison system doesn't work. Prisons are wrong in concept, wrong in application, wrong at their core.

CHAPTER EIGHTEEN

When Bill Weld was elected Governor of Massachusetts in 1990, he implemented sweeping changes within the Department of Correction as it stood and converted Walpole State Prison into a strictly punitive institution. An ex-federal prosecutor, Weld was well known for his tough talk against crime. With crack flooding the streets of Boston and violence rising at an exorbitant rate, his stance generated enormous public support.

"I'm of the belief that prison should be like a tour through the circles of hell," Weld said. "In making it so, however, our task is a formidable one since we have to undo many years in which Massachusetts treated crime as a social services matter rather than a public safety problem. So-called experts carried the day with their convoluted claims about addressing the 'needs' of criminals, all the while forgetting about the victims of crime and rendering our law enforcement and corrections systems toothless...

During my campaign for Governor, I was adamant about the fact that for too long Massachusetts prisons were seemingly run under the premise that inmates were victims rather than victimizers. There was an unfortunate lack of focus on punishment and protecting the public, and instead an emphasis on explaining away criminals' misdeeds against society.

Add to this the fact that the administration preceding ours allowed prison overcrowding to escalate to the point where overcrowding became the favored excuse for those who preferred flaccid counseling programs to address the so-called 'root causes' of crime. Doing hard time fell out of fashion, as it seemed the corrections system was more concerned with easy furloughs, parole, and commutations than providing for our public safety.

Further, as a check on the problem of recidivism, prison should, as I said during my campaign, 'reintroduce inmates to the joys of busting rocks.' Doing time should be a hard experience that prisoners are loathe to repeat. And so while we have taken away perks, such as the three-hole golf course at one of our prisons, we also have put inmates to work. Inmate labor makes prison life a bit more punitive, as it should be."

When Weld came into office, he devastated the Department of Corrections. People have no comprehension of the damage that idiot did. The correctional people that knew about the concepts of rehabilitation, he pushed out of the system. There is nobody in the Department of Correction trained in re-entry, trained in rehabilitation. They have what they call the unit manager concept, where one guy managed say two or three blocks. He called the shots. They found out after years and years that doesn't work, so they scrap the unit manager concept. And guess what they did with the unit managers? They didn't fire them or lay them off; they are now labeled 're-entry experts.' That's their title. They were incompetent unit managers and now they become re-entry experts. They don't have any idea what re-entry is. They know how to copy the terminology from the National Institution of Corrections and parrot the words, but they don't know how to implement it in the prison, and they don't know how to implement it on the street. They suck up money paying these idiots humongous salaries doing something that they don't know how to do. And it's very important, re-entry. If you successfully re-enter somebody, he is not coming back to prison. But that's the crux of the problem, he's not coming back into prison. That threatens job security. Of course you gotta come back to the prison, or we lose our jobs. There's a conflict of interest there. That's a huge problem in the correctional system.

They give you a statistic, forty percent recidivism rate, which is really a dishonest presentation because that's an average. Minimum level institutions are seventeen percent. Walpole prison, over sixty-eight percent recidivism rate. So when you hear a corrections officer say, 'I'm a professional,' I agree, he is a professional. He's a professional failure, nurtured by a system that's been a failure for over two hundred years. And they don't spend the money there; they spend the money in the minimum end. With a recidivism rate of seventeen percent, you could let most of them go, the highest degree of probability is the masses of them aren't returning to prison. Why are you spending money on them? The money belongs in the maximum security prisons. These are the guys that are going out raping, robbing, and plundering the community. That's going to be the guy you have to rehabilitate.

There are very few who should not return to the street, rehabilitation doesn't work for certain individuals. An example is Julian Stone, the military labeled him psychotic, schizophrenic. He has issues in his case that he could overturn his conviction, so we did a lot of legal work together. He's putting his case together, he's got a strong case but he's not moving on it. I say, 'Julian, why are you stalling? There's nothing else you can do to this case. You own it. There was a conflict of interest with the lawyers, and you have been ruled to be a legally certified schizophrenic. You're psychotic, there's no way you could have been found guilty.' I had cornered him, it was just him and me. He finally says, 'Bobby, I don't want to go to the street. I don't have any control out there. I go on the street, that person that comes out of me, I have no control over him. The only control I have is in the prison. I don't have any problems here. I'm happy right where I am, I don't want to go to the street.' I said, 'Say no more. I will never push you again. Keep playing your game with your case.' Backed away from it. There were several other guys with the same situation; didn't want to go to the street, they know they can't make it. I don't know what the answer is to dealing with people like that. But we definitely don't need them in a prison. This individual is sick, he belongs in a humane mental institution, not some barbaric snake pit like Walpole State Prison. Walpole has a sixty-eight percent recidivism rate. They're going out worse than they came in, if that's what your return rate is. You may as well not even put them in the prison. The crime rate is not going to rise significantly and you're gonna save huge sums of money that you can invest in other things inside the prison system and rehabilitate people.

Walpole under Weld was a punitive institution. You get GED, you don't get good time. Any other Massachusetts prison you take GED, you get 2 ½ days good time. Doesn't anyone see a due process violation? Whatever you give to one prison, this prison is entitled to the same thing. Except in Walpole. Walpole is made a punitive prison, that's a violation of law. DOC's not accountable. The statute says very plainly that DOC is required by law to rehabilitate prisoners. It's statutorily mandated, that's the law, but they're not doing that. The DOC has over a half-billion dollar annual budget, but most of it pays salaries. Less than two percent goes toward rehabilitation. But we don't have lawyers that will step up to the plate and force them to follow the law. It's understandable to some extent because DOC has a full staff of attorneys and they know how to drag a case out. They know how to burn lawyers out. You don't have the time and energy to play DOC's games, you gotta pay the rent. They know how to burn you out, that's the problem.

322

We're trying to figure out a way to fix the problem, and the devil's in the details. A start would be to take every MA court and take all the records, every transcript of prisoners vs. DOC and examine them. DOC in this court is saying one thing, and in this court saying the diametrically opposite thing. That's a violation of law. If we can document this all around the state, we can turn around now and get DOC attorneys disbarred. If we could do that we would make big changes at DOC. The biggest problem with DOC is their legal staff. When I win a case on a CMR (Code of Massachusetts Regulations), the judge rules in my favor, these attorneys circumvent the judge's decision by changing the CMR. Excuse me? That's not obeying a judge's order. If we could set up a program where we could pull all this information and go after DOC lawyers and get them disbarred. Quite a few of them should be, because what they're doing is patently illegal. They are the problem in the correctional system. Because when you talk to DOC they say we gotta talk to the lawyers. What does corrections got to do with the lawyers? They should be doing something on the vendors and all this other stuff, not circumventing court decisions and getting around what the law is. That's a big problem.

Prisons don't work. You must force them to follow the law. When you say prisons don't work, your abolitionists and reformers, we're not saying is that you're instantly going to change and shut prisons. But through attrition, you're going to bring them down. If you can force the Department of Correction to follow the statutes and be responsible, be accountable. The law says you must rehabilitate prisoners, if you're not doing that, you're in violation of the law. What are the consequences? There are none right now. Then we can get a judge to say you pay X amount of dollars, you put these programs in place. If that means you've have to cut the salaries by ten percent, then you cut the salaries by ten percent. You put the money into the rehabilitation. And you can force them to do that.

*   *   *

DOC's side of the equation, when a prisoner comes into Walpole that's when the re-entry starts. He has to be classified, he has to be given a barrage of psychological tests. After two tests, you gotta find out where this individual is at. And there isn't one plan that fits all. Some individuals were born addicted to drugs, mother was a hooker, father was a drug addict. A guy from suburbia, made an error in judgment. You've got all extremes in there. You have guys in there that are violent, and when you study them you find out they can't read or write. We have found out, when we did the educational programs in there, that when you taught these individuals to read and write, that violence disappeared. They could communicate with fists but they couldn't verbally communicate. Once you educated them, that violence disappeared. That was the school system's fault, you didn't teach this kid. You have to identify this kid. A kid can't read and write so you've got to get him a GED, teach him to read and write. So this is basically DOC's job to identify the individual's problem, find out what got him in jail, what are the issues. Guy comes into jail, he's a killer...it's not your job to torture this man for law enforcement. Your job is to rehabilitate everybody that comes to within your grasp. That culture's gotta change.

The Parole Board overlaps. Their job is more than just going in there and guessing whether this guy or that guy should gets parole. A year to six months before this guy gets released, whether it's by parole or wrap up, the parole board's job is to come in and *check this guy out, see what he did in the prison. DOC does the classification, Parole Board now has the classification, now they track the guy, and did he take care of any of these issues? Now you can make a rational decision as to whether to parole this guy or not. Plus we still got the furloughs. A guy has got to be brought out on furloughs by the Parole Board to get his paperwork to get his MA Health, to get his driver's license, to get whatever paperwork this guy needs to operate out on the street. They gotta get him a home, a job. The federal government will give bonding to ex-offenders, the Parole Board has to get commerce and the business community, sit them down and say listen, we got guys that are coming out that are qualified. We can bond them for $10,000 through the federal government, we won't bring you screwballs. We'll bring you guys that can become members of the union, whatever's necessary. But that's the Parole Boards job, so DOC and the Parole Board overlap at a certain point, which is six months to a year before a guy gets released. When they're considering you, the Parole Board, they have to have the background. If when they're looking at you, DOC hasn't done its job, they have to blow the whistle and say didn't do your job on this guy, what's going on? Force them to do their job. It's a little simplistic, but you can see if that's in place, they're going to rehabilitate prisoners. So what's going to happen, prison population is going to start going down. Prison population goes down, you can start closing prisons. The over half-billion dollars you're giving to DOC you can take away and put somewhere else. You can now get people out of those shelters and into homes. We spend more money on corrections than we do on higher education. You can now kind of reverse that equation. You can bring the colleges and universities into the prison system, and the vocational training, give them tax certificates, tax breaks. They'll gladly come in there and take that*

325

on. *That won't cost you an arm and leg. Not going to cripple the state. We don't do it because the DOC doesn't have a vested interest in rehabilitating prisoners, it's about job security. That's the nature of the beast. That's what we keep have to pound away in teaching people...listen, we're throwing money into an abyss, we need that money elsewhere.*

Most prison abolition groups don't know about NIC and its power. You need to look at the law that created them, shows their duties and responsibilities created by statute. In theory, reformers could create and propose a valid re-entry program for prisoners, and obtain grant money from NIC for that purpose. If the reform movement were to go this route, it would be crucial to have ex-offenders involved. They are the experts and know how to make rehabilitation work properly and efficiently. Without ex-offenders involved, it will not work.

There are alternatives. It is true that a prisoner cannot be forced to change, that he must want to be rehabilitated for it to be successful. But without being provided with the necessary tools, nobody has the chance to change for the better. Those who are in the best position to assist, support, and help direct an individual down a meaningful path of rehabilitation are not brought into the equation. Ex-prisoners, with little training, would be well-qualified to be part of the support network, helping inmates through the process of rehabilitation.

If we invested in these individuals, educated them, helped them get master's degrees and certification as teachers, trained them in vocational skills, got them certified as instructors in carpentry, plumbing, masonry, etc....With these skills prisoners could not only make a living wage on the street, but they could be used to maintain the institutions themselves, at huge savings to the state. And, of course, working at minimum wage, these prisoners would be paying taxes, which would help defray the cost of the correctional system.

Hire ex-offenders to participate in re-entry programs, these are jobs they can do well, gives them a job to support himself. Link recidivism rate of programs to funding, functionality. If it does well, keep it open, if not shut it down. Offenders understand the problem and know how to find the solutions. NIC should get more and more involved with the ex-offender. Their mission statement includes them, but in practice they do not.

We have an example here in Massachusetts. Boston University had a Master's degree program in Norfolk Prison. At one time, there was a three-year period that they had a zero recidivism rate. There were individuals who became law-abiding, taxpaying citizens. We can replicate this many, many times, and we can kill the pendulum concept. Because when you try to swing the pendulum, doesn't matter who the governor is. This works, the recidivism rate is going down, you're not going to push it up again. When Weld did the push to make it tough on crime, the recidivism rate was down. Guards don't have a vested interest in keeping it down, the Department of Correction doesn't have vested interest in it, but the community does. So we have to educate the community to have them understand these are your prisons. Ninety-seven percent of the people in prisons are coming back to the streets, to your community. Do you want them coming back better than when they went in, or do you want them coming back worse? Take your pick. It's that simple, it's black or white.

There used to be a concept; you got a guy in the drug block and he gets busted for having drugs. You throw him out of the drug block. Excuse me? He's in there because he's a drug addict. You catch him with drugs and all of a sudden you're offended? He's already told you, he's a drug addict, that's his problem, drugs. You're gonna throw him out in population, you think that's going to stop him from using drugs in population? You got him in the drug block, he's voluntarily in there, and you're controlling the drugs. Surely people are going to relapse. They're drug addicts, they're supposed to relapse, and that's the nature of the beast. But as long as you've got him in that controlled environment you have the ability to manipulate and control and get him off drugs. So he bounces back and forth, but he doesn't get out of the program until he straightens out. He's in the drug program until he meets a certain criteria that you say ok you've successfully maintained the program, participated in this stuff. Now we're going to move you from here to the next block, aftercare. Can he relapse in aftercare? Yeah. He relapses, what do you do with him, send him into population? No, you send them back into the drug block to try again. If you do that five, six, ten times it doesn't matter, because in the end, if you turn this guy around that's the purpose of the block.

A guy named Brian Sylvester detoxed over 20,000 people. This guy's a professional, he was with the MA Health Department. Murphy comes in and turns his aftercare cellblock into a regular cellblock with no conversation, no forewarning. So Sylvester quit. He walked out of there and right into the MA Department of Health to a better paying job than what he was getting there. But he would have stayed because that was what his job and function was, that was his lifestyle. Murphy went and played those games, took his aftercare block away without even saying anything, no option left, that was my decision. They cut down all the banquets and activities we had. They were supposed to have gotten twenty computers, but Murphy's crew stole five of them, so all that went into the program was fifteen of them. That was Paul Murphy. If there was something that helped prisoners, he took it away.

Rehabilitation works. Ignoring its benefits is a colossal failure. We continue, at great expense, to invest in a system that merely warehouses criminals and returns them to the street to commit more crime. High recidivism rates show that prison, by itself, is not deterrence to crime. We continue to throw money after a broken system where no benefit is derived, and where society is ultimately less safe, and more dangerous.

* * *

Right now, the law enforcement voting block and their funds are stronger than the CORI (Criminal Offender Record Information) people fighting for the change in CORI. Everybody knows that the CORI stuff that they're talking about is legitimate. It's outrageous what's going on. The public support for it is swelling. The public doesn't know that when they arrest a guy, he goes to court, gets arraigned, that generates the CORI record. The guy's found not guilty by a jury of his peers, the guy's still got a CORI. The Commonwealth charges this guy, gets him indicted. Finds out they got the wrong guy, drops the indictment, this guy still has a CORI. Why would you not erase that from this man's record? It's used against him and he's not guilty of anything. Who resists it? The prosecutors. Law enforcement. They insist that they need this information. For what? He was not guilty of this crime, what relevance does that have for any future behavior? If anything, using that to say because he did this over here or could have done this over here, he's guilty of this. That's against the law to do that. Why would you keep this on the record? It's because law enforcement doesn't want any part of the record to be destroyed. When people see that, they get outraged. And we've had situations where people killed themselves. One kid jumped off the roof. Not guilty of the crime, he lost his job, couldn't get any job anywhere, because that kept coming up in his face. He finally just leaped off the roof. It's outrageous. It has to be changed. But the politics that control it...law enforcement.

Let's say a guy has an A and B sentence. He goes from Walpole to Norfolk. Serves the A sentence, the B sentence is supposed to kick in. Norfolk lets him go. The guy had like fifty more years to do. The courts, I go into Suffolk County on a traffic violation. Middlesex County got serious bank robbery, murders, or whatever indictments on me. Suffolk County, when I pay the fines, lets me go. That's what generates the CORI law. The only people that create a CORI are the Criminal History System Board. So that each court logs in all the stuff about people, all that information. The only people that have access to it are law enforcement, prosecutors, the court, probation, and the Department of Corrections. Nobody else can get it. Anybody else, the law strictly protects that information to those five agencies. If you get your hands on CORI, it's a violation of the law.

Now, it's working. The A and B situation no longer exists. When a guy comes into court to pay his fine, right there on the computer it says Middlesex wants this guy for bank robbery. You can't let him go, you call, say listen I got this guy here, they come pick him up.

So everything, it works. Now that it's working, we had to fix it so we can break the thing. You have situations like with the home. Public housing is now required to do a CORI check. Go back a page, if I get public housing, I rape, rob, and plunder and public housing can't get sued. Go back a page again, because they're required to do CORI checks, if they give me housing then they're responsible. I rape, rob, or plunder, they can now get sued.

They get a million and a half requests for CORI's a year in Massachusetts. Where the resistance again is, it costs $25 or $30 a copy. So 1.5 million times twenty-five or thirty dollars, they don't want to give that money up. If you now restrict it back to where it was, you lose those millions and millions of dollars. That's what's killing us.

What really hurts people too, you try to explain to them, every time there's a court appearance, you're logging it in the book. You can get three pages talking about the same goddamn offense. You look at it and say, 'Look at this guy's record!' You're going back and forth into court, and then it eventually gets dismissed. So actually there's nothing there.

But the other thing that people don't understand is there's this big push for sealing the record earlier. If you have access to the record and you see a record sealed, what's your first impression? Sex offense. You know, 'Why is this here?' It hurts you, not helps you. The issue is if you're talking about housing and talking about jobs...what we need, and they fought it tooth and nail, we actually need a law that says you cannot be discriminated against based on CORI unless there's a nexus. Which means that if you're a child molester, you can't drive a school bus, you can't work in a daycare center. If you're a bank robber, you can't be a teller in a bank. That's a given. But the problem is if you say a child molester can't work. This guy's gonna hurt children. This guy's gonna go back to old behavior, you're forcing him if he can't get housing and can't get employment. I know I wouldn't wait around to starve in the street. That's being stupid on crime.

Now they're referring to shelters as housing. Shelters are not housing, a shelter is an emergency situation. They have people in there for years. You go into some of these shelters and they stink. There's vomit, piss smell and stuff. I mean a lot of these guys are alcoholics. Some of them are going to throw up all over the place. I'm not going into a shelter. The choice is either go to the shelter or sleep in the gutter; I'd rather sleep in the gutter. But I'm not going to do either. I'm going into your bank. You're forcing me to commit crimes by denying me access to housing and denying me access to a job.

They have these other little games...they want to pass a law that I have to be on the street under supervision for at least six months after the crime. Everybody's like, 'Oh that's a great idea.' And it's not a great idea. If you want me to be on the streets for six months, you don't add that on after my sentence. If you're sincere about having control over me for six months, parole me to the street six months before I wrap up. And you have the exact same situation. If I violate parole, I go back into jail. But that law and order nonsense mentality wants it attached in addition to your crime.

My attitude, and it's the attitude of a lot of people, is I get out in six months, I got a parole in six months, I wrap my sentence up. Report to you? See you later; I'm not coming to you. But if I was six months on parole, I'll probably come and report to you. But you're not running six months up my ass after I did my sentence. What are going to do? What are you going to violate me on? You're gonna violate me for that six month period? If I do that six months and I get out you're gonna add another six months? You're gonna give me a life sentence?

Here's another problem. Over one-third of all sitting judges in Massachusetts are ex-prosecutors. Some of them make good judges, but what put them on the chair was conservative right-wing governors. And that's the problem, these law and order governors are putting political conservatives on the bench. And that's destroying the judicial system. And you see some of the decisions these guys make, I mean it's just absurd. Over one-third of all sitting judges are prosecutors. If you play with the numbers, what percentage of all lawyers are prosecutors? It's gotta be less than ten percent of all lawyers. Where's that other percentage on the bench? One-third is disproportional. Something is wrong, it doesn't belong that way.

We have other problems. How do innocent people go to jail? In Suffolk County in about a two-year period they had twenty or so guys that they found out were innocent. The DA, he had to cut people loose after DNA testing. We know this when people go to jail. Civil liberties and other organizations claim that twenty-five percent of the people in prison are innocent. How does that happen? It's simple. Suffolk County DA has a success rate of convictions of forty-five percent. Guess what's happening in the next election? He's going to get knocked out of office, because his opponent is going to guarantee no less than eighty percent. You're gonna go on a law and order ticket, terrorize the community, all these dangers out there, and I'm going to steal the election.

So what happens, how do you maintain a high success rate? You put innocent people in jail. It's the conviction, that's the feather in the cap. That's the driving force, not justice. You're not looking for the truth. So you will accept, and you will see it, they take witness testimony, which we now know is highly unreliable. You know it's not true. So your choice is either let the guy go, or go forward with this bogus information. That's how innocent people go to jail. What's the solution? I don't know. I know what the problem is, how innocent people go to jail. Cops falsify information. You know cops get on the stand and lie. I mean it's not like now and then; the major amount of time that they get up there they lie. They try to solidify the case to get the conviction. So even if you get an honest prosecutor, you've got lying cops. This guy can be as honest as he wants to be, this puts an innocent man in jail.

So when they say we've got the best system in the world, no we don't, it's not true. That's pure propaganda. We're putting innocent people in jail. Now with DNA we now know that on death row were innocent people. You've been killing innocent people. Statistically, we don't know what the number might be, but the bottom line is you've killed people on death row because we now know that ID witness testimony is unreliable. Now with DNA, it proves it.

In the United States the basic philosophy was that it is better to let a guilty man go than put in innocent man in jail. But now isn't it...if you following that logic, that principle of law, isn't it better to put someone in jail for natural life than killing an innocent person? I mean if this is true here, that should be true up there. Once you kill somebody it's final. Give him a natural life sentence, if the truth ever comes out you have a person you can let go. You can't let a dead man go. We still have capital punishment in this country. Take all these filaments and put them together, that's why we got a problem in this country.

But we can't change all that, we can just focus on our area of expertise. So I focus on the idea that we have to abolish prisons. And the best way abolish prisons is by rehabilitating prisoners. If you educate prisoners, they become true experts, they become true professionals. They can turn around and tell you why this doesn't work and what a solution to that problem could be. That infection can spread out to all these other problems we've been talking about.

Abolish prisons!

CHAPTER NINETEEN

That's the sum total of all that experience, now I'm sitting here and this is what I see based on my experiences. Today, we are in a police state. It's gonna get really bad and you can see the reasons why. If you don't, you're blind because here it comes. People have got to learn how to survive in a police state. You're going to see in your lifetime people dying. Hopefully, as a direct consequence of that outrageous behavior by the Prison Industrial Complex, there will be a revolution. As a consequence of that, people rising up against that, the end result of that will be awesome because they won't allow that to occur again. It's like the revolution that got this country where it is today, but then everything went off the edge again. It's been said the tree of liberty now and then has got to be nourished with the blood of tyrants. Well, it's getting close to getting the blood of the tyrants on the tree to make it grow; it's going in that direction.

The prison was a microcosm of the macrocosm world. I saw that in there, once I got educated, and was able to look at the world instead of the little world I was living in, and started an appreciation and watching what was happening in the prison and how that translated into the streets. How laws against crime were used to suppress the general public. Now that stuff starts to become visible.

It began in the reform schools, they were terrible places. What they were producing was an abomination. Miller closing those institutions put an end to that and people don't seem to recognize that. And how the prison culture is constantly altering, it's not the same thing year after year. At one time you only had a few drug addicts in the prison; now you have eighty-five percent or better of the individuals in the prison have some form of substance abuse issues. Twenty years from now what's it going to look like...we don't know. But one thing you can bet on is we now have a national prison system. We have it in place, it's right there.

Evolution brought us in this direction. Jerome Miller demonstrated with his kind of concept, we can resolve this. It isn't a dead end street; we're going to go down bumps in the road. Until we hit the bumps we don't know there's a problem. So before we can make a smooth road we must hit the bumps to know what we have to straighten out. And when we straighten out something, we've got to learn how to capitalize on that.

*   *   *

Looking back, I don't say I spent all those years in a bad place. I was negotiating with the Governor of the state through his aides. I was negotiating with the Secretary of Human Services. I was a prisoner. How many regular citizens get to do things like that? So I don't look at it in the context that I lived in an evil place. The world that I lived in, I took control of. I didn't have freedom as far as mobility, but I did escape a few times! But as far as being free, I was free inside the prison. I did not accept my chains. I controlled the environment that I lived in, and I forced respect from the administration. They may have hated my guts, but they certainly respected me. And when I said something, they listened.

When we were doing the stuff in Walpole, the battle was inside the four walls. What you did out on the street was irrelevant, the battle is in here, you gotta step up to the plate. They learned from that experience, to control the inside environment, take that power away from us. Prisoners have forgotten that prisons only run at the consent of the prisoners.

337

Without that consent, the prison stops functioning. Prisoners have forgotten that, and that's how they took control away from us. The situation now and the whole political picture is the same thing—and this is the beef I have with the radicals, talking all that revolutionary nonsense—you cannot beat the system from the outside in. It's too big, it's too powerful, it's too rich. You have to beat it from the inside out. You have to get into the system, become part of the system and change the policies.

Using reason and rationality, I have the chance of changing somebody's mind. You got the opportunity to give them another view instead of that steel and concrete mentality. That's how we beat the system, is we get inside of it. We put the truth, the rational thoughts, and say listen this is the consequence of this behavior. This is what I was teaching them and I got a lot of surprised looks. But I feel good doing that. Going to the state house and doing all that talking, I was spitting in the wind, wasting energy talking to a bunch of politicians. Nothing's happening there. I'm not wasting my time with that nonsense anymore; I turn those things down now. But when I have a real audience, I have no problem going out there and educating their minds and if all I do is turn one head, I'm a success as far as I'm concerned.

In the prison system, emotions are suppressed and intellect increases. You become really sharp. When I come out on the street, people don't stand a chance. I can sit down with a person; I know his whole life story. He has no clue the things he's telling me. Because I learned how to analyze and listen to what people were saying because I had to in that environment in order to survive. I didn't take what you said as gold, I questioned why you said it and why are you coming near me with this. Once you come on the street, it's amazing, people on the street play the same game. But the problem is, and I still have that problem now, is the emotional side is still suppressed and I still operate on the intellectual. So I get in certain situations out here now, I recognize that the emotion is gone, or it's not in there, and I should be responding. I've tried it but it doesn't work out because you're faking the move, you're faking the emotion. If it doesn't come up, I just leave it alone and I operate on the intellect.

But my intellect is the ruler, not my emotions. And that's still the same way on the street. It's difficult to become emotionally involved with people, because I don't meet people that way. I don't meet them emotionally; I meet them intellectually at first. It's the idea of keeping your friends close and your enemies closer. That's the old school thought, you're going to have to be near us for three or four years before you get anywhere near us. We want to know what your mud is. And that doesn't happen just because you drop this name and that name, and act like a good guy. We want to see you under pressure and how you handle it. That's the mindset I still have. So when I meet people, I still do that. I was trying to balance the emotions, but dealing with a lot of these outside groups it reinforced the intellect because a lot of them are phony bastards and a lot of them are self-serving. They've got paying jobs and they're running their organization not so much for the organization aspect but for the money. It's a job. I learned real quickly that you can't trust everybody. Same thing as in the prison, intellect rules. I've suppressed a lot of emotions all these years, after forty years. I've got to work on that.

It's like me right now, I don't need crime in my life. I'm content. I get $825 a month, and I pay $250 a month for rent. I can live on that comfortably. My

*place I live in, it's not bad, certainly beats a jail cell!
I got a car, and even without the car I can survive
well. I have food stamps. I have a card for the train,
going and coming, for 80 cents I can go wherever I
want. Commuter rail I pay half price, boats across
the harbor I pay half price. I can live with that.
There's lots of guys that I know, they're good thieves,
they're in the same position I'm in. Why would I
gamble what I have? I really don't need the money.
The idea of a multi-million dollar snatch, that's nice
and entertaining, but I don't need it. That's what the
situation is, the guys are capable of doing just don't
do it anymore. They're usually old enough that
they're getting social security, they get senior
housing. You want to get smart on crime? There are
a lot of people that are capable of doing criminal
things, help them out a little and you stop all kinds
of crime. That's being smart on crime!*

*Coming out, doing all the hearings, talking with the
legislatures, is a big eye opener for me. I see a bunch
of phony bastards, double talking liars. What I'm
doing now is filtering a lot of that out, I'm finding a
direction. It's like why do I keep doing this? Look,
it's a little too late in my life to become a nuclear
physicist. What am I going to go with? I'm going to
go with what I know. And I still got friends in the
joint that are getting screwed by the system. So to
me, it's payback for forty years of torture, that's why I
do this. I have a sense of direction of where to go.*

*Since I've been out I've started to see all this shit. I'm
not burning energy in that direction any more. I'm
not going to curl up and go lay down in a corner
somewhere. So basically I won't say that's who I am,
but that's what I'm about right now. Whatever's in
that direction, I'll go there. I don't have a problem
with change. You want to make me an associate
commissioner of corrections on re-entry, I'll accept*

the job. I won't help you build your wall but I'll certainly help take it the fuck down.

EPILOGUE

Prior to 2003, Bobby Dellelo existed in my consciousness as a mythical figure. Although he's part of my extended family, I knew almost nothing about him until I was a teenager. Even then, my knowledge was limited to a few basic details: I was told that he was a very intelligent man and that he was living out a life sentence in Walpole State Prison for his role in a robbery many years earlier. That was it. I was always curious to know more about him but it never seemed to be a good topic to introduce at the dinner table. The years passed and he remained a mystery.

In college, my interest in the legal field began to blossom and I became interested in finding out more about Bobby's story. Researching old microfilm in a university basement (this was pre-internet days) I discovered the facts of his case through articles in the Boston newspapers. I learned that Bobby was about my age at the time of his crime, that a partner was involved, and that a police detective died. I learned about the felony murder rule—something I'd never heard of—and found that Bobby was convicted of a murder although he never actually killed anyone himself. I learned that he avoided the death penalty but was given a natural life sentence with no possibility of parole. Some of the articles had photos of him, which gave me a face to match the name for the first time. I had a clearer picture of the crime and some specific details to fill in some of the basic facts I'd already known, but remained unsatisfied. I wanted to know more.

One of my undergraduate law professors, Dr. Jones, openly informed us that he had served over a decade at Walpole for offenses he hinted at though never directly revealed. He had achieved most of his formal education within prison walls, a fact often evidenced by his unique classroom intensity. He had *been there and done that* many times over, and had undeniable credibility and an authenticity that many of my other professors seemed to lack. His style and experience-based knowledge blew me away; I took every criminal justice class he offered and loved them all. It was through those classes that I began to seriously consider attending law school after college. I approached him in hope of him providing me with a letter of recommendation.

We met for coffee to discuss academic matters when I hesitantly name-dropped Robert Dellelo. His eyes got wide, and he broke into a grin, "Bobby?" I didn't know him so informally, but confirmed yes, Bobby. "Everyone knows Bobby." This statement piqued my interest, as I figured it was a longshot that they'd crossed paths. When I asked why, Professor Jones made a comment to the effect, "He ran the show." He said it in a way that indicated this was something I should have already known, some kind of obvious truth. In fact I did not know this, and it was the first time I began to understand that Bobby's story was unique, that his story was not just that of the average criminal serving time. There was some follow up talk of Bobby's NPRA activity, of which I was also unaware, but then conversation turned back to academics. I was happy to have gained some new information about Bobby, but was left with more unanswered questions. If anything, it seemed that the more pieces of knowledge I gained, the harder it was to put the whole picture together. Who was this man?

I decided to write him a letter. Immediately, I realized that the process was going to be incredibly challenging and, even worse, socially awkward. For all I knew, my intention to communicate was entirely inappropriate. I was writing to a man I'd never met and was struggling to initiate a one-sided conversation. Television and movies had taught me that prisoners do not trust anyone, so I knew I had to be both credible and trustworthy to receive a reply.   My goal was to open up a dialogue, one which would enable me to ask the many questions I had in my head.   I needed him to know that my interest and curiosity was genuine, that I was someone he could talk to.   But for all I knew, he was a cold-blooded convict, uninterested in discussing anything with anyone.

Still, I figured that the worst that could happen was he wouldn't reply, and eventually I was able to complete a draft of the letter. It was terrible. I revised it several times; still terrible. The letter was never sent.

Several months later, having finished college, I was watching a football game with family members when breaking news interrupted the broadcast with a report of two convicted killers escaping from Bridgewater State Prison. We were shocked when Bobby's mugshot appeared on the screen.   In the days following the escape, I read every news article and discovered new details about his previous escapes and prison activism. As a fugitive, his life was now at risk; the state police fugitive apprehension team had been given shoot-on-sight orders. I found myself rooting for Bobby, hoping he would not hurt anyone or be harmed himself, but also hoping maybe he'd actually pull this off, disappear and never get sent back to jail.   For several weeks I was intensely curious as to his whereabouts, and I scrutinized faces when I was in public. *Is that him?* When he was captured a few weeks later I felt a mix of relief and disappointment.

While Bobby served five years in solitary confinement for the escape, I worked my way through law school. During that time I worked in a public defender's office as a student intern, hoping to make inroads to a career as a defense lawyer.   I pursued the idea that maybe one day I'd fight for truth and justice in the hallowed halls of the American legal system. With the promise of the opportunity to attend court daily, I quickly became enraptured. It seemed important, adult, and serious. The setting, the ceremony, the excitement; I felt certain that I had made the right choice and that I was on the path to a fulfilling career.

Unfortunately, attending court in person proved to be a very different experience than television had led me to believe. I learned much through my observations, but in an unexpected way. One morning I watched the closing arguments in a first-degree murder case. The defendant was an eighteen-year-old drug dealer and he looked every bit the part: baggy jeans, oversized shirt, cornrows, hard demeanor. The victim, a friend of the defendant, had told friends that he had always wanted to die "with a blunt in his mouth." As it turned out, the victim's casual comment of street bravado served as inspiration for the method and manner of his own death, as his killer had remembered those words and honored the request by shooting him point blank in the back of the head as he smoked weed. Apparently, the defendant killed his friend because he felt disrespected by an unpaid drug debt. After the jury returned with a guilty verdict, I watched the judge dispassionately sentence the defendant to life in prison without the possibility of parole. The kid appeared bored and indifferent, showing as much reaction as I would have if the judge just told me the sky was blue.

I was taken aback by the reality of the situation; the gravity of the sentence, the authority of the state. It was nearly impossible for me to comprehend the end of any kind of normal life at such a young age; this young man had just traded in his own life for that of his victim, and would probably never be free again. I tried to imagine the events and experiences I would miss out on in my life if my freedom were taken away at that moment.

It was too large to fully comprehend. From that exact moment forward, he would no longer *live*; he would merely *exist*. I wondered what his life was like before the murder. Was this a crime that was years in the making? What had his family life been like? What had brought him to the point where he just didn't care about human life, neither the victim's nor his own? There were, I knew, no answers to these questions to be found in that courtroom.

Some weeks later I was digging through boxes of files and came across a disturbing case. The defendant, a Hispanic male in his late twenties was accused of raping a child. As I poured over the police report and witness statements, I became anxious and uncomfortable. Until that time, I had not really been troubled by depictions of violence. My curiosity usually seemed to override my revulsion, and I had never had any kind of a problem watching violent movies or reading about the grim details of crimes or war. I've always been fascinated by the extremes of human behavior, by people who think and act so very differently from the majority of the world, both good and bad. I had been confident that I could handle any criminal case thrown my way without being impacted emotionally by the brutality or the violence.

Then I saw the photos.

A supervisor took out a series of 8"x10" color photographs and spread them across a conference table. Had I known what I was about to see, I would not have looked. My eyes draped over the images, taking a moment to process what I was seeing. The victim was not just a child, but a baby less than a year old. At the top of the photo was the baby's mouth and lower jaw, eyes cropped from the image. My eyes scrolled down across the droplets of blood splattered over her smooth chest, which morphed into a red smear as her torso appeared. Further down, her little body was unrecognizable. I felt sick.

"Bet you don't get this kind of education in law school, do you now?" the supervisor asked, seeming to enjoy my discomfort.

I didn't answer, but in that moment it became clear to me that I would not become a defense lawyer. I understand, respect, and admire that idea that everyone has a right to zealous legal representation when charged with a crime, and that for our system to function properly, everyone *needs* that representation; I just wasn't going to be the guy who was providing that zealous representation, especially for crimes like this. My allegiances would lay with the victims, especially child victims, not the perpetrators of crime.

I still held on to the ideal of using the law to help people, though. When I began practicing law I represented plaintiffs in civil lawsuits of all types, assisting those who had been wronged to obtain some sense of justice through the courts. While I experienced glimpses of justice and moments of satisfaction, there was much less of either of those than I had expected. In fact, true victims were a minority of my client base; there were many people I came to label as "tort-savvy plaintiffs," those who were looking for a payout without having suffered a real and compensable loss. The truth is, more often than not, I felt as if was I was doing was little more than legally assisting in insurance fraud.

I shifted into criminal law, and went to work as a prosecutor. Now, I believed, finally, I could truly help innocent victims. And it did feel satisfying to play a part in sending a domestic abuser to jail, helping to allow the victim to feel some semblance of safety and security again. It was nice to be able ensure that a victim would be repaid for their loss, or that a thief would be held accountable. Over time, though, I began to notice something. Most of the people who came through the courts were not necessarily classic criminals, not the "bad guy" who had made intentional decisions to commit illegal acts. Rather, I saw hundreds of people whose lives had spiraled out of their control. These were people whose actions, far more often than not, had resulted from a number of conditions they endured, everything from drug addiction to poverty to mental illness. Punishment for those people was a temporary remedy for society and an outright refusal to address the bigger problems causing the criminal behavior. It fixed nothing.

As part of my prosecutorial duties I also served as a community liaison, a duty which required going to local school districts to discuss with police and school administrators the behavior of certain students getting in trouble out on the street. It was essentially a time to share information in order to keep tabs on troubled kids, and, frankly, felt like a gossip session. Just about all of the kids needed help of some kind: drug rehab, financial assistance, academic support, peer mentorship, adult supervision, emotional counseling, and much more. My role in this situation, I quickly realized, played no real part in actually helping these kids. Instead, I was securing punishment and consequence after the damage was already done, none of which, of course, actually prevented the criminal behavior. I saw so many young people whose lives were a hopeless mess, and it was an inevitable and accepted conclusion that today's class cutters and cigarette smokers would become tomorrow's drug dealers and domestic abusers—and worse. For them, prison or early death was nearly a foregone conclusion. And nobody seemed to want to do anything about it; it was just *the way it is*—like homelessness or poverty— and therefore, acceptable.

This idea troubled me and I spent a lot of time thinking about it. Kids make mistakes. They feel invincible. They are impulsive. They don't think. As a result, kids easily stumble into trouble and the consequences can last well into adulthood. For so many of them, they had no guidance or adult help to understand these basic principles. I began wondering: If I worked with kids *before* trouble found them, would they have a shot to succeed? I wasn't sure, but I did know that meting out punishment after the fact was unsatisfying and unhelpful. From what I had seen, punishment provided no incentive for any individual to try harder or do better. It's only motivational value is for an individual to put more effort into not getting caught. Most of the "criminals" I saw didn't need punishment. They needed help. They needed education.

While still prosecuting cases, I had the opportunity to teach some law classes at a local community college, and instantly knew that it was the setting I had been looking for. Standing in front of a classroom filled with young people felt—and still feels—important, meaningful, and enjoyable. The experience was both amazing and scary, and it signaled for me a career change from practicing law to education. I began a new career as a high school teacher, and was able to continue using my legal background and training, as my assigned courses focused on constitutional and criminal law. I finally felt like I was on the right side of the equation.

Soon after I began teaching, I received surprising news: Bobby was getting out of prison. I was so wrapped up in my career change that I was unaware that he'd been pursuing an appeal and had won his motion for a new trial. The release details were being negotiated and he'd be out any time. This was something I hadn't thought even possible. *He's been in prison for forty years, life without parole, how did he flip his case after all these years? He's really getting out? What then?*

We met in person a week or so after he walked out of the federal courthouse in Boston as a free man. Since I had always assumed he would die in prison someday, it was a bit surreal to shake his hand and introduce myself. I didn't know what to say in this kind of situation. *Congratulations? Nice work?* I settled on "welcome home." He seemed to like that, smiling and nodding in acknowledgement. The first thing I noticed was that he was clearly in the process of readjusting to freedom. He moved slowly, dragging his feet in short strides as he walked, as if his ankles were still confined by shackles. He spoke carefully and thoughtfully and seemed hyper-aware aware of his surroundings. He used prison yard slang as he spoke, referring to marijuana as "grass" or prison as "the joint." His teeth were in poor shape, testifying to the dismal quality of dental and health care in the prison system.

But most striking to me was his demeanor; he didn't seem like the dangerous criminal I had read about. He was friendly, humorous, and polite. He laughed easily and often. I was surprised at his ability to have such a positive attitude after living in such horrible conditions for decades. The fact that he wasn't an angry, hardened convict went against all of my assumptions about prisoners. I quickly felt comfortable with him and began asking about the legal issues involved in his appeal, followed by dozens of other questions. I wanted to be respectful and go slow, but Bobby showed no hesitation. He seemed to appreciate that I had some knowledge and background to get into the legal nuances of his criminal appeal. He spoke openly and freely, and no topic seemed to be off limits. It was those early conversations that began laying the foundation of trust for our relationship.

While it was obvious that he enjoyed his freedom, there were frustrations. Bobby was fortunate enough to have a supportive and encouraging family but finding work was proving to be a huge obstacle. "I can't get a home. I can't get a job," he told a newspaper reporter. "I know how to rob banks. I know how to rob armored cars. What do you think I should do?" He'd been released directly to the street; there were no transition programs, no parole officers, and no support networks. One day he was in Walpole, and the next day he was home. Despite the difficulties, Bobby never seemed to feel sorry for himself; instead, he simply tried to move forward as best he could. He enrolled in classes and earned a paralegal certificate (though he was already a self-taught legal research whiz). He began working with American Friends Service Committee, advocating for prisoners' rights issues by speaking all over Massachusetts to civic groups, students, and even the state legislature. An understanding defense lawyer employed him as a legal research assistant, and he continues to work on appeals for numerous men behind bars today. It took a few years, but he eventually qualified for public housing and got his own studio apartment and a dog for companionship. It hasn't been easy, Bobby admits, but he's quick to point out his modest lifestyle is exponentially better than life in any prison.

The many years of prison rules and procedures that governed Bobby's every movement were now gone, and the effect was often overwhelming. Shortly after his release, his brother Louie took him to a Wal-Mart to buy some clothes and toiletries. Bobby stood in the aisle in awe at the vast selection of available toothbrushes. "How do I know which kind to get?" he asked. Louie told him that they were all the same, and to just pick his favorite color. While something as mundane as selecting a toothbrush would be a trivial matter to anyone else, the situation made Bobby extremely anxious. He became visibly upset and quickly left the store. Over his shoulder he said to his brother, "I can't do it. You pick." Today, "toothbrushes" is a code word his family understands to mean he is feeling overwhelmed. Open spaces and large crowds tend to rattle Bobby, overpowering him almost to the point of panic. Without the comfort of a gun, as he carried while an escapee, he had trouble feeling comfortable with people next to him, in front of him, behind him. During escape periods, he knew if any sort of trouble arose, the gun would be there to deal with it. Now, he was forced to think in an entirely new way, and the paranoia fostered by the prison experience made that transition incredibly difficult.

Physical changes in his hometown perplexed Bobby. He walked through the streets of his youth, Washington Street, Boylston Street, and the old Combat Zone. Nearly all of it was gone: the seedy bars, diners, and porn theaters, the clientele those establishments would attract, all gone. Entire city blocks had become completely unrecognizable with new high rise buildings offering top end condominiums and upscale shops and boutiques lining the district. The South Station terminal, now completely remodeled, resembled nothing of the station he recalled. The entire MBTA system, with its many stops and stations, had entirely transformed. Now, only grainy snapshots in his mind were left. Times had changed, and the old Boston that had been his playground was long gone.

Bobby's readjustment, his struggle for normalcy, is a continuous process that will last for the rest of his life. At his age, he understands now is not time to launch a career. He stays within his comfort zone by pursuing what he knows, what he has passion for. He knows what happens to people in prisons, and he holds himself out as living proof. He is an expert, an activist, and ultimately, an abolitionist. He continues to contribute, to try and give something back in whatever ways he can. Many of his friends are still on the inside, and their continued incarceration is what keeps him up late at night, reading, researching, and writing. His motivation remains high.

It was important to me that Bobby never proclaimed himself to be an innocent man. He didn't pretend to be a victim, and never once engaged in self-pity. He owned up to his actions and acknowledged that what happened never should have happened. Though Bobby and I come from very different backgrounds and experiences, it became clear that we agreed on many things. Here in America, ground zero for freedom and democracy, we have a system that locks up more people than anywhere else in the world, even as crime rates decline. We have a system that places politics and profit ahead of public safety. We have a system that supposedly rehabilitates prisoners while in actuality, recidivism rates continue at ludicrously high levels. We have a system that derives massive profit from human failure, and that is structured to encourage and facilitate that failure. We have a system that promotes control and violence. We have a system that is corrupt, financially unsustainable, and grossly inefficient. We have a system that is racist and stacked against the poor, a system where money and influence clearly and unarguably dictate leniency of punishment. We have a system that is irretrievably broken.

The prison system is a factory, one which creates and nurtures its end product: the criminal. Once a young kid is caught up in that system, the chances of emerging unscathed are incredibly low. He will be taught how to be a criminal, how to be violent, and how to manipulate. He will then be thrown back out onto the streets without skills, education, money, or any means of legitimate support. He will fail and he will eventually end up right back in prison where he started. He will pass through this cycle again and again throughout his life. He is a product of the factory.

Bobby Dellelo's journey is a compelling story for a number of reasons, perhaps mostly because he is a living exception to the rule. He escaped when confined, kept his sanity in an insane environment, fought for his dignity in the face of hopeless circumstances, educated himself despite a lack of resources, succeeded in court when lawyers failed him, and did not return to crime after his release into society. Most exceptional of all has been his ability throughout to maintain a positive outlook on life, and to carry forward in his post-prison life with a meaningful agenda. Very few individuals have travelled an even remotely similar path.

Bobby has said many times that education is the key to meaningful change, a point I couldn't agree with more. We tend to not care about the things that we know nothing about, to remain indifferent with aspects of life that we never have to come into direct contact with. In our own individual ways, Bobby and I have made efforts to promote thinking and discussion, and sometimes arguing, and sometimes simply informing to help others understand what's going on behind prison walls. It's very basic and grassroots, but that's where it all begins.

Eventually, I invited Bobby to speak to my high school students. He showed up with information sheets filled with facts and figures to support his lecture. As he handed them out, I looked across the room filled with young faces, kids with an entire lifetime of experiences yet to happen. Bobby was not much older than them when he received a life sentence, and went on to serve well over twice their lifetimes in prison. I thought about reform school, and how at age thirteen Bobby entered a system from which there was no turning back. It was a room full of students casually indifferent toward their own freedom; it struck me that Bobby was once one of these kids.

Now, here he was, fifty years removed from the 21-year-old kid with a gun in downtown Boston, standing a few feet away at my teaching podium. Sixty students sat attentively as Bobby gathered his thoughts and flipped through his notes. Finally, he took a sip of water and began his story.

My name is Robert Dellelo. I was released from Walpole State Prison after serving over forty years of a natural life sentence. I've spent over two-thirds of my life in some kind of confinement...

Notes

Chapter 1

"I got banned...attention to authority." All quotes by Robert Dellelo have been transcribed from interviews spanning 2008-2014 with co-author Christopher Lordan.

Chapter 2

"The housemaster called...softly to myself." Mark Devlin, *Stubborn Child* (Macmillan Pub. Co. 1985), 66-67.

"Vincent "Jimmy the Bear" Flemmi...life sentence anyway." Casey Sherman, *The Animal* (Northeastern University Press, 2013), 76.

"Flemmi's close personal...Witness Protection Program." For Joe Barboza's biography and criminal history, see generally Casey Sherman, *The Animal* (Northeastern University Press, 2013).

"Barboza's own lawyer...suffered a great loss." Anglin, Robert J., "Barboza Death Tied to Dispute on West Coast," *Boston Globe,* February 13, 1976.

Chapter 3

"Miller's vision was...and apply them." Jerome G. Miller, *Last One Over the Wall* (Ohio State University Press, 1991). In his book, Miller recounts the political battles he engaged in as head of the Massachusetts juvenile system, and the closing of all state reform schools.

Chapter 6

"Bobby's lawyer, Helen...within the department." "No Brutality—McNamara," *Boston Globe*, November 10, 1963, p. 3.

"How long were...never saw Yasian." *Commonwealth of Massachusetts v. Robert G. Dellelo*, Suffolk Superior Court Nos. 8803-8809, 1964, Trial transcript 161-162.

"Did you hear…turning onto Winter." Ibid., 230-231.

"The Commonwealth presented…forty-seven dollars." Ibid., 1055-1057.

"Now Mr. Foreman…do your duty." Ibid., 1149-1150.

Chapter 7

"Bobby D. and I…that it is so." Unpublished letter from Ralph Hamm to Christopher Lordan, November 2013.

"One of the most…what went on." Michael McLaughlin, Russell S. Dydna, & Warren Jamison, *Screw: The Truth About Walpole* (New Horizon Press, 1989) 86-87.

Chapter 9

"Nearly half of…given out upon request." Jamie Bissonette, *When the Prisoners Ran Walpole* (South End Press, 2008) 74-75.

Chapter 10

"The old Massachusetts…guns and surrendered. "The Siege of Cherry Hill," *Time Magazine*, January 31, 1955.

"The National Prisoners'…lives of all inmates." Jamie Bissonette, *When the Prisoners Ran Walpole.* Chapters 6 through 8 discuss the establishment and rise of the National Prisoner's Reform Association.

"During later negotiations…act like an animal!" F.B. Taylor, Jr., "Walpole inmates, officials talk 8 hours; results inconclusive," *Boston Globe*, October 13, 1971, p. 39.

"I became…cause of abolition." Unpublished letter from Ralph Hamm to Christopher Lordan, July 2014.

"The guys have…he'll react like one." Jerry Taylor, "Guard unions ask top state court to declare Cmr. Boone unqualified," *Boston Globe*, August 9, 1972, p. 21.

"In an effort...Boone the Coon." *Boston Herald*, March 9, 1973, p. 1.

"Rehabilitative programs... to better himself." Jerry Taylor, "Walpole inmates buoyed by reform act," *Boston Globe*, October 4, 1972, p. 60.

"Prior to this...it's *our* food." *Three Thousand Years and Life*, documentary film by Randall Conrad (1973).

"Albert DeSalvo himself...we are unity." Ray Richard and Al Larkin, "Walpole guards given chance to return," *Boston Globe*, March 17, 1973, p 1.

"NPRA Treasurer...this is our home." Jerry Taylor, "Full collective bargaining rights sought by Walpole inmates," *Boston Globe*, April 30, 1973, p. 4.

Chapter 11

"Former Commissioner...organization of 440 men." Robert L. Ward and Joe Pilati, "Police press hunt for Walpole 'lifer' who escaped armed from hospital," *Boston Globe*, October 5, 1973, p. 3.

Chapter 12

"We were locked...smelled like shit." *When the Prisoners Ran Walpole*, p. 113.

"Let's think about... that's not my job." Jonathan Saltzman and Thomas Farragher, "Guards, inmates a volatile dynamic," *Boston Globe*, December 11, 2007.

"You accept if...a problem dealing with." Court TV, The Investigators, "Maximum Security," aired June 1999.

"In my opinion...the broader prison environment." *Madrid v. Gomez*, 889 F. Supp. 1146 (N.D. Cal. 1995).

"Grassian described symptoms...obsessional thoughts of death." Stuart Grassian, M.D., *"Psychiatric Effects of Solitary Confinement,"* September, 1993.

"The paradigm in...thrown into solitary confinement." Bruce Porter, "Is Solitary Confinement Driving Charlie Chase Crazy?" *New York Times*, November 8, 1998.

Chapter 13

"While the motion...long-term repair plan." Ed Hayward, "Silenced alarm aided prisoners in break from Bridgewater facility," *Boston Herald*, November 4, 1993.

"Some guards called...months later in New Jersey." Ed Hayward, "Escaped convicts no stranger to life on lam," *Boston Herald*, November 1, 1993.

"Following their escape...Wood said." David Arnold, "Captured escapees were planning robbery, authorities say," *Boston Globe*, November 27, 1993.

"Robert Dellelo...to his life sentence." Bobby Dellelo interview with WCVB-TV reporter Ron Gollobin, December 1993.

Chapter 14

"You ought to...couldn't hide from Bobby." Susannah Sheffer and Dwight Harrison, *In a Dark Time*, (Stone Lion Press, 2005), pgs. 88-89.

"Somewhere along the way...that's not what happened." All Susannah Sheffer quotes taken from an interview with Christopher Lordan, December 2010, Amherst, MA.

Chapter 15

"The jury...a single brief transaction." *Commonwealth v. Dellelo*, 349 Mass. 525 [209 N.E. 2d 303] (1965).

"Please be advised...the Main Law Library." Letter to Robert Dellelo from Allison Hallett, Director of Treatment at Walpole State Prison, September 25, 1997.

"In 1979...the *Sandstrom* decision." *Sandstrom v. Montana*, 442 U.S. 510 (1979).

"A defendant need...to prove him guilty." Trial transcript, pgs. 1164-65.

"Now, whose idea...this load of ammunition." Trial transcript, pgs. 1141-42.

"Now, Officer...he could have." Trial transcript, pg. 160.

"Those of you...abused by the police." Trial transcript, pgs. 1142-44.

"Now, Mr. Foreman...this situation on Yasaian." Trial transcript, pg. 1151-53.

"While not in...the Commonwealth's closing argument." *Commonwealth v. Dellelo*, Suffolk Superior Court Nos. 8803-8809, Memorandum of Decision and Order on Defendant's Motion for New Trial, Superior Court Justice Carol S. Ball, June 9, 2003.

Chapter 17

"While the U.S....the 1980s and 1990s." See *Gaming the System: How the Political Strategies of Private Prison Companies Promote Ineffective Incarceration Policies,* Justice Policy Institute, June 2011.

"This conjunction of...to all current difficulties." Dwight Eisenhower, Farewell Address to the Nation, January 17, 1961.

"On September 8th...the Attica uprising." Tom Wicker, *A Time to Die* (Quadrangle/The New York Times Book Co., 1975).

"The business profiteers...thirty-five states nationwide." See *Gaming the System*, pgs, 21-25.

"Private prison corporations...thrive in those states." *Banking on Bondage: Private Prisons and Mass Incarceration*, American Civil Liberties Union, November 2011.

"Our growth is...incarceration at correctional facilities." Corrections Corporation of America Annual Report, 2010.

"In 2006...depression to schizophrenia." U.S. Bureau of Justice Statistics, 2006.

"Bureau of Justice...to the criminal behavior." U.S. Bureau of Justice Statistics, 2006.

"More recently...any particular day." *Banking on Bondage: Private Prisons and Mass Incarceration*, American Civil Liberties Union, November 2011.

"Under the federal...or risk arrest." Illegal Immigration Reform and Immigrant Responsibility Act of 1996, 110 Stat. 3009.

"Bureau of Justice...by mainstream media sources." U.S. Bureau of Justice Statistics, 2006.

"Tough on Crime...corresponding increase in crime." *Incarceration and Crime: A Complex Relationship*, The Sentencing Project, 2005.

Chapter 18

"I'm of the belief... it should be." Remarks by Governor William F. Weld, The Attorney General's Summit on Corrections, April 27, 1992, Washington, D.C.

Epilogue

"I can't get...think I should do?" Meghan Tench, "Debt paid, they want a chance to rebuild lives," *Boston Globe*, April 20, 2006, pg. B1.

Appendix

18 U.S. Code § 4352 National Institution of Corrections:

(a) In addition to the other powers, express and implied, the National Institute of Corrections shall have authority—

(1) to receive from or make grants to and enter into contracts with Federal, State, tribal, and general units of local government, public and private agencies, educational institutions, organizations, and individuals to carry out the purposes of this chapter;

(2) to serve as a clearinghouse and information center for the collection, preparation, and dissemination of information on corrections, including, but not limited to, programs for prevention of crime and recidivism, training of corrections personnel, and rehabilitation and treatment of criminal and juvenile offenders;

(3) to assist and serve in a consulting capacity to Federal, State, tribal, and local courts, departments, and agencies in the development, maintenance, and coordination of programs, facilities, and services, training, treatment, and rehabilitation with respect to criminal and juvenile offenders;

(4) to encourage and assist Federal, State, tribal, and local government programs and services, and programs and services of other public and private agencies, institutions, and organizations in their efforts to develop and implement improved corrections programs;

(5) to devise and conduct, in various geographical locations, seminars, workshops, and training programs for law enforcement officers, judges, and judicial personnel, probation and parole personnel, correctional personnel, welfare workers, and other

persons, including lay ex-offenders, and paraprofessional personnel, connected with the treatment and rehabilitation of criminal and juvenile offenders;

(6) to develop technical training teams to aid in the development of seminars, workshops, and training programs within the several States and tribal communities, and with the State, tribal, and local agencies which work with prisoners, parolees, probationers, and other offenders;

(7) to conduct, encourage, and coordinate research relating to corrections, including the causes, prevention, diagnosis, and treatment of criminal offenders;

(8) to formulate and disseminate correctional policy, goals, standards, and recommendations for Federal, State, tribal, and local correctional agencies, organizations, institutions, and personnel;

(9) to conduct evaluation programs which study the effectiveness of new approaches, techniques, systems, programs, and devices employed to improve the corrections system;

(10) to receive from any Federal department or agency such statistics, data, program reports, and other material as the Institute deems necessary to carry out its functions. Each such department or agency is authorized to cooperate with the Institute and shall, to the maximum extent practicable, consult with and furnish information to the Institute;

(11) to arrange with and reimburse the heads of Federal departments and agencies for the use of personnel, facilities, or equipment of such departments and agencies;

(12) to confer with and avail itself of the assistance, services, records, and facilities of State, tribal, and local governments or other public or private agencies, organizations, or individuals;

(13) to enter into contracts with public or private agencies, organizations, or individuals, for the performance of any of the functions of the Institute; and

(14) to procure the services of experts and consultants in accordance with section 3109 of title 5 of the United States Code, at rates of compensation not to exceed the daily equivalent of the rate authorized for GS–18 by section 5332 of title 5 of the United States Code.

About the Authors

Robert G. Dellelo spent over two-thirds of his life in some form of confinement, from reform schools to state prison. In April of 1964 he entered Walpole State Prison with a natural life sentence and a seventh-grade education. While at Walpole, he was the first president of the Prisoner's Union (National Prisoners Reform Association), and chairman of the Inmate Council that preceded the NPRA. In November of 2003, having overturned his sentence, he left prison with a bachelor's degree, having majored in sociology. He became a Certified Paralegal shortly after his release to the street. Now, having over 50 years of field experience in the "causes and effects" of confinement, having spent many years in solitary confinement, and having watched brats turned into killers and having seen sane citizens turned into violent, hard core, insane criminals, all in the name of "corrections," he holds himself out to be an expert in rehabilitation and corrections. Since his release, he has spoken about prison issues in a variety of venues: he testified before the Governor's Commission on Corrections Reform, addressed lawmakers at the Legislative Education Day at the State House, and testified at numerous legislative hearings. He has spoken to audiences at Harvard Law School, Boston College Law School, Northeastern University School of Law, and at various church groups and advocacy organizations. Dellelo has been profiled in numerous publications, including *The Boston Globe Magazine* ("Solitary Men") and *The New Yorker* ("Hellhole" by Dr. Atul Gawande). He is a co-author of the book "When the Prisoners Ran Walpole" (South End Press).

Christopher Lordan earned a *juris doctor* degree from Roger Williams University in 1999. After working as a civil litigator handling discrimination and sexual harassment cases, Lordan served as an Assistant District Attorney in Middlesex County. There, he handled both juvenile and adult criminal cases with a concentration on drug-related offenses, additionally serving as a community liason. Since that time, he has earned a Master's degree in Education Curriculum and Instruction and has taught Criminal Law, Constitutional Law, and Tort Law at both the public secondary and college levels. He also spent years as an alternative school educator in Boston, working with incarcerated, homeless, addicted, and other disadvantaged youth. Lordan continues to actively research and write in the areas of education and criminal law.

Made in the USA
Middletown, DE
23 February 2016